THE PARADOXICAL RATIONALITY
OF SØREN KIERKEGAARD

INDIANA SERIES IN THE
PHILOSOPHY OF RELIGION

Merold Westphal, editor

THE
PARADOXICAL
RATIONALITY
OF
SØREN
KIERKEGAARD

RICHARD McCOMBS

Indiana University Press

Bloomington & Indianapolis

This book is a publication of

Indiana University Press
601 North Morton Street
Bloomington, Indiana 47404-3797 USA

iupress.indiana.edu

Telephone orders 800-842-6796
Fax orders 812-855-7931

♾ The paper used in this publication
meets the minimum requirements of
the American National Standard for
Information Sciences—Permanence
of Paper for Printed Library Materials,
ANSI Z39.48-1992.

*Manufactured in the
United States of America*

*Library of Congress
Cataloging-in-Publication Data*

McCombs, Richard Phillip.
  The paradoxical rationality of Søren
Kierkegaard / Richard McCombs.
    pages cm. — (Indiana series in the
philosophy of religion)
  Includes bibliographical references
(pages   ) and index.
  ISBN 978-0-253-00647-9 (cloth : alk.
paper) — ISBN 978-0-253-00657-8
(electronic book) 1. Kierkegaard, Søren,
1813–1855. 2. Faith and reason—
Christianity. 3. Philosophical theology.
I. Title.
  BX4827.K5M33 2013
  198'.9—dc23

                          2012039961

        1 2 3 4 5 18 17 16 15 14 13

TO MY PARENTS

RICHARD AND SANDRA McCOMBS

CONTENTS

ACKNOWLEDGMENTS

Many people gave helpful criticisms and suggestions on drafts of this book. Jim Carey minutely critiqued an early draft. James Cutsinger gave helpful suggestions on parts of the manuscript and, more importantly, helped me with superlative Socratic art to learn a way of reading and thinking that led to the writing of this book. John Cornell, Joseph Smith, Steven Taylor, and Llyd Wells read portions of the manuscript and gave useful advice and criticisms. Sandra McCombs proofread the last draft and pointed out many errors. Walter Sterling read all of the manuscript and gave excellent advice both on the organization of the book as a whole and on the beginning of the book in particular. Merold Westphal, my mentor on Kierkegaard, gave very valuable advice on the manuscript as a whole and also made crucial suggestions on additions to the manuscript. Finally, my wife, Acacia, read the entire manuscript once, and many parts of it several times, and discovered many obscurities, inconsistencies of voice, and infelicities of style, and, more importantly, patiently supported and encouraged me in the writing of this book. Of course, any remaining errors in the text are to be attributed to its author.

ABBREVIATIONS

CA	*The Concept of Anxiety*
CD	*Christian Discourses, Etc.*
CI	*The Concept of Irony*
COR	*The Corsair Affair and Articles Related to the Writings*
CUP	*Concluding Unscientific Postscript*
EBD	*Early Buddhist Discourses*
EO, 1	*Either/Or*
EO, 2	
EUD	*Eighteen Upbuilding Discourses*
FPOSL	*From the Papers of One Still Living*
FSE	*For Self-Examination*
FT	*Fear and Trembling*
JC	*Johannes Climacus or De omnibus dubitandum est*
JFY	*Judge for Yourself!*
JP	*Søren Kierkegaard's Journals and Papers*
M	*The Moment and Late Writings*
MLD	*The Teachings of the Buddha, the Middle Length Discourses of the Buddha*
PC	*Practice in Christianity*
PF	*Philosophical Fragments*
PV	*The Point of View for My Work as an Author*
R	*Repetition*

SLW	*Stages on Life's Way*
SUD	*The Sickness unto Death*
TA	*Two Ages*
UDVS	*Upbuilding Discourses in Various Spirits*
WA	*Without Authority*
WL	*Works of Love*

THE PARADOXICAL RATIONALITY
OF SØREN KIERKEGAARD

ONE

A Pretense of Irrationalism

Be ready always to give an answer to every man that asks
you a reason for the hope that is in you. (1 Peter 3:15)

The noble lie [is] useful to human beings as a
sort of remedy. (*Republic* 414c, 389b)

What I have wanted has been to contribute . . . to bringing, if possible,
into these incomplete lives as we lead them a little more truth. (PV, 17)

The truth must never become an object of pity; serve it as long
as you can, to the best of your ability with unconditioned
recklessness; squander everything in its service. (PV, 211)

Temporarily suppressing something precisely in order that the
true can become more true . . . is a plain duty to the truth and
is part and parcel of a person's responsibility to God for the
reflection [thinking capacity, reason] granted to him. (PV, 89)

[Sometimes the wise teacher] thinks it most appropriate to say that he
does not understand something that he really does understand. (PV, 49)

One can deceive a person out of what is true, and—to recall old
Socrates—one can deceive a person into what is true. (PV, 53)

This was sometime a paradox, but now the time
gives it proof. (Shakespeare, *Hamlet*)

Søren Kierkegaard often seems to reject reason, but in fact he affirms it.[1] There are two principal causes of his appearance of irrationalism. First, his conception and use of reason, which he calls *subjectivity,* is so different from conventional versions of rationality that it often seems irrational, especially at first sight.[2] Second, and more importantly, Kierkegaard does not attempt to correct his misleading appearance of irrationalism, but instead deliberately cultivates it, precisely because he thinks that he needs such deception in order to assist his readers to become more rational. Thus it might be said that Kierkegaard pretends to be irrational in order to communicate rationality.[3] In his own colorful words, he is a *spy* "in the service of the truth" with the *absurd* or irrational as his *incognito* (CUP, 467; PV, 72; FT, 34; CUP, 500).

Kierkegaard's strategy of feigning irrationality in the service of reason has both divine and human models and is grounded in both faith and reason. The divine prototype is the incarnation of God in the man Jesus Christ. As God humbled himself to become an individual human being so that individual human beings might become divine, so Kierkegaard humbles himself to appear irrational so that his readers might become (more) rational. Whereas the incarnation is the "absolute paradox," because it transcends reason and therefore cannot be explained, comprehended, or demonstrated, Kierkegaard's serving reason by seeming unreasonable is only a "relative paradox," because it initially seems absurd, but can be explained, understood, and justified.[4]

The human model for Kierkegaard's incognito of irrationalism is Socrates. If Socrates ironically feigned ignorance in the service of knowledge, Kierkegaard "goes further" and ironically feigns irrationality in the service of reason. Rarely has any thinker conceded so much with an *argumentum ex concessis.*

Just as Kierkegaard's pretense of irrationalism is derived in part from Socrates' profession of ignorance, so, more generally, his *indirect* mode of *communication* is derived in part from Socratic *midwifery.* Even more generally, Kierkegaard's whole conception and use of reason—which includes his "indirect communication"—is modeled on Socratic rationality.

Like Kierkegaardian communication, Kierkegaardian rationality is paradoxical. What I am calling *paradoxical rationality,* Kierkegaard himself calls *subjectivity.* Subjectivity is paradoxical in that it strategically expresses itself in ways that make it seem irrational, at least initially, and in that it is an imitation by the finite, temporal, particular, and conditioned human being of an infinite, eternal, universal, and absolute ideal. Subjectivity is rational in that it uses the human mind to discover these opposites within human nature and strives to live and act consistently with this discovery. Thus subjectivity, like all rationality, is consistency. But, unlike some versions of rationality, it is a consistency not just of thought with thought, but of the whole person. More fully, it is an "existence-attempt" at "infinite self-consistency," an uncompromising striving to integrate in one project all the elements of the self, including *thinking, feeling, willing, acting,* and *communicating* (CUP, 318; SUD, 107).

Insofar as subjectivity is an attempt to apply one's convictions to life and action, it bears a strong resemblance to what is often called "practical reason."[5] Indeed, Climacus strongly implies that he sees subjectivity as "*usus instrumentalis* of reason," an instrumental use of reason (CUP, 377). Nevertheless, insofar as subjectivity does not narrowly focus on action, but endeavors to embrace and do justice to the whole human person, it is more accurate to call it *holistic* or *humane rationality.*

Most great thinkers who value reason desire to seem reasonable, and more or less effortlessly succeed in fulfilling this desire. Moreover, if they have a message to communicate that they know will initially seem unreasonable, they explain that the rationality of their message will become apparent if only their readers will bear with them for a while. Therefore, the fact that Kierkegaard neither seems reasonable to most people nor explains that he aims to be reasonable is an indication of how much Kierkegaard's conception and use of reason differs from those of other thinkers and of how much most people stand to learn from him about rationality and communication—if, that is, he is correct about these things. This present book represents an attempt to learn from Kierkegaard important and essential truths about the character and communication of rationality.

If Kierkegaard's method of communicating rationality by pretending to be irrational were entirely correct, it would be meddling foolishness to expose and explain it. Conversely, if Kierkegaard's feigning of irrationality were wholly misguided, then studying it would scarcely be worth the effort. But in fact, as I will argue, his pretense of irrationality is rational enough to be instructive and mistaken enough to need correction. Alternatively, Kierkegaard's strategy of feigning irrationality is a good idea in principle and is often so in practice, but it has succeeded so well—in that many readers who sincerely try to be open and receptive to Kierkegaard's writings never (adequately) discover his rationality—that it needs to be explained. Hence I will dare to explicate the method in Kierkegaard's mad stratagem of pretending to be irrational in order to communicate rationality.

Prospectus

In this first chapter, I argue that Kierkegaard is committed to reason and that he often pretends to be irrational in order to communicate rationality. In the second chapter, I follow up this argument by explaining not only Kierkegaard's conception and use of reason, but also why he thinks feigning unreasonableness is required for the communication of rationality. Each of the remaining chapters explicates a paradox that is a part of the paradox that Kierkegaard feigns irrationalism in the service of reason, or derived from this paradox, or analogous to it. In chapter 3, we will investigate why Kierkegaard thinks that the best way to reveal the goal of paradoxical reason is artfully preserving silence about it. In chapter 4, we will look into Kierkegaard's claim that the most psychologically subtle and the most powerful means to the goal of paradoxical reason is simply to try as hard as one can to attain it. Chapter 5 evaluates Kierkegaard's claim that the simple means of paradoxical reason must be communicated with bewildering complexity and indirection. In chapter 6, we will investigate why Kierkegaard thinks that the most artfully drawn limits to human reason form a ladder to transcendence. Chapter 7 explicates the Kierkegaardian assertion that the downfall of reason is its perfection. And, finally, chapter 8 examines and defends Kierkegaard's claim that the most cogent demonstration of ethics, religion, and Christianity is not a philosophical argument, but a life.

The Relation of Kierkegaard and Johannes Climacus

This present book is about the paradoxical rationality, not just of Kierkegaard, but also of Johannes Climacus, the persona created by Kierkegaard to be the pseudonymous author of *Philosophical Fragments* and *Concluding Unscientific Postscript to Philosophical Fragments*. Climacus's conception and use of reason are similar to Kierkegaard's, but with an important difference: Climacus's rationality is more philosophical than his creator's is. Kierkegaard creates Climacus specifically to address and appeal to philosophical readers, or, as Kierkegaard might say, in order to *find* such readers "where they are" so as then to *lead* them to subjectivity (PV, 45).

Since Climacus is more philosophical than Kierkegaard, he is also less rational—at least in Kierkegaard's estimation. For Kierkegaard believes that philosophy tends to be abstract, incomplete, and inconsistent, or that philosophers overemphasize thinking to the neglect of enacting or applying what they think. Climacus himself is very concerned about putting thought to the trial of action. That is to say, he writes a lot about it and heartily recommends it. But, as a self-professed *humorist,* Climacus fails to put into practice the highest things that he understands and admires and is consequently inconsistent and irrational by his own standards (CUP, 451). Therefore, in addressing his readers through the persona of the (partially) irrational Climacus, Kierkegaard in a way pretends to be irrational—since readers naturally tend to suppose that Climacus speaks for Kierkegaard.

It would be cumbersome always to be explicitly marking the agreements and disagreements of Kierkegaard either with Climacus or with his other pseudonymous authors by writing "Kierkegaard and Climacus agree about this or that," or "Climacus thinks this, but Kierkegaard disagrees and thinks this other thing." Therefore, I propose the following convention. The reader is to assume that I think Kierkegaard agrees with his pseudonymous authors, unless the context makes it clear that he disagrees with them, or unless I explicitly call attention to their disagreement. Sometimes, when I think that it is uncontroversial that Kierkegaard agrees with a pseudonym, I will even go so far as to attribute opinions quoted from a book he wrote pseudonymously to Kierkegaard himself. The previous paragraph should make it clear that I do not adopt this policy in the opinion that the distinction between Kierkegaard and his pseudonymous authors is unimportant.

Evidence That Kierkegaard Is an Irrationalist

There is no denying that Kierkegaard often presents a quite convincing appearance of irrationalism. Consequently, the first step in the argument for the thesis *that in order to communicate rationality Kierkegaard pretends to be irrational* is to describe Kierkegaard's irrational appearance.

Kierkegaard often appears to deny the power of reason or of the human mind to know things that he thinks are immensely important. For instance, in *Philosophical Fragments,* Climacus denies the power of reason to *demonstrate* the "existence of God" (PF, 39–44). Similarly, another pseudonymous author of Kierkegaard, Anti-Climacus, claims that "one cannot *know* anything at all about *Christ*" (PC, 25; cf. 23, 35).

Sometimes Kierkegaard appears to deny the value or relevance of rational arguments or of knowledge, or even to assert that seeking rational evidence is foolish, perverse, or evil. For example, Anti-Climacus dubs the person who first practiced apologetics, which is the attempt to *defend* Christianity with *reasons,* "Judas No. 2" (SUD, 87, 102–103).

Kierkegaard sometimes appears to go farther than denying the power and value of rational evidence, by suggesting that human excellence consists in believing or acting contrary to reason. For example, Climacus, who regards Christian faith as an attractive possibility, claims that if a person is to become a Christian, his *understanding,* that is, his reason, must "will its own downfall," step *aside,* be *discharged,* be *surrendered,* or even *crucify* itself (PF, 37–39, 59, 54; CUP, 559). Moreover, he claims that one *believes* in Christ "against the understanding," or "in direct opposition to all human understanding" (CUP, 568, 211). He even calls the Christian claim that God was made man in the person of Jesus Christ a *contradiction,* thereby giving the impression that it is a logical contradiction (PF, 87). Obviously, if the doctrine of the incarnation is logically self-contradictory, then faith in Christ involves a violation of the most basic principle of reason. It is not surprising, therefore, that another pseudonymous author, Johannes de Silentio, frequently claims that one has "faith by virtue of the absurd" (FT, 35).

Kierkegaard's elevation of the "single individual," or of the *particular,* above the *universal* also seems to constitute a rejection or demotion of reason, since reason typically if not always emphasizes the universal over the particular. Similarly, the *Postscript's* polemic against *objectivity* and *objective truth* often looks like a denial of rational norms and goals, while its panegyric of *subjectivity* and *subjective truth* frequently appears to be subjectivism, individualism, or relativism.

Evidence That Kierkegaard Is Rational

Lessing, a thinker whom Kierkegaard greatly admired, trenchantly criticized the apologetics of a certain Pastor Goeze of Hamburg in the following words: "Herr Pastor! Herr Pastor! Does the whole *rationality* of the Christian religion consist only in not being *irrational*? Does your theological heart feel no shame at writing such a thing?"[6] It seems to me that Lessing is right: A defense of the rationality of anything or of anyone that argues only that it or he is not irrational is not yet a sufficient defense of their rationality. Therefore I will argue not only that Kierkegaard is not an irrationalist, but that he is a robustly rational thinker, even though he is not a rationalist in any ordinary sense of the word, and maybe not even a philosopher.[7] Though I will begin arguing for the robust rationality of Kierkegaard here in this chapter, the argument will not be complete until the end of the next chapter.

While it is easy to find evidence that Kierkegaard and his pseudonymous authors are irrationalists or skeptics, the evidence they that affirm reason and knowledge is unspectacular, inconspicuous, and sometimes even hidden—which is exactly what we should expect, if Kierkegaard often pretends to be irrational.

Kierkegaard and his pseudonymous authors occasionally affirm *reason* (JFY, 91, 96; CUP, 41, 145, 161, 377) and *knowledge* by name, but more often than not, they affirm them by way of euphemisms: *dialectic, reflection,* or *thinking,* for reason; and *understanding, awareness, consciousness,* or *clear conception* for knowledge. Moreover, these affirmations of reason and knowledge tend to be hidden away in the less exciting, and therefore less read, portions of Kierkegaard's authorship, that is, either in the books to which he signed his own name—what I call *alethonymous* books—or in the two books by the pseudonymous author named Anti-Climacus. Finally, these affirmations are often only implicit and consequently in need of explication. Our present task therefore is to uncover and unfold the evidence that Kierkegaard and (many of) his pseudonymous authors affirm both reason and knowledge.

Kierkegaard values knowledge very highly, as the following passage indicates:

> Believe me, it is very important for a person that his language be precise
> and true, because that means his thinking is that also. Furthermore,
> even though understanding and speaking correctly are not everything,
> since acting correctly is indeed also required, yet understanding in rela-
> tion to acting is like the springboard from which the diver makes his
> leap—the clearer, the more precise, the more passionate (in the good
> sense) the understanding is, the more it rises to action. (PC, 158)

In this passage, Anti-Climacus asserts that *understanding,* or knowledge, is "very important"—not, however, for its own sake, but insofar
as it supports and informs *action.* In other words, Kierkegaard values
practical understanding, or practical knowledge.

Kierkegaard similarly affirms practical knowledge and rational
thinking in the service of practice when he writes that "the condition
for having had benefit [of a practical sort] is always first and foremost
to become aware," and "no earnest person . . . wearies of tracking down
illusions, because . . . he fears most to be in error" (WL, 85, 124).

Kierkegaard values practical understanding in part because he
thinks human dignity requires that a person be responsible both for
his or her actions and for being the sort of person one has made of
oneself, and because he thinks responsibility in turn requires knowing
what one ought to do and the *freedom* to do or not to do it (SUD, 21,
29). Thus he conceives of freedom, not as individualistic and arbitrary
self-creation, but as the capacity to strive or not to strive to conform to
a known *criterion,* or to an "unconditioned requirement," or to an *ideal,*
or, in short, to the dictates of *conscience* (SUD, 79; PC, 67, 90; FSE, 21, 40;
JFY, 91, 166–167). This conception of freedom comes to light in Anti-
Climacus's definition of *sin* as to *understand* or to know "what is right,"
and nonetheless either to "refrain from doing" it or else to do "what is
wrong" (SUD, 95).

Given the fact that Kierkegaard and his pseudonymous authors
think that ethical and religious action requires knowledge, we should
expect to find them affirming knowledge of ethical and religious norms
or ideals. We are not disappointed in this expectation. For example,
Anti-Climacus speaks of his *knowledge* of what is "humanly the true
good" and of his "awareness of the holy" (PC, 139). More specifically,
Kierkegaard claims that "every human being knows the ethical," and,
more generally, he claims that "basically we all understand the highest"

(JP 1:649, 11; WL, 78). Ethical knowledge, moreover, is according to Climacus knowledge to a very high degree, since he claims that "the ethical" is "co-knowledge with God" (CUP, 155; cf. PV, 75). Presumably one knows something rather well when one knows it "with God." Thus the ethical is "secure knowledge" and *certainty* (CUP, 152).

Knowledge of ideals is not only knowledge to a high degree, it is also knowledge of high things. For when one becomes *aware* of ethical and religious ideals, one becomes aware of them as *infinite, eternal,* and *absolute* (CUP, 143; SUD, 30; PF, 64; FT, 70). Anti-Climacus even claims that one can "become aware of God," the infinite and eternal source of ideals, and the highest of all beings (SUD, 41).

Since ethical and religious striving demand that one *examine* oneself in order to assess one's character and actions in the light of the ideal, it is not surprising that Kierkegaard and his pseudonymous authors affirm both the value and the possibility of *self-knowledge,* whose object is both human nature in general and oneself as a particular individual (SUD, 31; JP, 1:649, 5; PF, 37; and all of FSE and JFY). This emphasis on self-knowledge is also apparent in the fact that Kierkegaard constantly stresses the importance of *honesty,* especially with oneself. For honesty is possible only to the degree that one can become aware of the truth about one's feelings, actions, and convictions.

One of the more remarkable aspects of the human capacity for self-knowledge is, according to Climacus, that all people can know the limits of their actual knowledge: "Every human being, the wisest and the simplest, can just as essentially ... draw the distinction qualitatively between what he understands and what he does not understand" (CUP, 558; cf. CA, 3). This knowledge of one's limits is valuable because it helps one to be *humble* and receptive to God and truth, and because it helps to prevent one from getting lost in vain *speculation.* Although self-knowledge is vitally important, not many seek it, at least according to Kierkegaard, who knows "only all too well ... how true it is that the world wants to be deceived" (JFY, 91).

Kierkegaard and his pseudonymous authors often seem to deny the value and possibility of knowledge in relation to Christ and Christianity: "one cannot *know* anything at all about Christ"; there "is nothing at all that can be 'known' about him"; and "no one *knows*" "who Christ is" (PC, 25, 23, 36). Nevertheless, they end up affirming knowledge of

Christianity and of Christ in many ways: They claim that they "know what Christianity is," that they "know what it means to be a Christian," and that they are "more aware of what Christianity is, [and] know how to describe it better" than their contemporaries (PV, 15, 138; FSE, 21). Kierkegaard has a very high estimation of his knowledge of Christianity: "My activity . . . is to nail down the Christian qualifications in such a way that no doubt . . . shall be able to get hold of them" (JP, 1:522). It is hard to see how Kierkegaard and his pseudonyms could know what Christianity is, or what it means to be an imitator of Christ, without their also knowing something about Christ too. For in order to know how to imitate Christ as an ethical and religious exemplar one must have some understanding of who he is and of the principles of his actions. Therefore, not surprisingly, Anti-Climacus speaks of the "knowledge of Christ" as both desirable and possible (SUD, 113).

Although Kierkegaard often seems to think that he alone of his contemporaries knows what Christianity is, nonetheless he does not claim that such knowledge requires exceptional intelligence or a special, divine dispensation. Anti-Climacus writes that whereas in the "modern age" people do "not even know what the issue is" about Christ and Christianity, in the "first period of Christendom" people in general knew this (PC, 123; cf. CUP, 31, 24). And even now, according to Climacus, "one can know what Christianity is without being a Christian" merely by making a sincere and honest effort to discover these things (CUP, 372; cf. 373–375).

Among the more surprising suggestions of knowledge in Kierkegaard's authorship are Anti-Climacus's repeated claims that this or that does or does not belong *essentially* to Christ, thus implying that he thinks he knows the essence of Christ, at least in part (PC, 24–25, 34–35, 40, 153). Most surprisingly of all, Anti-Climacus asserts several times that God *cannot* do this or *must* do that (PC, 136–137, 142–143; cf. 131–132, 134–135, 184–185). Since Anti-Climacus presumes to assert that which limits or binds God, he must be fairly confident in his knowledge of the divine essence and its capacity.

The long list of things that Kierkegaard and his pseudonymous authors claim that they know, or that all people know or could know, might be expanded even more. For example, Kierkegaard claims that "every human being can come to know everything about love, just as every human being can come to know that he, just like every human being, is loved by God" (WL, 364). But I will bring the list of Kierkegaardian intelligibles to a close with some things that he and his pseudonyms say about their writing. Anti-Climacus claims that he "knows very well what he is doing" as an author (PC, 40, 52). By this assertion he seems to mean that he knows the "dialectical presuppositions" of indirect *communication,* and why these presuppositions require an oblique manner of writing (JP, 1:645; CUP, 72). Kierkegaard also claims that he knows the *dialectical* "problems . . . involved" in using "direct communication to make" people "aware of indirect communication," that is, to explain indirect communication directly (JP, 1:656). And, most generally, he claims that Christianity needs a "new science [or systematic knowledge] of arms" and implies that he himself has developed that science, at least in part (PV, 52; cf. PC, 138–139, 178, 183; CUP, 381).

Kierkegaard's affirmation of reason is less obvious than his affirmation of knowledge—though whenever he claims to know something without recourse to revelation he also implicitly affirms the human mind or human reason as the organ of that knowledge. He and his pseudonymous authors sometimes use the word *reason* and its cognates as terms of approval, but not very often (TA, 5; JFY, 91, 96; CUP, 41, 145, 161, 377). Similarly, they sometimes complain about the *irrationality* of the *times* (TA, 21). However, they often speak approvingly of reason by way of euphemisms for it like *thinking, dialectic,* and *reflection.* For instance, according to Climacus, "every human being is by nature designed to become a thinker," because "God . . . created man in his image" (CUP, 47). Thus Climacus claims that the principal basis of human dignity, namely, likeness to God, consists at least in part in the fact that human beings are *thinkers,* that is, rational beings.

Kierkegaard and his pseudonymous authors often affirm *dialectic* and claim to be *dialecticians* (PV, 132; PF, 108). A *dialectician* is someone who is "capable of pushing a point to its logical conclusion," someone who uses logic to make "absolute distinctions" (CUP, 40; PF, 108). Dialectic is not just an artificial logical game played with linguistic tokens, but a means of discerning the structure and essence of reality. For "everything has its dialectic," structure, or essence, which dialecticians use their reason to discover (CUP, 525; PC, 27–29). Thus Kierkegaard and his pseudonymous authors often use dialectic to argue that their opponents have not respected "qualitative" or essential differences between things, or that their opponents have made an unfounded, illicit "change of genus" in their thinking (PC, 27, 29; PF, 73; JP, 6:6780; CUP, 113; SUD, 97). Among the things whose dialectic Kierkegaard claims to discover and articulate are the incarnate *God, Christianity, faith, communication,* the "single individual," the *stages* or *spheres* of human *existence, contemptibleness,* "the relationship of prayer," and *power* (PC, 132; PF and FT in general; CUP, 72–93; PV, 123; CUP, 387–586; COR, 160; CUP, 162; JP, 2:1251).

There are many surprisingly argumentative passages in Kierkegaard's books. The "Interlude" in *Philosophical Fragments* contains an impressive dialectical or logical analysis of *possibility, necessity, time, eternity, freedom,* and the inter-relations of all these things (PF, 72–88). It might almost be said that this section evinces as much confidence in metaphysical reason as any text of Aristotle or of Thomas Aquinas. Similarly, in the *Postscript,* Climacus does not just dismiss Hegelian objectivity in a fit of subjective passion, he subjects it to a lengthy logical critique (CUP, 301–343). Again, he uses dialectic to criticize various views and defenses of Christianity (CUP, 23–57; PC, 26–35). Finally, Climacus gives an example of how a "subjective thinker" uses dialectic in an effort to explore and answer several existential questions in a personal manner (CUP, 165–181).

Another sign that Kierkegaard and his pseudonymous authors respect logic and reason is that they constantly criticize their opponents for being *confused.* Similarly, but less often, they berate an opponent for being *thoughtless, stupid,* an *idiot,* or a *fool* (CUP, 91; PF, 82; CUP, 306; CUP, 280). And since it is logic or reason that discovers confusions and other stupidities, Kierkegaard's sanguine mockery of confused thought implies much confidence in reason.

Although Kierkegaard affirms reason and logic in many ways, it must be admitted that his commitment to them is called seriously into question by the fact that he sometimes appears to deny the principle of contradiction. For instance, Climacus calls the incarnation a *self-contradiction,* but does not regard its self-contradictoriness as a decisive objection to it, and even seems to see its contradictory character as constituting a bracing test of faith (PF, 87). Moreover, Silentio and other pseudonymous authors refer to the incarnation as *absurd* and seem to recommend having "faith by virtue of the absurd" as an attractive possibility. Therefore, to establish Kierkegaard's commitment to reason, it is necessary to show that his endorsements of contradictions and of the absurd are not, as they seem to be, rejections of reason.

Although Climacus sometimes indicates that he regards "the paradox," or the incarnation, as a contradiction, he also argues that it is precisely because the "single individual's relation to the god contains no self-contradiction" that "thought can become preoccupied with it as with the strangest thing of all" (PF, 101). And since a paradox is, if nothing else, something *strange* with which one becomes *preoccupied* and at which one wonders, it follows that Climacus does not think that the paradox is a logical self-contradiction; otherwise one could not wonder at it as the highest and strangest thing of all. Furthermore, to know that the incarnation of God was a contradiction, one would need a thorough understanding of the essence of God and of temporal, finite human existence, so as to see that divine and human existence were utterly incompatible. But this is quite a lot of knowledge. Therefore, Climacus could claim that the paradox was a logical contradiction only if he also claimed to thoroughly understand God, time, and human nature; yet his reason for calling the incarnation the Paradox in the first place is to emphasize its incomprehensibility.[8]

If Kierkegaard and his pseudonymous authors do not in fact deny the logical principle of noncontradiction, why then do they so often seem to? A large part of the explanation is that they frequently use *contradiction* in a nonlogical sense to mean a tension or an unresolved opposition (PC, 39, 59, 60, 76, 82, 110, 113–116, 120, 124–125, 129, 131).[9] Oddly, Kierkegaard seems to have learned this use of *contradiction* from Hegel, whom Kierkegaard criticizes for using words in confusingly *volatized* senses (CA, 35). Perhaps he imitates the confusing Hegelian usage of *contradiction* as part of his pretense of irrationality.

A crucial sign that Kierkegaard respects reason is that he claims a person strives to become *good*—and striving to become good is at the very core of subjectivity—"with the aid of reason" (CUP, 161). And since the traditional name for using reason to become good is *practical reason,* we may say that subjectivity is some sort of practical reason. Presumably part of the aid that reason contributes to becoming good is to know the good so as to do it. Climacus corroborates his opinion of the importance of reason when he refers to "Plutarch's splendid definition of virtue: 'Ethical virtue has the passions for its material, reason for its form'" (CUP, 161–162).

Another crucial sign that Kierkegaard respects reason is his great admiration for the rationalist Lessing, and even his greater admiration for Socrates, the prince of philosophers (CUP, 63–70, 368). It is very hard, if not impossible, to see how Kierkegaard could esteem Lessing and Socrates as highly as he does if he did not also have a great deal of respect for reason. For to esteem Socrates but not to respect reason would be like loving circles but detesting roundness.

One might suspect that, his respect for reason notwithstanding, Kierkegaard thinks that becoming a Christian in the end demands going beyond reason with an irrational leap of faith. In other words, one might think that Kierkegaard respects reason up to a point, or for some purposes, but that he thinks one must leave reason behind, and maybe even reject it, in order to become a Christian. Kierkegaard seems to confirm these suspicions in the following entry from his *Journal:*

> What I usually express by saying that Christianity consists of paradox, philosophy in mediation, Leibniz expresses by distinguishing what is above reason and what is against reason. Faith is above reason. By reason he understands, as he says in many places, a linking together of truths, a conclusion from causes. Faith therefore cannot be *proved, demonstrated, comprehended,* for the link which makes a linking together possible is missing, and what else does this say than that it is a paradox. This, precisely, is the irregularity in the paradox, continuity is lacking, or at any rate it has continuity only in reverse, that is, at the beginning it does not manifest itself as continuity. (JP, 3:3073)

In agreeing with Leibniz that "faith is above reason," but not "against reason," Kierkegaard seems to say that faith is nonrational or suprarational but not irrational. His explanation for his claim that faith is nonrational is that Christianity "cannot be *proved, demonstrated, comprehended.*" But to say that faith is nonrational because Christianity cannot be demonstrated is to hold faith and Christianity to a very high standard of rationality. One might have thought that a way of life can be rational in some sense even if its basis cannot be *demonstrated.* Otherwise few or no people would have a rational way of life. If so, Christianity's nonrationality would distinguish it from few or none of its rivals.

A second look at the preceding *Journal* entry reveals that it contains a very surprising implication, namely, that faith can be demonstrated—eventually. For the entry uses *continuity* as a synonym for *demonstration* or *proof* and then suggests that faith can achieve continuity, not indeed at the *beginning*, but "in reverse." This is to say that faith, or its object, can be demonstrated after some unspecified evidence, experience, or capacity has been acquired. Thus in the very place in which he asserts that faith is above reason because its object cannot be proved, Kierkegaard also implies that faith or its object can in fact be proven—eventually. What is more, in suggesting that faith can ultimately prove what is initially above reason, Kierkegaard intimates that faith can elevate reason and maybe even perfect it. Therefore, when Kierkegaard says that faith is above reason, he might fairly be interpreted as meaning that faith is "more reasonable than ordinary reason" or that it "elevates or perfects reason."

There are many indications in Kierkegaard's writings that he thinks faith perfects (or at least strengthens) reason. According to the B hypothesis in *Fragments,* human beings in their *fallen* state lack the *condition* for knowing "the truth" (PF, 13–14). But, Climacus claims, "the god" gives or offers the condition to human beings, and Climacus calls the acceptance and use of this condition for the truth *faith.* Thus, according to Climacus, faith is not a blind acceptance of Christian tenets, but an elevation of the mind's natural capacity to a condition in which it can understand or become deeply aware of what previously transcended it. In other words, faith involves the elevation or perfection of the mind's natural capacity, which capacity usually goes by the name of reason.

Climacus's comments about *autopsy* similarly show that he thinks faith is rational and even perfects reason. He explains that faith is or has *autopsy* (PF, 70, 102). In the drafts of *Fragments,* Climacus (or should I say Kierkegaard?) goes even further, writing that "all faith is *autopsy*" (PF, 198, 215). *Autopsy* literally means "seeing for oneself." And *seeing for oneself,* which is to say, *not accepting something blindly on someone else's authority,* is a rational norm. Therefore in calling faith autopsy Climacus implies that faith is rational. And since he thinks that the truth of which faith becomes aware is not just any truth but "the truth," that is, the highest truth, Climacus also implies that faith elevates or perfects reason.

Kierkegaard expresses his agreement with Climacus that faith is autopsy when he writes that "through the relationship of your conscience to God . . . you [the single individual, judging for yourself, are] eternally responsible for your relationship to this doctrine" of Christianity (WA, 97; cf. 105). Like Kant and St. Thomas Aquinas before him, Kierkegaard sees *conscience* as a *rational* faculty (JFY, 91). Playing on the etymology of *con-science,* Kierkegaard sometimes refers to his "co-knowledge with God" (CUP, 155; cf. PV, 75). Presumably Climacus thinks that "everyone knows the ethical" because he thinks that everyone has this co-knowledge with God. Thus, in claiming that Christianity appeals to conscience, Kierkegaard indicates that Christianity appeals to reason, and not just to feeling, imagination, or the heart. And since Kierkegaard thinks that the Christian truth of which one becomes aware through the rational faculty of conscience is the most important truth, it follows that Kierkegaard thinks that faith elevates or perfects reason.

Judge for Yourself contains yet another indication that Kierkegaard thinks that faith perfects reason. In this work, Kierkegaard imagines a dialogue in which "the Christian" says to the "secular mentality," "do become reasonable" (JFY, 96). This quotation obviously implies that becoming a Christian involves or requires becoming reasonable, or more reasonable, and thus an elevation or perfection of reason.

Kierkegaard's theory of the stages of human existence provides strong evidence that he thinks becoming a Christian is not only compatible with reason, but its perfection. The theory of the stages is an ambitious attempt to schematize all human ways of existing: "I have set forth the decisive qualifications of the *whole* existential arena with a dialectical acuteness and a primitivity not to be found in any other literature, as far as I know" (JP, 5:5914; emphasis added). It is hard to see how Kierkegaard could so confidently propound such a bold schematization if he did not have great confidence in reason's ability to understand all human existence, and Christianity's place within it.

One might suspect that his boldness in schematizing is based on a belief that the stages are revealed in the Christian scriptures. But in fact he implicitly denies that the scriptures reveal them, when he writes that the Bible's presentation of Christ as the *prototype* leaves out "all the middle terms" between Christ and typical human existence. According to Kierkegaard, these "middle terms" between the average human being and Christ must be supplied by "human interpretation," which presumably involves human reason. Furthermore, Kierkegaard adds that though the "essentially Christian" remains unchanged throughout the ages, it nonetheless sometimes needs *modifications* in order to "secure itself against," or adapt itself to, the *new* (PV, 131–132). Presumably this work of modifying Christianity to suit new times must also involve reason. Thus the theory of the stages is the result of Kierkegaard's efforts to use reason both to supply the middle terms between ordinary human life and Christianity, and, when necessary, to adapt Christianity to his own, modern age.

To supply the middle terms between the lowest stages of human development and Christ, and, when necessary, modify Christian doctrine so as to adapt it to the needs of one's particular historical situation, reason must be able to understand several things: Christ's actions, at least well enough to imitate them; therefore also the principles of his actions so as to be able to imitate them in new situations; which actions of Christ are to be imitated and which not; and the right way to adapt Christ's actions both to human capacity and to new historical conditions of humanity. Therefore Kierkegaard's attempt to supply middle terms and adapt Christianity to his own age evinces great confidence in human reason.

Even if Kierkegaard thought the only way to generate the theory of the stages was to begin from the scriptural revelation of Christ and then to interpolate a path leading from ordinary human existence up to a way of life characterized by faithful imitation of "the paradigm," he would still have to think that reason and faith are somehow akin or commensurable. But, as we have already begun to see, in fact Kierkegaard does not believe the theory of the stages needs revelation as its starting point. To be sure, he asserts that revelation is necessary for becoming aware of the specifically Christian stage. But he does not think that revelation is required to work out and through all the other stages that lead to and prepare for the distinctively Christian stage. For Climacus claims that the highest stage just before Christianity, called "Religiousness A," has only "universal human nature as its presupposition" (CUP, 559). This is to say that Religiousness A can be discovered and actualized by a capacity for knowledge and action that resides in human nature as such. Traditionally, such a universal faculty for knowledge and for action based on knowledge is called *reason*. Thus Climacus claims that reason (or human beings equipped with reason) unaided by revelation can discover and actualize Religiousness A, the last stage of human development before Christian faith. And this is to say that though unaided reason cannot discover Christ, it can discover the way to or toward Christ.

Climacus confirms that he thinks reason by itself can and should discover and actualize Religiousness A when he claims that "Socrates was an ethicist . . . bordering on the religious" (CUP, 503). If Climacus thinks that Socrates, who is a figure and hero of natural reason, "bordered on the religious," this means he also thinks that reason as it perfects itself tends toward the religious. And since Climacus regards Religiousness A as the last stage of human development before Christian faith, he also thinks reason in its perfecting of itself tends toward Christianity. That is why subjectivity, which as we have seen is practical reason, and Christianity "are a perfect fit" (CUP, 230).

Kierkegaard is convinced not only that Socrates worked his way toward Christianity; he is also "definitely . . . convinced that [Socrates] has become" a Christian (PV, 54). If Kierkegaard thinks that Socrates— who claimed that he was "such as to obey nothing else of what [was his] than that argument which appear[ed] best to [him] upon reasoning,"—has definitely become a Christian, then Kierkegaard must believe that the perfection of reason requires, or at least allows, converting to Christianity.[10] To put it starkly, to say that Socrates, the most rational man, has definitely become a Christian is to say that the *telos* of reason is Christianity.

Thus Kierkegaard thinks that reason, whether it uses only its own resources, or takes its goal from revelation and then interpolates a path from average human existence to Christianity, conceives of human development along the same lines. Hence he thinks that there is a very deep agreement between reason and revelation about the ethical and religious development of a human being, and that Christianity is the perfection and fulfillment of reason.

I shall add yet more arguments for the claim that Kierkegaard thinks that faith fulfils and perfects reason in a later chapter when I argue that Climacus sees the *downfall* of reason as the perfection of reason. But, for now, I shall quote a passage from *Practice in Christianity* that aptly epitomizes the cooperative relation of reason and revelation as it is understood by Kierkegaard: "I make an honest effort to use [my] knowledge" "of the secrets of existence" to "illuminate what is humanly true and what is humanly the true good. And this [knowledge] I use in turn to prompt, if possible, an awareness of the holy," which "no human being can comprehend" (PC, 139). I propose that this passage says that Kierkegaard uses rational knowledge of human things to point to Christianity, which cannot be *comprehended,* that is, fully understood, but can be understood in part.

Thus Kierkegaard's claim that faith is above reason is incomplete and misleading. For he also implies that reason leads to faith, that to acquire faith is to become (more) reasonable, and that faith is the perfection of reason. More fully, he thinks that becoming a Christian means becoming more honest, less self-deceived or more self-aware, more consistent and more adept at dialectic, more self-reliant in one's thinking, more clearly aware of what it means to be a human being and of what a human being's place in the world is, and therefore more in touch with the *universally human.* And since all of these changes make a person more rational, it must be acknowledged that Kierkegaard thinks becoming a Christian means becoming more rational.

More basically, since Kierkegaard cares deeply about such things as honesty, judging for oneself, consistency, dialectic, and knowledge, especially knowledge of the good, knowledge of oneself as an individual human being, and knowledge of what it means to be a human being in the world, and since honesty, autopsy, ethical knowledge, self-knowledge, and knowledge of universal human nature are rational norms, methods, or goals, it seems we must conclude that Kierkegaard is a rational thinker, perhaps a robustly rational thinker—though the full argument for this claim will not be complete until the end of the next chapter.

Pretending to Be Irrational

We are now in a position to gather together some of the evidence *that* Kierkegaard pretends to be irrational in order to communicate rationality, though we are not yet well placed to appreciate *why* he thinks artfully feigning irrationalism is a wise method of promoting rationality in his readers.

Although Kierkegaard very often seems to reject reason, he in fact affirms it. If we grant that he knows what he is about as an author and is therefore largely in control of the appearance he presents in his writings, then we must conclude that though he is rational he wishes to seem irrational, or at least that he knowingly consents to seeming unreasonable.

If Kierkegaard is rational but wishes to seem irrational, and takes measures to seem so, it follows that he pretends to be irrational. Alternatively, suppose that he does not actively feign irrationality but merely consents to seeming irrational. Even so, this consent virtually amounts to pretending to be irrational in the case of an author like Kierkegaard who so often rants against *confusion* and *dishonesty;* for Kierkegaard certainly occasions much confusion by consenting to seem irrational; and in consenting to seem irrational, he is dishonest by consenting to appear as what he is not—especially since it would be such an easy matter for him to say forthrightly that he is, or intends to be, rational. Therefore, based on what Kierkegaard is and what he seems to be, it is fair to say that Kierkegaard pretends to be irrational.

Kierkegaard explicitly claims that indirectly communicating something existential requires an appearance of *equivocalness* about that thing (PV, 33–35). This equivocalness brings "attack and defense into a unity in such a way that no one can directly say whether one is attacking or defending" the thing that one is indirectly communicating (PC, 133; cf. CUP, 65). Despite the equivocalness of his indirect communication, Kierkegaard claims that "the true explanation [of what he is attacking, what he is affirming, and why] is available to the person who is honestly seeking" (PV, 34). This description of the equivocation of indirect communication perfectly describes the way that Kierkegaard writes about reason: He seems irrational, he partly conceals, partly reveals his rationality, and he hints at—makes *available*—the explanation of this equivocation.

Kierkegaard claims that a bad *author* or *teacher* "fears that someone will think that he does not know much," and that instead of doing all he can to assist the learner, such an author "really aspires to be cited for excellence—by the learner" (JP, 1:637; PV, 49). This claim of Kierkegaard suggests that good teachers must be willing to seem less knowing, less wise, and less rational than they really are in order to aid their students to grow in knowledge, wisdom, and rationality.

Kierkegaard is professedly a great pretender. In writing pseudony-mously he pretends to be another person with ideas and attitudes that differ from his own. Moreover, he calls his "esthetic works," and the "esthetic in the works," an *incognito*, thereby indicating that he uses a disguise or pretends to be what he is not in some of his writings (PV, 24, 67). The pseudonymous authors themselves also claim that they are pretenders. Climacus, for example, uses the images of a *spy*, and Anti-Climacus uses the image of an "ingenious secret agent"—that is, figures who disguise themselves—to describe their work as authors. Finally, Climacus explains that an indirect communicator such as himself fre-quently needs to operate *incognito* in order to accomplish his purpose (CUP, 466, 410).

Kierkegaard does not just pretend to be authors *different* from him-self; he pretends to be authors he believes to be *inferior* to himself in important respects. For instance, in volume 1 of *Either/Or* he adopts the persona of the pseudonymous author named "A," who represents an esthetic way of living and thinking to which Kierkegaard clearly thinks his own thinking and way of life are superior.

He pretends to be someone inferior to himself in another way when he adopts the persona of Judge William, the pseudonymous author of volume 2 of *Either/Or*. Commenting on *Either/Or*, Climacus claims that "A," but not Judge William, "possesses all the seductive gifts of under-standing and intellect," and that "A" is "far superior" "as a dialectician" to Judge William. And yet Judge William is, according to Climacus, closer to the truth than "A" is (CUP, 253). Thus Climacus intimates that Kierkegaard pretends, for the purposes of indirect communication, to have far less dialectical skill than he actually has even as he defends truth against error—and this despite the fact that he identifies himself as a dia-lectician and is obviously proud of his dialectical prowess. Kierkegaard himself also explicitly says that he locates himself "higher than Johannes Climacus," thereby indicating that in writing as Climacus he pretends to be someone less than himself (JP, 6:6433).

The strategy of selling oneself short is so important to Climacus that he has technical terms for people who adopt a persona inferior to their own in order to communicate subjectivity. Thus *irony* is the *incognito* of ethicists who conceal their ethical commitments and attainments as they indirectly communicate the ethical, and *humor* is the *incognito* of indirect communicators of the religious who strategically obscure their religious convictions and achievements (CUP, 503, 505–506).

Kierkegaard explicitly calls his adopting an incognito in some of his writings a *deception* (PV, 24). Moreover, he explains that he attempts to *deceive* his readers "into what is true" (PV, 53). Thus he indicates that he attempts to deceive his readers into what is true by pretending to be what he is not, that is, by being untruthful. And since deception is contrary to the highest goals of reason, while truth is, or is among, the highest goals of reason, deceiving a person into what is true consists in using the irrational in order to bring about the rational.

According to Alastair MacKinnon, who performed word-counts of important terms in Kierkegaard's authorship, the pseudonymous authors very frequently use *absurd* to describe faith and its object, but Kierkegaard himself scarcely ever does this.[11] Moreover, Kierkegaard himself states that "when the believer has faith, the absurd is not the absurd—faith transforms it" (JP, 1:10). Thus Kierkegaard creates pseudonymous authors who disagree with him in that they think, suspect, or at least say that Christianity is absurd. And since readers naturally suppose that the pseudonymous authors represent the opinions of Kierkegaard himself, and since readers also generally assume that Kierkegaard is himself a Christian, by having his pseudonymous authors call faith absurd Kierkegaard in effect misrepresents himself as having rejected reason in favor of the absurdity of faith. Thus yet another way emerges in which Kierkegaard pretends to be irrational in and through his pseudonymous authors.

In the *Postscript,* Climacus writes that Socrates, in his efforts to help the learner, "initially speaks like a madman" (CUP, 83). Since Socrates is a figure of reason, and madness is a failure of rationality, Climacus implies that Socrates pretends to be irrational in order to communicate rationality. And since Kierkegaard sees his indirect communication as an imitation and appropriation of Socratic pedagogy, the implication is that he also pretends to be irrational in order to communicate rationality. He confirms this implication when he says of himself that "I chose . . . to seem to be the most frivolous person of all, to 'become a fool in the world'" (PC, 228).

Similarly, Kierkegaard writes that helping a deluded person requires "taking the other's delusion at face value" (PV, 54). But a delusion is a self-deception, a case of irrationally tricking oneself out of the truth, and taking the other's delusion at face value means seeming to share his delusion, which is to say, pretending to be irrational. Thus Kierkegaard almost explicitly says that he pretends to be irrational in order to bring about the rational improvement of an undeception.

An Example of Pretending to Be Irrational
from *Fear and Trembling*

Kierkegaard pretends to be irrational in *Fear and Trembling* by adopting the persona and point of view of Johannes de Silentio, the book's pseudonymous author, who is partly irrational in that he practices self-deception to evade acting on his convictions about faith.

Silentio repeatedly claims that he "cannot make" "the movement of faith"—an incapacity that must weigh heavily on him, since he regards faith as the "true greatness" of a human being (FT, 36–37, 51–52, 81). As we shall see, his claim that faith is beyond his reach is extremely dubious.

Silentio gives only one reason, and that a very unconvincing one, to explain his inability to make the movement of faith. He cannot make this movement, he claims, because he "continually use[s] all [his] strength in resigning everything"—that is, he uses all his strength on the first movement of faith so that he has none left for faith's second and decisive movement (FT, 49–50). More plainly, faith is "just too hard" for him. Any parent, teacher, or coach quickly learns to be suspicious of the excuse that something is just too hard for the learner. Certainly Kierkegaard himself does not tolerate this excuse. In his *Journals,* he explains that "if the learner says: I can't, then the teacher answers: Nonsense, do it as well as you can, in order to get to know the task better and better" (JP, 1:653, 4). Thus Kierkegaard himself would not accept Silentio's justification for his lack of faith.

Silentio writes that "every time I want to make this movement [of faith], I almost faint" (FT, 48). Wanting to make the movement of faith is not the same as actually trying to make it. One can want to do something, but not attempt to do it, because one is not willing to endure the consequences of making a serious effort. Tellingly, Silentio never claims that he has attempted to make the movement of faith. But, supposing he has never even tried to make this movement, it is highly doubtful that he could know that he is incapable of it.

It is possible that Silentio makes (or has attempted to make) the movement of faith, but for some reason remains silent about his achievements (or about his frustrated heroic efforts). But whether he really neglects to strive for faith or merely pretends to be neglectful, in either case he presents a convincing appearance of evading the task of faith. And it will be instructive for us to study this appearance, whether it be feigned or accurate.

Kierkegaard would admit that there is some truth in Silentio's claim that he *cannot* make the movement of faith, since Kierkegaard thinks that "without God's help" "a person is capable of nothing . . . at all," and that "to need God is a human being's highest perfection" (EUD, 322, 297, 307). But, Kierkegaard might add, since Silentio realizes that he cannot attain faith "by [his] own strength" (FT, 49), Silentio should ask for God's help, rely on God's assistance, and thus attain faith by accepting divine grace.

Silentio himself seems to understand that one becomes faithful not through one's own strength but through God's. For he writes that Abraham, whom he regards as the father and exemplar of faith, "conquered God by his powerlessness" and was "great by that power whose strength is powerlessness" (FT, 16). But if Silentio understands that faith requires reliance on divine might, his claim that by his own power he cannot make the movement of faith turns out to be an irrelevant excuse. Another pseudonymous author, Anti-Climacus, gives a description of a "poet-existence verging on the religious" that very well describes Silentio with his despair of acquiring faith. Judging by this description, the reason that Silentio fails to avail himself of divine assistance is that he will not "humble himself" to receive it (SUD, 77–78). This judgment is confirmed by Silentio when he repeatedly suggests that *humility* is what distinguishes faith from infinite resignation (FT, 34, 42, 44, 45, 49, 73).

Silentio also tells us that if only he could find a "knight of faith," "I would watch him every minute to see how he made the movements; I . . . would divide my time between watching him and practicing myself, and thus spend all my time in admiring him" (FT, 38). This claim that he "would practice" the movements of faith "if only" is highly suspicious. Since Silentio, by his own admission, already "can describe the movements of faith," surely he does not need a knight of faith to teach him these movements (FT, 37). Moreover, Silentio claims that by appearances it is "impossible to distinguish" the knight of faith "from the rest of the crowd," or, as Climacus would put it, that faith is an "essential secret" (FT, 39; CUP, 79–80). Therefore Silentio could never know that he had found a genuine knight of faith, nor could he observe the hidden, inner movements of the knight's faith even if an obliging angel were to point such a knight out to him. Furthermore, according to Climacus no one is ever "assisted in doing the good by someone else's actually having done it," so that (if Climacus is right) seeing an example of faith would not help Silentio actually to acquire faith himself (CUP, 359). Consequently, since Silentio can already describe the movements of faith without having found a knight of faith, and since in any case he could not find a knight of faith, nor, if he could find one, could he observe the knight's hidden movements of faith, nor, if he could observe these hidden movements, could he be inspired or helped to faith by this observation, his claim that he *would* practice faith *if only* he could find a knight of faith is basically an oblique confession that he has no intention to attempt the movements of faith, thank you very much.

It is also highly suspicious that Silentio says that if he found a knight of faith he would "spend all his time in admiring him," since one can very well admire something without making the least effort at imitating it, and even use admiration as an evasion of imitation—a point stressed by Anti-Climacus, as we shall see.

Silentio's claim that he cannot make the movement of faith loses all credibility when we reflect on the fact that he says that "no human being is excluded from" faith, and that "true greatness," which he identifies with faith, "is equally accessible to all" people (FT, 67, 81). If all people can make the movement of faith, then surely Silentio can make it too, unless perhaps he were to beg off with the technicality that he is not a real person, but merely a fictitious pseudonymous persona. Therefore, to be blunt, his claim that he cannot make the movement of faith is a lie that he knows or ought to know for a lie; and, it seems, he deceives himself about his capacity for faith in order to evade faith, or as Kierkegaard might put it, because he "want[s] to make excuses and look for excuses" (JP, 1:649, 10).

"Poeticizing" faith "instead of being" faithful is perhaps the main way that Silentio evades faith (SUD, 77). In other words, Silentio substitutes poetically celebrating faith, or *admiration,* for existentially striving to be faithful, or *imitation.* There are several passages in *Fear and Trembling* in which Silentio indirectly confesses that he desires to praise Abraham and his faith, but not to imitate him. For example, Silentio describes a man, suspiciously like himself, whose "one wish," or "one longing," was not to be like Abraham, but "to see" him and "to have witnessed that event" in which God tried Abraham (FT, 9). This suggests that Silentio's one wish is to see and to *contemplate* the greatness of Abraham, but not to attempt such greatness himself. Similarly, Silentio claims that the poet —and, notwithstanding his protests to the contrary, Silentio very much seems to be a poet—is *happy* that the hero whom he admires is "not himself, that his love can be admiration" (FT, 15). In other words, Silentio the poet is quite happy not to imitate his hero.

Given that Silentio is content to praise the hero of faith without imitating him, it is not surprising that he tries to justify or excuse his praise *sans* imitation. Silentio claims that "God created" the "poet or orator," who "can do nothing the hero does; he can only admire, love, and delight in him"—a claim suspiciously at odds with his assertion that "no human being is excluded from the heroism of faith" (FT, 15). Furthermore, he says, *admiration* is the poet's "humble task" and "his faithful service in the house of the hero" (FT, 15). With these words, Silentio indirectly asserts that God created him as a poet commissioned to praise the faith of Abraham, but he is incapable of imitating it—a dubious assertion, as we have seen, but also an ironically apt assertion, since Kierkegaard does indeed create Silentio as just such a poet.

Even though Silentio admits that faith is "the greatest of all," it nonetheless seems that he attempts to suggest that doing the deeds of faith and observing faith are more or less equal, when he writes that "it is greater to have faith, more blessed to contemplate the man of faith" (FT, 17). Given Kierkegaard's myriad objections to mere contemplation and his countless warnings about the necessity of acting on what one knows or believes, there can be no doubt what Kierkegaard would say about Silentio's suggestion concerning the equality of seeing and doing.

Silentio completes his brazen and blustering substitution of poeticizing faith for being faithful when he writes that if the poet "remains true to his love" for the hero, "then he has fulfilled his task, then he is gathered together with the hero" (FT, 15–16). Thus Silentio asserts that he and his collaborator the poet share the heavenly reward of their hero, even though they have not dared what the hero dares, endured what the hero endures, and struggled and suffered as the hero struggles and suffers. Kierkegaard himself strongly disagrees with Silentio's estimation of the value of poeticizing, writing that "it seems a flagrant wrong" for the suffering imitator of Christ and anyone else to "be equally blessed" (FSE, 23).

Our suspicions concerning Silentio are corroborated by Anti-Climacus, who in many places analyzes and exposes "the sin of poetizing instead of being" in a way that calls Silentio to mind (SUD, 77–78, 30–33, 35–37; PC, 233–255). Anti-Climacus explains that whereas "an imitator *is* or strives *to be* what he admires . . . an admirer keeps himself personally detached," that is, objective (PC, 241). Anti-Climacus also explains why the admirer poeticizes the hero: "in every individual . . . there resides . . . a profound cunning . . . that is of evil" that wants to "sneak away from the *requirement*" by means of poetic *admiration,* which is essentially "excuse and evasion" (PC, 239–240). When imitation is not added to admiration, the latter is a "deceit, a cunning that seeks evasion and excuse" (PC, 242). Thus the admirer "is only spinelessly or selfishly infatuated with greatness" (PC, 246). Needless to say, it can hardly be an accident that Anti-Climacus's description of the poet-admirer so closely resembles Silentio.

Lest there be any doubt about this resemblance, compare the following utterances: Anti-Climacus says that the poet-admirer of the religious "loves God above all, God who is his only consolation in his secret anguish, and yet he loves the anguish and will not give it up"; and Silentio says that his "eternal consciousness is" his "love for God," and that he "find[s] joy and peace and rest in [the] pain" of his infinite resignation, which is based on his love for God (SUD, 77; FT, 48–49). The similarity of these two descriptions is striking: Silentio and Anti-Climacus's poet both suffer for God whom they love, and they both love and find consolation in their sufferings for God. Therefore, I conclude, Silentio is created by Kierkegaard (partly) to exemplify the sins of poetic admiration.

Silentio evades the task of being faithful not just by poeticizing faith and claiming that faith is too hard for him, but also by making out that he does not understand faith well enough to perform its movements. Sometimes he claims that he cannot understand faith; sometimes he doubts that anyone can understand it; and sometimes he even claims that it is absurd. And yet both Kierkegaard and his pseudonym Anti-Climacus describe faith simply and without any hint that the difficulty of faith is that it is hard to understand. Indeed, Kierkegaard writes: "Ah, this matter of the essentially Christian is so strange; in a certain sense it is so indescribably easy to understand, and on the other hand it actually becomes difficult only when it is that which must be believed" (CD, 146). This is to say that the faith itself is not hard to understand well enough to enact it, but that people make it so in order to evade the task of having faith. Therefore, if Silentio finds faith hard to understand, this seems to be because he himself has complicated it. Incidentally, I do not mean to deny here that faith is a mystery that cannot be comprehended; rather, I mean to assert that one can understand it well enough to put it into practice, if one is willing—at least according to Kierkegaard.

Silentio disagrees not only with Kierkegaard and Anti-Climacus about the difficulty of understanding faith, but he also disagrees with himself. For if, as he claims, everyone is capable of faith, then understanding faith *well enough to be faithful* cannot require unusual intelligence. Moreover, Silentio does in fact describe some movements of faith fairly clearly, and admits that he can do this, but surely he could not do this if he did not understand faith with some clarity. Finally, he says or implies in many places that he does understand faith, most notably at the end of his book, where he writes the following: "Here again it is apparent that one can perhaps understand Abraham"—and therefore faith as well, since Abraham represents faith for Silentio—"but only in the way one understands the paradox. I, for my part, can perhaps understand Abraham, but I also realize that I do not have the courage to speak in this way, no more than I have the courage to act as Abraham did" (FT, 119–120). Here he seems clearly to admit that his problem is not finding the wit to understand the faith of Abraham, but finding the courage to imitate it. It is as if Silentio were thinking with himself thus: I am duty-bound to imitate the faith of Abraham only if I understand it. Can I help it that every time I try to understand it, difficulties, complications, and absurdities arise? Good question, Silentio. Perhaps readers who, like me, find their own way of thinking similar to his, should ask themselves the same question.

To understand why Kierkegaard presents Silentio as a self-deceiving evader of the task of faith, let us begin by noting that the basic function of the Silentio pseudonym is to help readers become *aware* of and *admire* "the greatness of faith": "the point is to perceive the greatness of what Abraham did so that the person can judge for himself whether he has the vocation and the courage to be tried in something like this," that is, in the struggles and ordeals of faith (FT, 53). Similarly, Silentio, who, despite his protests, acts or writes like a poet, says that the "humble task" of the poet is to use his *song* "so that all may admire the hero as he does, may be proud of the hero as he is" (FT, 15).

In *Works of Love,* Kierkegaard explains that the best praiser of love proceeds in the "fear that someone will think that he was speaking about himself" when he praises what he admires (WL, 372). In other words, the best praiser of spiritual greatness fears that his audience will refuse to admire the greatness that he is celebrating because they suspect that he has the ulterior motive of wishing to be admired as an example of this greatness. More simply, he fears that they will dismiss his praise as unreliable, or not even listen to it, because they suspect that it is proudly praising himself. Therefore, Kierkegaard concludes, the best praiser of love or of faith must present himself as lacking the love or the faith that he celebrates. Thus it is necessary for Silentio, if he is to be the best poet of faith that Kierkegaard can make him to be, to present himself as lacking faith. Incidentally, by claiming that he has achieved the heroic greatness of "infinite resignation," but denying that he has faith and thus placing himself below faith, Silentio gives an artful a fortiori argument for the loftiness and sublimity of faith.

Silentio's claim that he cannot make the movements of faith is a crucial tactic for fulfilling his goal of assisting readers to become aware of and admire the greatness of faith. Kierkegaard thinks that faith is a task, or an "absolute requirement," to which all human beings are summoned by God. But, he thinks, it would be bad strategy for him as a writer immediately to inform his readers of their unconditional duty to strive for faith. For faith is a difficult, dangerous, strenuous, and painful duty, and human beings will do virtually anything to evade such a duty. Therefore, if he were to begin his praise of faith by announcing that faith is a requirement for all human beings, it is likely that his readers would refuse to listen to him so as to avoid becoming personally aware of the requirement. As a countermeasure to this defense and others like it, Kierkegaard separates the greatness of faith from the requirement of faith and tries to make his readers aware of the greatness before he tries to make them aware of the requirement. And to do this, he presents Silentio as excusing himself from the task of faith, as saying that faith is too hard for him. Because Silentio excuses himself in this way, he does not pose a threat to readers. Instead he comforts them—they have no fear that such a man is going to demand faith of them. And, shielded from this fear, readers are freed up to acknowledge and admire the greatness of faith. As long as there is no question that faith is required of them, they may very well have the magnanimity to admit that faith is a supreme greatness achieved by a few exceptional human beings like Abraham. Thus Silentio's self-excusing, self-deceiving, task-evading admiration of faith is Kierkegaard's way of getting his readers to be as receptive as possible to learning to admire and acknowledge the greatness of faith. As Anti-Climacus puts it, "the misunderstanding that goes under the name of admiration . . . is even necessary in order to attract people" (PC, 245). In short, Kierkegaard first tries to get readers to admire the greatness of faith, and then later he breaks the distressing news to them that the faith that they admire is an absolute duty.

Thus in general Silentio functions as an intermediary between Kierkegaard, who admits the greatness of faith and personally strives for it, and the *intended* readers of *Fear and Trembling,* who neither admire faith nor strive for it. Silentio is Kierkegaard's way of reaching out to such readers, a concession or a compromise, his way of meeting or finding them (near to) where they live and think. That is to say, in the person of the irrationally self-deceived Silentio, Kierkegaard pretends to be irrational in order to induce his readers to give faith an honest hearing.

In order to see yet another function of Silentio's self-deceiving evasion of the task of faith, let us suppose that Silentio succeeds with some readers in helping them to become aware of the grandeur of faith. The next step for such readers is to realize that mere admiration of faith is not enough; they must also imitate the exemplars of faith. Kierkegaard thinks that this next step is immensely difficult, that overcoming the temptation to self-deceiving evasion of the task of faith is a heroic accomplishment. By presenting Silentio as a deluded shirker of faith and its tasks, Kierkegaard gives his readers the chance to discover this deluded shirking in a character other than themselves, where it is easier to detect than it would be closer to home. And, if they discover self-deceived evasion of faith in Silentio, then they will be better placed to discover it, or the temptation to it, or analogues to it, in themselves. Furthermore, by not accusing his readers directly of deluded dodges like those practiced by Silentio, but instead gently and indirectly inviting them to discover these things for themselves, Kierkegaard avoids provoking them to defend themselves irrationally, avoids tempting them to worm themselves deeper into a bog of self-deception. As Nathan the prophet first induced David to admit that the man who stole another person's beloved sheep was ignoble and despicable, and only then told him that in stealing Uriah's wife David was like that sheep-thief, so Kierkegaard invites his readers first to become aware of the artful dodging of faith in Silentio, and only then (indirectly) invites them to become aware of it in themselves.

Thus Kierkegaard has constructed *Fear and Trembling* so ingeniously that interpretation of it unexpectedly and disconcertingly turns into self-examination. Unsuspecting readers begin by thinking that they are reading "lyrical dialectic" about Abraham and his faith, and then to their dismay find that *Fear and Trembling* holds up a mirror to their own (possible) evasions, excuses, and self-deceptions. Consequently, *Fear and Trembling* has a triple meaning requiring a triple movement of interpretation: First one becomes aware of the greatness of faith; next one realizes that Silentio dishonestly and irrationally avoids the requirement of faith; and finally one compares him- or herself to Silentio to see whether Kierkegaard has cleverly and artfully maneuvered him or her, as Nathan maneuvered David, into the rhetorical trap that clamps down on a person with the distressing words: "Thou art the man."

Unfinished Business

I have argued that Kierkegaard is or sees himself as rational. But I have not explicated his version of rationality. In the next chapter I will explicate subjectivity as Kierkegaard's conception and use of reason and show how the case for the reasonableness of subjectivity emerges from Kierkegaard's critique of what he calls *objectivity*. Finally, in later chapters, especially the last one, I will critically assess subjectivity.

I have argued that in order to communicate rationality Kierkegaard pretends to be irrational. In the next chapter I will explain more fully why he thinks this strange strategy is necessary or useful. And in chapter 5, I will critically evaluate the "indirect communication" of which this strange strategy forms a major part.

Most of the remainder of this book, however, is dedicated to exploring the many paradoxes that emerge (partly) from Kierkegaard's communication of rationality through a pretense of irrationality.

TWO

Paradoxical Rationality

But thou, when thou fastest, anoint thine head, and wash thy face; that thou appear not unto men to fast, but unto thy Father which is in secret. (Matthew 6:17–18)

Most people have no intimation of this superiority over oneself . . . of wanting to be incognito in such a way that one seems lowlier than one is. (PC, 129)

How strange or odd some'er I bear myself (As I perchance hereafter shall think meet to put an antic disposition on). (Shakespeare, *Hamlet*)

Though this be madness, yet there is method in't. (*Hamlet*)

The play's the thing wherein I'll catch the conscience of the King. (*Hamlet*)

The reason he is pretending to be crazy is to enable another knight to recover his lost senses. (Cervantes, *Don Quixote*)

In *Judge for Yourself!* Kierkegaard stages the following dialogue: "'Do become reasonable, come to your senses, try to be sober'—thus does the secular mentality taunt the Christian. And the Christian says to the secular mentality, 'Do become reasonable, come to your senses, try to be sober'" (JFY, 96). There is a sense in which Kierkegaard's whole authorship is this little dialogue writ large. The voices of the dialogue are two rival versions of rationality, which Kierkegaard calls the "secular mentality" and "the Christian" in the quotation, but more generally, *objectivity* and *subjectivity*.

The purpose of this chapter is to explicate this conversation in Kierkegaard's authorship between objectivity and subjectivity. Or, to drop the metaphor, my present aim is to compare objectivity and subjectivity, to explain Kierkegaard's rational critique of objectivity, to unfold his implicit arguments for the reasonableness of subjectivity, and to show why Kierkegaard sees fit to communicate rationality to objective readers by pretending to be irrational.

A Preliminary Sketch of Objectivity and Subjectivity

Kierkegaard and his pseudonymous authors have many names for objectivity, its various modalities, and its analogues: *speculation, abstract thinking, pure thinking, probability, paganism, spiritlessness,* the *secular mentality,* and the *demonic.*[1]

Focused and fixated on the objects of thinking, the objective person is *abstract, absentminded, fantastical, forgetful* that he is an "individual human being" and therefore busily engaged in "canceling himself out." In other words, objectivity is a one-sided preoccupation with thinking and with the objects of thought, and a consequent neglect of oneself as the person who thinks. The chief aspects of the human person that objectivity neglects are *feeling, willing,* and *acting.* Objective people do not adequately understand what they feel, will, or do, nor do they adequately feel, will, or enact what they think. They avoid putting their ideas into practice partly by thinking impractical thoughts, partly by thinking thoughts that ought to be practical, but in a perversely impractical and impersonal manner, and partly by not thinking about themselves as human beings summoned to ethical and religious action. Thus objectivity is "neither more nor less than a lack of conscience" (FSE, 40). Or, more humorously, to be objective is to "erect . . . a huge, domed palace" in thought, but to live "in a shed alongside" that palace, "or in a doghouse, or at best in the janitor's quarters" (SUD, 43–44).

Although objective thinkers deem themselves eminently rational, Kierkegaard regards them as egregiously irrational. Therefore, if Kierkegaard is right about them, they are deluded about their own rationality, and their delusion compounds their irrationality.

Kierkegaard does not think that objectivity is utterly irrational, but diseased or compromised rationality. Indeed, if he judged objectivity to be wholly irrational, his practice of dialectically criticizing objective thinkers in the hope that they will see the justice of his critique would be pointless. Furthermore, Kierkegaard acknowledges that objectivity has a limited sphere of legitimacy, a sphere that includes mathematics and natural science. But he also thinks that math and science can be used to evade the ethical and the religious, and thereby they lose their legitimacy. We might also add that many things that Kierkegaard calls *objectivity* include a minimal subjectivity, but remain primarily objective because they do not amount to a serious effort to live according to ethical and religious ideals. In other words, Kierkegaard thinks that no or few people are wholly objective, but that many or most people are nonetheless primarily and pathologically so.

Kierkegaard and his pseudonymous authors also have many names for subjectivity, its modalities, and its analogues—*appropriation, striving, simplicity, existing, earnestness,* and *enthusiasm*—as well as words for specific forms of subjectivity, like *the ethical, irony, the religious, humor,* and *faith.*

To be subjective means consistently to relate oneself, the *subject* of thinking, to what one thinks. It is to think about life and action, especially one's own life and action, and to strive to feel, will, and act consistently with one's thoughts. In other words, subjectivity is inquiry into, striving after, and imitation of ethical and religious ideals, followed up by, or together with, conscientious self-examination in the light of those ideals.

Climacus and Kierkegaard think that subjectivity is "more true" and more *reasonable* than objectivity is, and not in a merely Pickwickian sense (CUP, 56, 201). They think this because they deem subjectivity to be more complete and more consistent than objectivity—more complete because, instead of pandering to philosophical curiosity, it aims to do justice to the whole human being and to the whole of human life, and because it conforms to reality, not just with the instrument of the speculative intellect, but with the symphony of the mind, emotions, will, and actions—and more consistent because it is not a cacophonous conflict of thinking and action, but a harmonious blending of them.

Although I will present detailed arguments that subjectivity is more true and more reasonable than objectivity is, I will not attempt to assess whether (or how accurately) Kierkegaard describes his specific objective opponents such as Hegel—though it seems to me that he is fair to Hegel, not indeed perfectly, but in a rough and ready way.[2] Nor do I propose to investigate whether Kierkegaard succeeds in refuting the sophisticated theories of Hegel or other objective thinkers. Since Kierkegaard intends to address each of his readers as a "single individual," the task of the reader is not to determine whether Kierkegaard accurately describes and trenchantly criticizes other people, or people in general, but to examine whether he accurately describes and trenchantly criticizes that most relevant of persons, oneself. Accordingly, I hope to aid readers in making this determination about themselves but not about irrelevant others.

Disinterestedness versus Concern

It is obvious that interest can pervert thinking. We can be so perverse as to think that something is true because we like it, or because it justifies our behavior, or because it legitimates our privileges, or because we fear to face the consequences of its falsity.

Recognizing the perverting power of interest, objective thinkers attempt, or claim, to be *disinterested* (CUP, 22, 55). In other words, their goal, or boast, is that they eliminate or sufficiently minimize every influence of desire, fear, and passion on their thinking, except the influence of the noble desire for truth.

Kierkegaard agrees with objectivity that interest can, and typically does, pervert thinking, and that this perversion must be addressed and if possible corrected. But he disagrees with objectivity about the solution to this problem. For he judges that thinking is unavoidably interested, since every human being naturally and inevitably desires to be happy; this is to say that when objective thinkers claim to be disinterested, they are dishonest or deceived about their own motives. Kierkegaard loves to satirize the pretensions of "assistant professors" who vaunt their putatively divine aloofness from human desires and passions, but who also eagerly seek out both the *security* of a "salaried position" in a "well-ordered state" and the glory of having made a *contribution* to *scholarship* and to the *System*.

Subjectivity differs crucially from objectivity in that it makes a serious effort, not to be disinterested, but to become aware of its own interests. And since subjectivity acknowledges its own interestedness, and examines its desires and motives rigorously, while objectivity hastily declares victory over interest without even making a serious effort at self-examination, subjectivity may justly claim to be more rational than objectivity with regard to the problem of interest.

Subjective thinkers strive not only to know their own interests, but also to shape and organize them in a way that is conducive to truth. For instance, they strive to cultivate *honesty, courage,* and *self-denial:* three obviously truth-promoting virtues that involve habits of desire and emotion. And they cultivate these virtues, not just when they are cozily ensconced with a book in their studies, but in their lives as a whole. Therefore, when they inquire into the truth they can draw on these truth-promoting virtues that they have striven to cultivate in their lives. And since objective thinkers work on the problem of interest only when they think, and work on it only with the questionable strategy of eradicating, or rather ignoring, interest, but subjective thinkers strive to cultivate emotions, desires, and virtues that promote truth, again it is arguable that subjectivity is more rational than objectivity in the way that it addresses the problem of the influence of interest on thinking.

Kierkegaard's belief that thinking is unavoidably interested has important consequences for his manner of writing. Instead of posturing as a divinely aloof mind serenely dispensing knowledge to dispassionate investigators, Kierkegaard attempts to exemplify in his writing the right relation of interest and thinking, and to this end, he expresses desire, longing, fear, passion, and various moods in ways that he thinks are apt and honest. One result of his writing in this way is that he often appears indulgently and irrationally emotional to objective readers accustomed to expect a pretense of transcendent tranquility from reputable and reasonable authors.

Theory versus Practice

Objective thinkers claim to be theoretical, or contemplative, or to pursue knowledge for its own sake. Less flatteringly, they ignore or neglect to meditate on the consequences of their thinking for their lives and actions, and they neglect to put these consequences into practice. In contrast to objectivity, subjectivity is practical, or holistic, in that it aims to understand and cultivate the whole human person in a sane and balanced manner.

Kierkegaard thinks that it is highly irrational for objectivity to proceed as if, or to assume without proof that, a human being is a *pure* and *eternal* mind whose *temporal* and *personal* aspects are unimportant, unessential, or negligible. In order to wake readers from this theoretical dream, he often satirizes the pretensions, hypocrisies, and weaknesses of "absent-minded" *professors*. For example, he quips that in objective thinking "observing has finally become falsified as if it were actuality" (CUP, 319). In other words, objectivity brazenly treats *thinking* as *being*: the "absent-minded" *professor* "writes something down on paper," and then pretends that by being written it is actual or already accomplished (CUP, 405). Kierkegaard adds plausible analysis to biting satire when he explains that the function of the professor's belief in his magic pen is a lazy and cowardly evasion of action: "What is a task for action" or *duty*, which "is what one ought to do," "has been turned into a question for thought" (CD, 205).

Climacus describes how a seemingly serious inquiry about whether to become a Christian can actually be a lazy and cowardly evasion of this momentous decision. Since "historical knowledge" is at best only an *approximation*, that is, uncertain, while the decision to become a Christian is of *eternal* and *infinite* importance, historical knowledge can never be a sufficient basis for a *decision* to accept or to reject Christianity (CUP, 23–49). And since this is so, historical inquiry into Christianity is very often a *parenthesis* in the process of deciding about Christianity. Moreover, since historical scholarship about Christianity is subject to constant reversals, and since there is always some new book that promises to cast the whole subject in a new light, the scholarly inquirer can prolong the parenthesis indefinitely and ad libidem (CUP, 28–29, 32, 52). But just as a never-ending parenthesis is bad grammar, so endless inquiry into a practical question is meaningless deliberation (CUP, 29). Therefore, when objective thinkers make out that they are engaged in a serious historical inquiry into Christianity so as either to accept or reject it, but in fact never reach a decision—unless quitting due to exhaustion, despair, or boredom counts as a decision—it is impossible not to suspect that the whole inquiry was from the beginning a charade intended to avoid a real decision and the striving, suffering, and responsibility that a real decision about Christianity might entail.

Kierkegaard describes a similar sort of evasion sometimes practiced by people who claim to study the Bible as a guide for life (FSE, 25–44). Their evasion consists in postponing any serious effort to live in accordance with scripture until they have worked out a solid interpretation of it. But since they never firmly establish the meaning of the difficult, "obscure passages"—indeed it may be that understanding the most difficult verses requires striving to live in accordance with easily understood passages—they can, if they wish, indefinitely evade living the Word whose guidance for life they profess to be seeking (FSE, 29). Thus *scholars* and people infected with *scholarliness* "[shift] the view of what earnestness is and" make "busyness with interpretations into real earnestness" (FSE, 34). For Kierkegaard, this busyness with interpretations is all the more censurable because "it is only all too easy to understand the requirement contained in God's word" (FSE, 34). "The most limited poor creature cannot truthfully deny being able to understand the requirement—but it is tough for flesh and blood to will to understand it and to have to act accordingly" (FSE, 34–35).

Another *sly* and *sagacious* way that theorizers avoid action is to claim that *knowledge* attained through philosophical inquiry is necessary and sufficient for right action: "It is assumed that if only the objective truth has been obtained, appropriation is an easy matter" (CUP, 22; cf. 37, 46). Kierkegaard does not think that he can demonstrate that this claim is false and seems to believe that we need revelation to teach us that knowledge of goodness is insufficient for being good. But, curiously, he suggests that Socrates, without the aid of revelation, had intimations of this bad news for theorizers (SUD, 93, 95). And he gives voice to reasonable objections to, or plausible suspicions about, the power of knowledge over action.

One obvious objection is that many people seem to know what they ought to do but fail to do it. Someone who holds that knowledge is sufficient for virtue may respond "that he didn't *really* know it" to any claim that he knew what was right but did not do it. But this response is suspiciously convenient for the objective thinker. For with the excuse, I mean the claim, that what is needed is not striving to do the good, but merely inquiring into it, one can avoid the strain and pain of ethical striving. Moreover, when someone never actually achieves a knowledge that radically transforms his life, but is always seeking such knowledge and postponing practical efforts at life transformation, it is hard to avoid the suspicion that his noble quest for knowledge is really just an ignoble flight from practice. Thus the chicanery of theorizing is to substitute the interesting activity of inquiring about the good for the painful task of striving to become good.

Even supposing that knowledge is sufficient for right action, or goodness, or virtue, it could still be true that coming to know the good requires first striving to do what one believes to be good. And if so, it would be wrong, both ethically and philosophically, to postpone seriously striving to become good until one knew the good.

We can sum up the last few paragraphs by saying that theorizing objectivity evades practice by making an *idol* of knowledge (CUP, 304). By substituting thinking for practice, objectivity ascribes to thinking the value and importance of practice itself, as if the plan were the execution. Similarly, thinking about practice is properly a part of practice, so that when objectivity settles for just thinking about practice without actually practicing, it treats the part as the whole. Finally, when objectivity regards knowledge as possessing the power by itself to transform life, action, and society, it superstitiously treats knowledge as a sort of magical charm. Thus objectivity makes an idol of thinking by ascribing to it a value, completeness, and power that it lacks.

Someone might object that Kierkegaard's practicality is just as extreme and unbalanced as the theorizing that he rejects—someone might object, in other words, that Kierkegaard makes an idol of practice. But this is not so. For subjectivity includes the love of and search for truth and rejects not inquiry as such, but only inquiry for its own sake or just for the sake of knowledge. Kierkegaard's broad inclusiveness is especially evident in the fact that he expresses deep admiration for the theorizing of Lessing and of the ancient Greeks, who, in their honesty and artful acuity, Kierkegaard thinks, expose the theorizing of his contemporaries as mendacious bungling.

Practicality and Indirect Communication

Kierkegaard's purpose as a writer—to communicate an uncompromising practicality or holism—deeply affects the way that he writes. He thinks of his books, not primarily as communications of *doctrine* to be interpreted and understood, but as "existence-communications" to be *used* (CUP, 379–380, 560; cf. 371). Thus Climacus calls an *author* who "misuses what he has borrowed" "from another author" "extremely bothersome," and he says that he is "pleased that the pseudonymous authors . . . have . . . not . . . misused a preface" (CUP, 8, 252). Similarly, he reproaches "speculative thinkers who . . . write that which, if it is to be *read with the aid of action* . . . proves to be nonsense," because their writing cannot be coherently put into action (CUP, 191, emphasis added). He even goes so far as to call communications that cannot be consistently lived *nonsense,* that is, self-contradictions (CUP, 191, 442). Thus he thinks reading with the aid of action can be a method of refutation. For example, Climacus describes a *youth* who, though incapable of refuting or "overcoming Hegel" dialectically, could nonetheless discover absurdity in Hegel's thought if he attempted to use or to live it (CUP, 310). Consequently, to read Kierkegaard and Climacus well requires a user's reading, or a practical hermeneutics.

Let us consider some examples of how Kierkegaard writes to be used or in order to encourage action or a practical attitude in his readers.

Sometimes he exemplifies a practical attitude toward a stock theoretical topic in order to reveal and challenge the theoretical tendency. In his *Journals,* he writes:

> What skeptics should really be caught in is the ethical. Since Descartes they have all thought that during the period in which they doubted they dared not to express anything definite with regard to knowledge, but on the other hand they dared to act, because in this respect they could be satisfied with probability. What an enormous contradiction! As if it

were not far more dreadful to do something about which one is doubtful (thereby incurring responsibility) than to make a statement. Or was
it because the ethical is in itself certain? But then there was something
which doubt could not reach! (JP, 1:774)

Although many people object to skepticism in the name of the practical,
few object to it, as Kierkegaard does in the preceding quotation, on the
grounds that skeptics *contradict themselves* in that they doubt what they
are to say and think but not how they are to act.

Once we see this objection posed, we might well wonder why we did
not think of it ourselves. The answer, perhaps, is that we tend to assume
unquestioningly that the significance of skepticism must be merely theoretical. We scarcely suspect that the most trenchant objections to doubt
might be practical—or, contrariwise, that one might seriously attempt to
live skepticism, even though the ancient Greek skeptics attempted to do
precisely this. And if we are surprised by Kierkegaard's serious, practical objection to skepticism, we might go on to consider whether we have
irrationally contracted our conception and execution of the practical.

The *Postscript* contains a paragraph that illustrates how Kierkegaard
aims artfully to induce his readers to shift their attention from theory
to practice (CUP, 312–313). It begins metaphysically with the problem
of *continuity* within *motion*. More clearly, its point of departure is the
metaphysical problem of how one thing stays the same thing even as it
changes, so that one and the same thing is changing. After discussing
this problem about *substance* in a metaphysical-philosophical mode for a
few lines, Climacus writes that "the difficulty for the existing person is to
give existence the continuity without which everything just disappears"
(CUP, 312). With this surprising change of direction and orientation,
Climacus converts the theoretical enigma of the metaphysical basis of
continuity within change into the existential task of giving one's own life
continuity by devoting oneself to a unifying ideal. Thus the existential
alchemy of Climacus transmutes metaphysical conundrums into practical imperatives.

The artistry with which Climacus constructs the paragraph under
consideration is marvelous. He begins it by appealing to the reader's
theoretical or philosophical interest in a metaphysical problem. He even
pretends to share that interest (cf. PV, 45–46). Then, without overtly rejecting the metaphysical impulse, he subtly redirects it toward a practi-

cal, existential task. To put it simply, he entices his readers with something metaphysical to be understood in order to catch them off guard with something practical to perform.

Kierkegaard's efforts to communicate practicality can give the misleading impression that he endorses irrationalism. Consider the following famous passage from the *Postscript*:

> If someone who lives in the midst of Christianity enters, with the knowledge of the true idea of God, the house of God, the house of the true God, and prays, but prays in untruth, and if someone who lives in an idolatrous land but prays with all the passion of infinity, although his eyes are resting upon the image of an idol—where, then, is there more truth? The one prays in truth to God although he is worshiping an idol; the other prays in untruth to the true God and is therefore in truth worshiping an idol. (CUP, 201)

On a first reading, this passage appears to reject, in the name of the "passion of infinity," the objective concern for knowing or accurately describing reality as it is. But this is a misreading. For the passage in question acknowledges that there is an important difference between the true God and a mere idol. And it does not say, as it might at first sight seem to say, that passionate idolatry is an adequate form of truth, but only that it is more true than passionless, objective correctness.

Consider now another passage about prayer, also from the *Postscript*:

> To pray is . . . a very simple matter. . . . And yet how difficult! Intellectually, I must have an altogether clear conception of God, of myself, and of my relationship with him, and of the dialectic of the relationship of prayer—lest I confuse God with something else so that I do not pray to God, and lest I confuse myself with something else so that I do not pray—so that in the relationship of prayer I maintain the distinction and the relationship. (CUP, 162)

This quotation shows that Climacus places a high value on having a correct conception of God—not for the sake of theoretical accuracy, but for the sake of praying adequately. Thus this easy-to-understand passage on prayer corrects the misleading impression of the preceding difficult passage on prayer. But, we might ask, if Climacus cares so much about having a correct conception of God, why does he irresponsibly give the misleading impression that he does not?

If one is treating people whose disease is that they always turn ideals to enact into theories to contemplate, it is unlikely that one will set them on the road to recovery by plainly explaining their disease to them—since more likely than not they will use the explanation as just more grist for the theoretical mill. A much better treatment might be a sort of shock therapy that disrupts and derails, or flouts and frustrates, their pathological habits of thinking. And if a little exaggeration, or some misleading misdirection is required for this therapy, so be it. Thus the passage on prayer that gives the impression that Kierkegaard does not care what God really is might be said to use a strategy of therapeutic disorientation.

Climacus very clearly explains the necessity of downplaying knowledge and conceptual correctness, even though he acknowledges their profound importance. "My main thought was that, because of the copiousness of knowledge, people in our day have forgotten what it means *to exist,* and what *inwardness* is." Moreover, if what it means to exist "is communicated as knowledge, the recipient is mistakenly induced to understand that he is gaining something to know." Therefore, "sensible communication" "consists in" taking his "copious knowledge" "away from him" either by showing that he does not know what he thinks he knows, or by stressing appropriation, or even by seeming to deny the existence or importance of knowledge, at least provisionally. "Only the person who has an idea of a misunderstanding's tenacity in assimilating even the most rigorous attempt at an explanation and yet remaining a misunderstanding, only he will be aware of the difficulty of an authorship in which care must be taken with every word" in order not to encourage the search for more knowledge (CUP, 249). It is easy to imagine that this care often requires denying the importance or existence of knowledge.

The passage that accuses skepticism of an enormous practical contradiction, the passage that initially seems metaphysical but quickly turns to the practical, and the passage on prayer that seems to disregard conceptual correctness in order to promote a complete response to divinity are not isolated, exceptional passages in Kierkegaard's writings, but are emblematic of the way that he writes in general. For Kierkegaard characteristically writes as a corrective to objectivity, challenging it, shocking it, and saying things that objective readers are likely to misinterpret as irrational or skeptical.

Objective Self-Deception Contrasted with
Subjective Self-Examination

As we have seen, Kierkegaard regards objectivity as an evasion of ethical and religious action. This evasion is both caused by and is in turn a cause of self-deception. To see how this might be so, let us examine the following passage from *Judge for Yourself!*

> This is the truth of the matter. In every human being there is a capacity, the capacity for knowledge. And every person—the most knowing and the most limited—is in his knowing far beyond what he is in his life or what his life expresses. Yet this misrelation is of little concern to us. On the contrary, we set a high price on knowledge, and everyone strives to develop his knowing more and more. (JFY, 118)

This passage begins with an echo of the claim we saw Kierkegaard making back in chapter 1 that all people have at least some ethical knowledge. Then it goes on to assert that all people's ethical action falls short of their ethical knowledge, or that all people fail in some way or another to put their ethical knowledge into practice. Finally, it concludes by saying that no one is sufficiently concerned about his failure to apply his ethical knowledge, even though "it is infinitely further from the clearest understanding to doing accordingly than it is from the profoundest ignorance to the clearest understanding" (JFY, 116). For, if we were genuinely concerned about the fact that our behavior does not measure up to the standard of our ethical understanding, we would try harder to enact what we understand. But instead of using this simple remedy, we typically seek instead to extend our understanding or knowledge. Thus arises the suspicion that we use the search for knowing as a way to delay or to evade ethical action.

Suppose for a moment that the ulterior motive of many inquiries is to evade action. If so, it is likely that our search for knowledge is often based on the delusion that we need to increase our knowledge before we begin to act in earnest. It is not hard to imagine why this might be so. Serious ethical action is often dangerous, or painful, or embarrassing, or laborious, or merely inconvenient; therefore it is frequently safer, more comfortable, and easier to inquire instead of acting. Surely we can all see that there is no harm in trying to get a little clearer about the issues before taking any dangerous or inconvenient action; surely one cannot "think too precisely on the point" (*Hamlet*)—right?

If it is true that inquiry is often based on self-deception, it would not be surprising to discover that inquiry often intensifies or compounds the self-deception from which it takes its start. One simple way that inquiry can lead to self-deception is by delaying action. Delay has much power to deceive. Anti-Climacus claims that if "a person does not do what is right at the very second he knows it—then, first of all, knowing simmers down" (SUD, 94). This is to say that not acting immediately on one's knowledge is a way of forgetting what one knows. Even a little self-examination confirms, in my own case at least, that a human being sometimes procrastinates in the hope that tomorrow his conscience will not be so urgent and insistent about some difficult task. Moreover, there are many ways to prolong inquiry so as to delay acting. One can create confusions and complications, or diversions and digressions. Therefore, when one already knows enough to act but instead of acting inquires further into what to do—or into something else altogether—the suspicion arises that the purpose of this investigation may well be to forget one's inconvenient knowledge so as to evade acting on it. And this is to say that inquiry, whose very definition is the search for truth, can be perverted into a search for *untruth*. Thus arises the rule that the "good must be done immediately," that is, before one has a chance to forget it (SUD, 94; cf. JFY, 116, 120; JP, 1:653, 4).

Inasmuch as self-deception by delay does not aggressively seek to destroy ethical knowledge, but sits by and waits for it to fade away, we might call it passive self-deception, or an ignorance of omission. One advantage of delusion by delay is that its very passiveness makes it difficult to detect, and, once detected, makes it seem more innocent than it is. Just as the forgetful and procrastinating servant is less conspicuously disobedient than the overtly rebellious one is, so fruitless and endless inquiry into the good is less conspicuously defiant of the good than an outright evil.

Kierkegaard also describes an active variety of self-deception, which more or less deliberately tries to destroy ethical and religious knowledge. Essentially, active self-deception consists in using thinking "to make excuses and look for excuses" (J, 1:649, 10). In other words, one can use the power of logical thinking to devise dishonest doubts and difficulties and to invent insincere objections and obfuscations so as to justify not doing what one knows, deep down, to be one's task. Owing to the fact that it does not camp safely behind the fortifications of delay, waiting for ethical and religious knowledge to starve and waste away, but takes the battle to the enemy, this kind of self-deception may be called active.

According to Kierkegaard, self-deception is not a rare phenomenon, but the main cause that many human beings are deficient in "ethical and religious comprehension." He puts the point thus:

> The great majority of men . . . work gradually at eclipsing their ethical and religious comprehension, which would lead them out into decisions and conclusions that their lower nature does not much care for, but they expand their esthetic and metaphysical comprehension, which is ethically a diversion. (SUD, 94)

Given that he sees self-deception as one of the most serious of human problems, Kierkegaard judges that the chief task of rational inquiry is to detect and to overcome delusion. This is why so many of his books have *psychological, psychology,* or *psychologically* in their subtitles or in the titles of their subsections, why he constantly stresses the need for honesty, and why he writes a whole book entitled *For Self-Examination.*[3] Kierkegaard's conviction that the task of reason is to search out and expose delusion goes a long way toward explaining the great difference between his conception and use of reason and most philosophical versions of rationality.

According to Kierkegaard, ethical and religious self-examination is the only sort of investigation that almost no one gets too much of. In other words, although he is suspicious about other forms of inquiry on the grounds that they can be used to evade ethical and religious action, he does not think that ethical and religious self-examination is susceptible to the same perversion. For almost no one thinks carefully and honestly about his faults and failings for the mere pleasure of it.[4] Indeed there are times when it would be a relief to cease contemplating the ill deed one has done and to go out and attempt to act better. Therefore, whereas most inquiry tends to be evasion of action, self-examination tends to promote action.

Pretending to Be Irrational as a Tactic of Undeception

In the last chapter I argued that in order to communicate rationality Kierkegaard pretends to be irrational. I will now use his ideas about self-deception to explain why he thinks this pretense is necessary.

According to Kierkegaard, the ideal makes its appearance in the world as its opposite, analogously to the way objects appear *inverted* in a mirror (PC, 198).[5] Similarly, he thinks, when people strive to imitate the ideal, to the world they will appear as the contrary of what they are striving to be. Thus the person who tries truly to "love the neighbor" looks *selfish* and is accused of *selfishness* (WL, 113, 128; TA, 89). And the person who genuinely attempts to be *humble* and to practice *self-denial* appears to be proud and is accused of *pride* (PV, 25). A major cause of this inversion is self-deception. Self-loving, proud, and selfish people want to feel good about themselves and their way of life and therefore feel threatened by a single individual who strives to be truly loving, humble, and selfless. The simplest way to deal with this threat to their comfortable self-complacency is to "band together" in agreement that the striving single individual is a hypocrite who is so proud and self-loving that he or she wants to seem better than everyone else. But if, as Kierkegaard thinks, the single individual is in fact in the right, then the agreement of the many vicious folk is a collective self-deception designed to dismiss the threat of the single individual. We will look into this collective self-deception in detail in the next section.

Let us suppose for a moment that Kierkegaard is exceptionally rational in that he strives to be uncompromisingly consistent. If so, the law of inversion predicts that Kierkegaard will appear irrational to most people (who prefer to be *moderately* and *compromisingly* rational), even if he should vehemently insist that he is rational or indignantly protest that he is not irrational.

Kierkegaard's pretending to be irrational is largely a result of the fact that he accepts the law of inversion and its consequences with good grace. In other words, he does not himself artificially create the illusion that he is irrational, but he humbly and strategically plays along with his readers' delusions that he is.

In *The Point of View for My Work as an Author*, Kierkegaard explains why playing along with an *illusion*[6] is or can be the most effective way of curing it. A "direct attack" on an *illusion,* he says, only makes people *defensive* and *strengthens* them in their illusion, or it *infuriates* them and makes them *shut* themselves "off from you" in their "innermost being" (PV, 43, 45). In other words, a direct attack on an illusion challenges and invigorates the very same forces in the soul that created the illusion in the first place. Therefore, when a person comes face to face with a powerful and direct attack on his delusion, it is likely that he will attempt to preserve it in the only way that he can: by elaborating and strengthening it, thus sinking further into self-deception. Presumably we have all had the frustrating experience of speaking bluntly to someone in order to enlighten him about his faults, only to find that we have made matters worse by provoking him to defend himself irrationally. It was by thinking about such experiences more thoroughly than most of us do that Kierkegaard developed his theory of indirect communication.

Since attacking an illusion directly is likely only to intensify it, Kierkegaard thinks that one must approach an illusion "from behind" (PV, 43). In other words, an illusion can be "removed . . . only indirectly"; one must *deceive* a self-deceived person "into what is true" (PV, 43, 53). To deceive someone into the truth, "one must first and foremost take care to find" the person under the illusion "where he is and begin there" (PV, 45). Meeting a deluded person where he is means "*taking his delusion at face-value,*" that is, pretending his delusion is true or pretending to share it (PV, 54, emphasis added). And since Kierkegaard thinks that his readers have the delusion that he and subjectivity are irrational, he begins his efforts to enlighten them by taking their delusion at face value, that is, by pretending to be irrational. You might say that he "humors them" in order to sober them.

Let us consider an example. Kierkegaard thought that many of his Danish contemporaries suffered from the double illusion that they knew what it meant to be Christians and that they were Christians. This being their illusion, they also would think that true Christians were not Christians and that people who understood Christianity misunderstood it. Therefore, proceeding in conformity with the rules of his "new science" for indirectly communicating Christianity, Kierkegaard did not, he explains, directly attack his contemporaries' illusion that they were well-informed Christians. Instead he took their illusion at face value, by saying to them: As you wish. "You are a Christian, I am not a Christian"

(PV, 54). And then, with this concession as his starting point, he worked slowly, patiently, and indirectly to help his contemporaries discover the true meaning of being a Christian.

Although he does not explicitly admit it, Kierkegaard communicates rationality in the same way that he communicates Christianity, and for the same reasons. In the one case, he was convinced that his contemporaries mistakenly thought that they, and not he, were Christians and that they, and not he, knew what it meant to be Christians. In the other case, he was convinced that his contemporaries mistakenly thought that they, and not he, were rational and that they, not he, knew what it meant to be rational. To correct his contemporaries' delusion about Christianity Kierkegaard pretended that they, and not he, were Christians. Similarly, to correct his contemporaries' delusion about rationality Kierkegaard pretended that they, and not he, were rational. And in each case, he pretended to be something that he was not because he thought that presenting himself in his true form would have been a counterproductive provocation of the delusion he aimed to dispel.

Kierkegaard thinks that the basis for his pretense of irrationality is or ought to be love. For "to love is to be transformed into likeness to the beloved" (JP 3:2450).[7] Therefore, if the beloved is irrational, love transforms itself into something irrational in order to be transformed into the likeness of the beloved. Incidentally, being transformed into the likeness of someone is obviously a very effective way, perhaps the most effective way, of meeting that person where he is. Therefore, as God transformed himself into a human being out of love in order to meet humanity where it is, so Kierkegaard transforms himself out of love into an irrational writer in order to meet his irrational readers where they are.[8]

Let us sum up the recent line of argument. Kierkegaard's pretense of irrationalism is based on both dialectics and on psychology. Dialectically, this pretense is an application of Socratic pedagogy, which begins with the learner's own assumptions and from these assumptions attempts to find a path to the truth. Since Kierkegaard thinks that his readers believe that both he and genuine Christianity are absurd and irrational, he begins precisely with this belief. In other words, he employs what is sometimes called "immanent criticism" on his readers, which is immanent in that it works as much as possible from within his readers' own mentality in order to transform it from within.

Psychologically, Kierkegaard is aware that his message is hard to take, challenging, unflattering, and even downright offensive. He is further aware that to begin with a forthright statement of his offensive message would not only be ineffective, but it would provoke or intensify in his readers self-deception and other irrational evasions of his message. Therefore he begins where his readers are in order to disarm them, make them feel more at ease, and thus win a hearing from them so as to be in a position to lead them to where he wants them to go. One psychological strategy that he employs, and which we saw in his use of the pseudonymous persona of Johannes de Silentio, is to mirror his readers to themselves, so that they may see themselves and their own irrationality external to themselves, where it is easier to begin to see it, in the hope that they will then discover the same thing closer to home.

A large part of the purpose of both the dialectical and the psychological dimensions of Kierkegaard's pedagogical pretense of irrationalism is to induce readers as much as possible to discover by their own self-activity both their own irrationality and the greater rationality of subjectivity and Christianity. For if readers discover the truth for themselves, they will understand it better; accept, own, and value it more deeply; and therefore be more likely to apply it to their own lives.

The Universal versus the Single Individual

In this section we will explore Kierkegaard's account of the social and political dimensions of objectivity's self-deceiving evasion of ethical and religious action.

According to Kierkegaard, "in our age the principle of association ... is an evasion, a dissipation, and illusion," or self-deception (TA, 106). By "lumping together" in the "established order" or "the public" or in the *mob, mass, crowd,* or *herd,* people try to evade their ethical and religious *responsibility* (TA, 106; PC, 85–90; TA, 90, 93; PC, 17; SUD, 34; TA, 62; PV, 106–107). Thus objective people cease to regard themselves as personally responsible for what they do or think. They feel responsible neither for the good that is yet undone, to do it, nor for the evil that they have done, to repent of it. Instead, if anyone or anything is responsible, it is some *abstraction* such as the *public*.

Objectivity contrives not only to transfer responsibility from single individuals to the collective, but also to lower the standards of behavior. Feeling that the *ideal* or the "unconditional requirement" of ethics and religion is "too rigorous," the group "scales down" the requirement and, as much as possible, abolishes *guilt* and *repentance* as morbidity and extremism. Objective people's chief means of scaling down the absolute requirement is to judge themselves by *comparison* with "the others" (PV, 134). If a person meets the mediocre norm of the majority, which he helps to set by his own paltry efforts, then why should he worry about the absolute requirement? Better to adhere to that safe and comfortable adage, "nothing too much," and thereby *exempt* oneself "from the least little decision," than to "torture and torment" oneself "with the enormous criterion of ideality" (PC, 90).

One might suppose that only uneducated or unthinking people shirk personal responsibility and lose themselves by accepting the *authority* of the crowd, the public, or the established order. But, according to Kierkegaard, all people are tempted to disavow their responsibility, and all people do in fact disavow it to some degree or another, even famous philosophers. The "mass-man" does this naïvely, while a philosopher such as Hegel does it with sophistication. For Hegel thinks that "the rational" must arise from and be instantiated in social and political customs and institutions. In other words, he thinks that the reason of a single individual cannot transcend the historical, political, and social conditions in which it is embedded. Since Kierkegaard thinks that single individuals can discover and criticize the irrationality of the established order, and ought in fact to judge for themselves, it might be said that he has more confidence than the extreme rationalist Hegel in the reason of single individuals, while Hegel has higher esteem than Kierkegaard does for the rationality of the established order. Thus the difference between them consists not so much in the fact that the one respects reason and the other does not, but in their conception and use of reason, especially in their ideas about the bearer or agent of rationality.

One of the main principles of objectivity is that the truth is *the universal*. Although Kierkegaard often seems to reject the universal, he in fact thinks that one and the same truth stands over all people and demands their allegiance (see chapter 1). Furthermore, he thinks, all people would agree about the truth that overarches them if they were sufficiently honest and courageous, and if they had put themselves in a position to experience it through ethical and religious striving. But he disagrees with objectivity's claim that the established order is or can be *the rational*, or the standard and arbiter of rationality. For, he thinks, since there are truths that many people do not want to know, do not try to know, and even do their best not to know, it is therefore unreasonable to determine the truth by *voting*, whether one does this naïvely like the mass-man or in the super-sophisticated style of Hegel.

Kierkegaard thinks that the attempt to evade responsibility by join-ing the "human throng" is the result of many ignoble interests and irrational vices. There is *cowardice,* which craves "total peace and secu-rity" and therefore avoids the dangers and *suffering* entailed by striving to fulfill the absolute requirement, and which fears to stand alone in opposition to the opinions and disapproval of the public, who deem the "single individual" to be irrational or insane (PC, 88). There is the *laziness* that wants to evade "strenuous tasks" and that craves ease and comfort (PC, 88). There is the *dishonesty* that does not examine itself in order to find its own deepest convictions, but instead gets its be-liefs ready-made from the factory of public opinion and thus "always live[s] by adaptation and comparison" (JP, 1:654). There is the *envy* of the *mediocre majority,* which invents that "monstrous abstraction," that *phantom* called "*the public,*" which the majority uses for *leveling,* that is, for negating the distinction between excellence and heroic striving for the ideal on the one hand, and its own complacent contentment with mediocrity, on the other (TA, 63, 84, 90). And there is *pride,* which leads people to "join forces and abandon themselves in order to become something *en masse*"; "they dare to live only in great herds and cling to-gether *en masse* in order to be at least something" (CUP, 346, 356; original emphasis).

This pride culminates in the "deification of the established order," which wants to "fancy that . . . now we have achieved the highest" (PC, 88). "Under the guise of worshiping and adoring God, they worship and adore their own invention . . . in self-complacent joy, since they them-selves are the inventors" (PC, 92). In the literal sense of the word, this self-deifying monstrous abstraction called the *public* is an *idol.*

Thus people constitute themselves as a public in order to evade personal responsibility, to scale down ethical and religious requirements, and to have a substitute for the individual greatness that they forfeit. One might say that a public is a sort of conspiracy to indulge in ignoble irrationality and call it normalcy.

Once constituted, a public escapes the control of the conspirators who created it and becomes "an abstract power," or a *demon,* "which no individual can control" and which tends to *level* all important human distinctions in its wake (TA, 86). Thus a public is doubly decadent, first by deliberate choice, then by a sort of possession; this is why "not even the most cowardly of all the individuals was ever as cowardly as the crowd always is" (PV, 108).

The public is not content merely to excuse or secure indulgence of its vices and irrationality, but it goes further, justifying itself, legitimating itself, and brazenly proclaiming that its vices are virtues, that its irrationality is rationality. As Anti-Climacus puts it, in its own eyes the "established order is the rational" and "always insists on being the objective" (PC, 90, 86). But in order to pull this off it must also regard the truly reasonable as unreasonable. Being *mediocre,* it calls striving to fulfill the ideal *insanity, exaggeration,* and extremism. Being cowardly, it calls *courage foolishness* and *rashness.* Being *cowardly* and *proud,* it calls *humble courage arrogance* and *pride.* Being *selfish,* it calls true *self-denial* and *true love selfishness* and *self-love.* And in short, being irrational, objectivity calls itself the rational and the objective and calls true reason unreasonable and *absurd.*

To transpose a point made in the last section, Kierkegaard often deals with objectivity's perversion of names by initially conceding to it honorifics like *reason.* Similarly, following Hegel's lead, he often uses *universal* to refer to the established order and to its ideas about what is true and good. Thus when Kierkegaard or his pseudonymous authors claim that the "single individual is higher than the universal," they mean that the single individual is higher than the established order, not that there is no intelligible truth that stands over all people (FT, 56). For, as Climacus puts it, "existence . . . is a system . . . for God" (CUP, 118).

Climacus explicitly claims that subjective thinkers communicate the universal (meaning, in this case, something that transcends all established orders), but indirectly, so that the universal in their hands looks irrationally individualistic (CUP, 73). Therefore, when Kierkegaard and his pseudonymous authors assert the primacy of the single individual over the universal they are not rejecting reason, or universal truth, but the mob-mentality of objectivity and affirming, like Socrates, that the reason of the single individual is a better judge of truth than a crowd. And if it is true that the reason of every single individual who stands alone before God is a better judge of the truth than a crowd, then subjectivity, which requires standing alone, is more rational than objectivity with its group-thinking and its reliance on the authority of the established order.

Some of Kierkegaard's formulations of the idea of standing alone are virtually identical to Enlightenment ideas of reason. For instance, Climacus praises the rationalist Lessing for his *autopsy*, which is literally seeing for oneself, and claims that "faith is autopsy," thus presenting faith as conforming to the Enlightenment and rationalist ideal of judging for oneself (CUP, 64; PF, 70, 102). Similarly, Kierkegaard insists that a thinker must achieve *primitivity*, which in part means overcoming custom, tradition, and prejudice in order to ask and answer fundamental ethical and religious questions for oneself (JP, 1:657). This idea of primitivity sounds like it could have originated with Descartes, the father and epitome of Enlightenment rationalism. And since standing alone before God is autopsy and primitivity, it is an affirmation of reason, which, ironically, is often taken for a rejection of reason.

Despite these arguments, it is undeniable that Kierkegaard's promotion of the individual and demotion of the universal nonetheless seem at times a lot like relativistic irrationalism. Furthermore, it might be objected that inasmuch as every human being is finite and fallible, not seeking correction or confirmation from one's fellow human beings in rational dialogue is a recipe for persisting in delusion, or even for becoming a kook. Finally, one might object that in rejecting the authority of the established order Kierkegaard goes to the opposite extreme, when he could have adopted the middle and moderate way of Socrates, who said that while he did not know how to persuade "the many," he knew how to use dialectic to "provide one witness" for what he said, namely, the person with whom he was conversing.[9] Thus, instead of the single individual, Socrates has the idea of two individuals who transcend their individuality in and by rational dialogue.

I will respond to these objections, not with the purpose of establishing that Kierkegaard is entirely right about single individuality, but only to support my claim that he intends the idea of the single individual as a rational ideal, and that this ideal is rationally defensible.

The irrational extreme of single individuality is a relativism that gives every individual an equal share in the truth. Climacus rejects this extreme when he calls the claim that "everything is relative," "Protagoras's sophism" (CUP, 33). Thus Climacus indicates that he rejects the irrationally extreme version of single individuality.

In an important sense all of us, willy-nilly, are single individuals. Climacus argues at length that everyone, even someone who thinks that he regards the voice of religion or revelation as more authoritative than his own, must *trust himself* in deciding to trust this or that authority and trusts what he trusts on the authority of his own reason or conscience (CUP, 24, 34–46). In other words, the person who trusts something else, even God, more than he trusts himself cannot avoid first trusting himself to assess the other whom he decides to trust "more than himself." Therefore, the idea of an authority that abolishes the need for self-reliance is an illusion. And since Kierkegaard knows this and argues for it, it would be a mistake for us to think that he rejects the self-reliance proper to reason in favor of religious authority or revelation.

Kierkegaard admits, even insists, that we are all finite and fallible human beings, especially when it comes to matters of faith (CUP, 426, 611). And though he thinks there are many irrational ways of treating others as authorities, he is not entirely against taking counsel with others as a correction to one's finitude and fallibility. Indeed, sometimes he explicitly invites his readers to refute him if they can. Moreover, if being a single individual meant refusing altogether to consult with others, then Kierkegaard would contradict himself by writing for others, even maieutically, and by reading and learning from Lessing, Hamann, and Socrates. Therefore Kierkegaard thinks that consultation with others is acceptable and even required, as long as one consults in the right way, that is, without irrationally attempting to foist the responsibility for one's beliefs and decisions onto them. Furthermore, Kierkegaard could urge that if, as he believes, there is a God before whom one can and ought to stand alone, then in "standing alone before God" one is in fact taking counsel with the highest mind and asking for its assistance, illumination, and revelation. This is why he sometimes speaks of *knowing* this or that "with God." Thus Kierkegaard is aware of and takes measures to correct for the problem of human finitude and fallibility.

He is also aware of the danger of becoming a kook or of going mad if one cultivates radical solitude. That is partly why he emphasizes that one stands alone before God in "fear and trembling." But, he would add, standing with others by conforming to the established order is always a form of madness and irrationality, even though the world affirms and rewards this madness, so that taking one's stand by oneself is one's only chance at true sanity and rationality—though it also risks a spectacular madness that is sure to be punished by the scorn and ostracism of the world.

To the claim that Socrates found a middle way between irrational collectivism and single individuality, Kierkegaard might respond that it is debatable whether Socrates often succeeded in securing the serious agreement of his solitary examinees. Socrates did, to be sure, often show that his interlocutors held confused and self-contradictory ideas, but this is not the same as winning their approval of his own convictions. In any case, Kierkegaard thinks that Socrates himself was a single individual and used the *category* of *"the single individual . . .* in a decisively dialectical way . . . in order to disintegrate paganism. In Christendom it will be used a second time in the opposite way, to make people (the Christians) Christians" (PV, 123; original emphasis). Kierkegaard's claim that the greatest hero of reason accepted the ideal of the single individual alone before God indicates that Kierkegaard himself sees single individuality as a kind of rationality that may or even must engage in dialogue with other human beings.

Kierkegaard's conviction that being rational requires being a single individual goes a long way toward explaining why he often appears, and even pretends to be, irrational in his writings, many of which he dedicates to "that single individual." As a single individual writing for single individuals he has the paradoxical task of *setting* his readers *free,* of *helping* them "to stand alone" (CUP, 74; WL, 274). A paradoxical task calls for a paradoxical solution. Accordingly, in order to get readers to rely on their own reason, Kierkegaard thinks that he must take measures to "decline partnership" with them and thus to *repel* them (CUP, 69, 383–384). Chief among these repelling measures is that he presents himself as a dubious and unreasonable character, so that his readers cannot comically contradict themselves by attempting to be self-reliant on his authority. As St. Thomas Aquinas informs us, Boethius deemed the argument from authority to be the weakest of arguments.

Many people claim to teach Socratically and to practice the art of midwifery. But almost every self-styled midwife at some point or in some way loses faith in the learners and then obtrudes on their freedom by trying to implant knowledge in them. Few imitators of Socrates evince as much consistency in their maieutic practice as Kierkegaard does when he pretends to be irrational so as to invite learners to be rational in the only way they can—on their own *responsibility,* at their own *risk,* and by their own *self-activity.*

Kierkegaard pretends to be irrational not only to *communicate* rationality, but also *to be* rational. For he thinks that the person who eagerly tries to convince others of something usually needs (or develops the need for) others to endorse his ideas and actions. Alternatively, he thinks that the person who sets up to be an authority for others more often than not ends up conferring on them authority over himself. Therefore, in order to be rational it is arguably necessary to take steps to divest oneself of authority.

Kierkegaard's ideas about Christian suffering help to explain why a reasonable person should avoid becoming an authority. He claims that specifically Christian suffering means "to do good and then to have to suffer for it" (JFY, 169). Such suffering suggests that one loves the good for its own sake, and not for the sake of the world's reward, or that one loves the reality of the ideal, and not an appearance of ideality. Similarly, by enduring the lesser martyrdom of being thought irrational because one is rational, a subjective thinker such as Kierkegaard unobtrusively declares that he values reason for its own sake. But "most people have no intimation of this superiority over oneself . . . of wanting to be incognito in such a way that one seems lowlier than one is" (PC, 129).

Two Rival Versions of Dialectic

Kierkegaard analyzes objectivity as idolatry of logic. According to his analysis, objective thinkers do not adequately acknowledge the limits of logic, do not face up to logic's liability to perversion, and consequently do not take adequate measures to detect, correct for, or prevent this perversion; they fail to seek, develop, and use sources of knowledge other than logic; they typically overestimate how much they have accomplished by means of their logical investigations; and, finally, they neglect or avoid ways of relating to the truth other than logically cognizing it, so that the ulterior motive of their obsession with logic is to avoid the subjective task of striving to conform to the truth as whole persons.

All logical thinking rests on premises. Although you can take any given premise and attempt to prove it logically, without arguing in a circle it is not possible logically to prove *all* of your premises, so that logical thinking is essentially either hypothetical or circular. Therefore, if you wish to move beyond mere hypotheses or fallacious circularity in your thinking, you must either make use of nonlogical means of knowing premises or concoct a potion to transmute vicious circularity into a virtue.

In Kierkegaard's estimation, philosophical solutions to the problem of premises are almost always comically inadequate. All too often philosophers proceed like the foolish builder who tried to compensate for his skyscraper's lack of a solid foundation by firmly joining together all its stories or like the fantastic architect who designed an edifice which was to be founded on its own roof. For example, Descartes—whether seriously or in jest—relies on "clear and distinct perception" to prove the existence of God and uses the existence of God to prove the reliability of clear and distinct perception. Thus goes the comedy of the "Cartesian circle."

According to Climacus, Hegel proposed what is perhaps the most ludicrous solution ever to the problem of premises when he claimed to begin the *System* of "absolute knowledge" *"without presuppositions,"* and then to use *mediation,* the logical movement of his *dialectic,* to transform this immediacy into absolute knowledge (CUP, 111–117, emphasis added). Thus, Hegel (as interpreted by Climacus) superstitiously ascribes to logic a magical power to create knowledge virtually out of nothing, or at least without premises, and his boast that he begins the System dialectically, but without presuppositions, betrays an egregious self-deception by which he and his followers hide their real assumptions from themselves, with the result that these assumptions exert a secret, irrational influence on their thinking. Better to be aware of one's assumptions as assumptions, than to be wholly unaware of them, or to be under the illusion that they are more than assumptions.

Logic can be used as a cosmetic to plaster over its own shaky foundations. Take the case of public argumentation, whose ostensible purpose is to refute error, explore possibility, and prove truth. Though the official intention is noble, the actual execution is often base. As Kierkegaard points out, very often what is really going on in public argumentation is that the participants are seeking confirmation or affirmation from others, and thus setting up others as authorities over themselves. Furthermore, people use the fact that they have *proven* something to someone else who shares their assumptions as a way of forgetting that what they have proven rests on questionable premises. When one shares an idea with others, it feels somehow more *probable,* to use a term of art from Kierkegaard's analysis of ideology. Thus public argumentation might be a good idea in principle, but in practice it is often a collaborative effort at self-deception, even when every inference is rock-solid.

Despite its many successes, logic does not always live up to its potential for clarity and rigor. The very existence of the word *sophistry* bears witness both to logic's liability to perversion and to the gullibility of human beings in the face of fallacious reasoning. We are especially susceptible to sophistry when we reason about ethical matters. Thus the word *casuistry,* originally coined to describe skillful ethical reasoning about specifics, has become virtually synonymous with ethical sophistry. The corruptibility of ethical thinking is a result of the fact that ethical truths often demand the frustration or moderation of deep and powerful desires, such as the desires for safety, comfort, wealth, honor, sex, and other pleasures. When these desires are threatened by the strenuous requirements of ethics, they fight back with astonishing cunning and sagacity, by co-opting the powers of logic for specious reasoning and for self-deception.

Extensive training and practice in logical thinking is no sure protection against sophistry. Well-known philosophers often accuse one another of faulty reasoning about the most trifling matters. And if philosophers err in their reasoning when little is at stake, how much more will they stray from the narrow path of truth when ethics calls their whole way of life into question and demands the denial of deeply rooted desires—desires which, moreover, have repeatedly proven their capacity to interfere with the delicate operations of logic. Finally, if philosophers slip in their public reasonings when their reputation is at stake and when they know that rivals lurk here and there to expose and ridicule their blunders, how much more will they err when they reason alone with themselves, with no fear of being pilloried, about things that they may be reluctant to think about in the first place.

Some professional philosophers insist that the purpose of philosophy is not to discover how to lead a better life or even that philosophy has nothing to do with this.[10] Given their opinion about the function of philosophy, consistency demands that such professionals not submit the ideas grounding their lives to the criticisms and objections of others in philosophical dialogue, but presumably they will use the skills of their trade to justify *to themselves* how they live and act. This insulated self-justification is surely a recipe for highly effective self-deception.

Though one sensible motive for acquiring competence in logical analysis is to protect oneself against sophistry, it is arguable that the more skill one has at logic, the better one will be at using it to deceive oneself. Just as the devil can quote scripture for his own ends, so self-deception can co-opt logic for rationalizing its delusions. And the self-deceiving sophistry that we perpetrate on ourselves is often the most effective and least detected fallacy.

Outright fallacy is not the only perversion of logic. Even valid reasoning can be used to "find and to make excuses" or for evading one's ethical responsibility. The better the logic, the better the excuse. The formula of excuse making is widely known: just use one's dialectical skill to create complications, confusions, doubts, and objections; or to raise difficult and subtle questions; or to make *quibbling irrelevant* distinctions (FSE, 43); or to elaborate on barely relevant extenuating circumstances; or, in short, to devise digressions and diversions. After all, one must think things through very carefully before one acts. Intellectual integrity and philosophical responsibility require it, as Hamlet is my witness.

If, despite these arguments, readers remain doubtful about the corruptibility of logic, I ask them to make the following thought experiment. Imagine that you are married to a philosopher who is an especially acute and astute reasoner. Imagine further that you yourself are neither philosophically trained nor naturally adept at logic. Imagine, finally, that though your philosopher-spouse is not a scoundrel, has some noble ideals, etc., he or she also has the not uncommon weakness of wanting a little too much to be in the right in marital conflicts. On the assumption that you will sometimes be defenselessly correct in disagreements with such a spouse, how would you like to argue with him or her about your life together? If the prospect of living and arguing with such a person seems worrisome to you, then perhaps you will agree that the more adept a person is at logic, the more cunning will he or she be in subtly perverting it, whether intentionally or unintentionally.

Despite the many ways that logical thinking can be perverted in the service of self-deception, objective thinkers do not, according to Kierkegaard, take adequate measures to detect, correct, or prevent this perversion. And because they do not turn to themselves as single individuals in the reflection of earnest self-examination, they in effect consent to delusion, even court or cultivate it, and are thus irrational.

Given objectivity's vulnerability to self-deception, we should expect to find many delusions in the claims that it makes for itself when it sets out to understand the world. In the next section of this chapter we shall consider the objective delusion of systematicity, and now we shall consider the dialectical delusion of objectivity.

When we make serious attempts to understand ourselves and our world, we discover opposites indissolubly bound up with one another. For example, we find that material things are both continuous and discrete, or that human beings are both objects in the world and subjects and agents who are conscious of the world and act in it, or that human beings are both particular and universal—particular in perhaps an obvious way, and universal in that they have a capacity to conceive universals and to instantiate them in their actions. Both objectivity and subjectivity agree that these things are so, and that they are puzzling. But (Hegelian) objectivity and (Kierkegaardian) subjectivity differ in that the former claims that it can comprehend the unity of opposites in theory, and, consequently, reconcile them in practice, while the latter claims that the unity of these opposites can be understood only in part, and consequently remain mysteries or paradoxes that defy comprehension. To take the distinction further, the function of the Hegelian dialectic is to unite opposites in thought, and the function of the Kierkegaardian dialectic is to show that the relation of many key pairs of opposites is paradoxical, and that these paradoxes pose a practical task for human beings, thereby exposing the fallacies and pretensions of Hegelian dialectic.

Even if logical thinking were ever so clever at explaining paradoxes, instead of being a dunce about them, and ever so pure, instead of being liable to perversion, and ever so powerful, instead of being conditioned and limited by its premises, Kierkegaard would still diagnose objectivity's obsession with logical thinking as a disease compromising the integrity of the human person. For objectivity is hypertrophy of the logical faculty, atrophy of the imaginative, emotive, volitive, and active faculties, and a disintegration of all human faculties. It is obvious that there can be little health in this objective constitution, being as it is a disequilibrium and conflict of the faculties—nor much rationality, unless we human beings really are pure minds called on to ignore or neglect everything except academic dialectic.

Logic's role in subjectivity is very different from its role in objectivity. Subjective thinkers such as Kierkegaard respect logic immensely and use it extensively. Climacus even claims that it has the authority to make "absolute distinctions," or eternally valid inferences (PF, 108). Despite their respect for logical thinking, however, subjective thinkers use it warily, or with an eye to its limits and its possible perversions. They also develop and artfully use sources of knowledge other than logic. And, most importantly, they integrate logical thinking within a holistic striving to conform to truth.

Subjective thinkers use logic, or dialectic, to think clearly and rigorously about life—how one actually lives, how one might live, and how one ought to live. Every person's life is based on ideas or ideals. But, Kierkegaard thinks, for most people the ideas grounding their lives are a confused and incoherent mishmash. Thus arises the subjective function of logic: to articulate the ideas grounding various ways of life, to show what it means to live each of these ways of life consistently and without confusion, and thereby to distinguish these ways of life from one another. The chief fruit of Kierkegaard's subjective dialectic is his theory of the "stages on life's way," which is an articulation of distinct modes of life set out in a developmental progression. Thus, in a nutshell, the work of dialectic is to expose and to clear up *confusions* about modes of living for the sake of living well. Judging by the constant complaints in Kierkegaard's authorship about the *confusions* of his contemporaries, he thinks that dialectic has a lot of work to do.

As I already indicated, Kierkegaard thinks that honest and perspicacious pondering about human life discovers many paradoxes, or opposites in tension with one another. Consequently Kierkegaard's writings abound in dialectically revealed paradoxes: in order to actualize universal human nature, one must become a single individual who both submits to and transcends the universal; God is both infinitely strict and infinitely lenient; the incarnate God is both lofty and lowly, while the believers who imitate him are both great and humble (they have "paradoxical and humble courage"); human beings in general are both free and bound, or have both possibility and necessity, and therefore must be both respected and manipulated by the teacher of subjectivity; subjective thinking is both positive and negative, and must be communicated by an artful combination of both direct and indirect communication; and the list goes on.

Although Kierkegaard thinks that the highest paradox is the "absolute paradox"—the incarnation of God as an individual human being—it is arguable that the central paradox in the Kierkegaardian corpus is that a human being is a *synthesis* of the *temporal* and the *eternal*, of the *finite* and the *infinite*, of the *necessary* and the *possible*, and of the *particular* and the *universal* (SUD, 29–42; CA, 28, 78; CUP, 56). As he sees it, this paradox presents the *task*, not of theoretically explaining the reconciliation of the opposites, but of actually striving to put the opposites together as well as one can in thought, action, and life (CA, 28, 80). Indeed, subjectivity may be defined as the attempt to become aware of an eternal and infinite goal and to imitate that goal within the limits of one's temporal and socially situated becoming. And since there is no theoretical explanation of how to do this, neither is there a scientific method for achieving it. Instead, putting the opposites together is an *art:* the subjective thinker is an *artist* with *style;* and *existence* itself is an *art* (CUP, 77–80, 86, 277, 349, 351).

Another subjective use of dialectic is the detection and correction of self-deception. Self-deception involves a perversion of logical thinking. Therefore the process of undeception requires that the self-deceived person use logic to discover the sophistries and casuistries that he has been practicing on himself. As Climacus explains, the task of the objective person is not to free himself from objectivity by one heroic effort, but to "work himself through and out of objectivity" (CUP, 67). And since objectivity is a perversion of logic, working one's way through and out of objectivity does not mean ignoring logic, but rectifying one's use of it.

Subjectivity thinks there is such a thing as an overuse of logic. For thinking is more than logic, and life is more than thinking. Not only health, but also rationality requires the development, activity, and integration of all the parts of a person. Therefore logic must neither overgrow its proper size nor overstep its proper role within the organism or economy of personhood.

It might seem that subjectivity's moderation of logic means a sacrifice of truth at the level of cognition. Kierkegaard, however, denies this. Instead, he thinks, logic performs its proper function most effectively when it refrains from meddling in tasks that do not rightly belong to it. Just as the pectoral muscles and triceps perform the bench press more effectively when other muscles, not directly involved in the pressing itself, support the body in the correct posture, so logic seeks the truth most effectively when virtues involving emotions, will, and actions support the human person in the correct posture for knowing the truth. If the postural muscles are neglected, a person becomes injured and unfit for pressing. Similarly, if the ethical virtues are neglected, a person becomes unfit for knowing the most important human truths. For self-deception is a result, not so much of bad thinking, as of vices that cause bad thinking.

Kierkegaard thinks that logic is not the only source of knowledge for a human being. Recognizing that logical thinking ultimately rests on principles that logic itself cannot prove, subjective thinkers strive to develop capacities for knowledge other than dialectic. In chapter 8, I will argue that these noninferential capacities are like logic in that they work best when they are supported by ethical and religious virtues that a person develops by practice. If this is true, then subjectivity's holism is not a compromise of the aim of truth-seeking, but its perfection. A poet said to his mistress: "I could not love thee, dear, so much, loved I not honor more." Similarly, the subjective thinker says to the truth: "I could not *know* you so well if I did not strive to be true to you in my actions."

The ideas about logic discussed in this section help to explain why Kierkegaard rejects *apologetics,* the project of defending and arguing for Christianity with logical thinking. The basic reason that Kierkegaard rejects apologetics is that he thinks it does not produce the sort of awareness of Christ required for making a responsible decision about Christianity, and in some crucial ways, it even obstructs this awareness.

Kierkegaard claims that the right *relation* of a person to Christianity "is not to doubt or to believe, but to be offended or to believe." Therefore the *discussion* in "modern philosophy" about Christianity is *confused* when it speaks of *doubt* instead of *offense* or *despair* (PC, 81). He goes further when he says that "one never comes to faith except from the possibility of offense," and when he suggests that "only two kinds of people can know something about [Christianity]: those who are impassionedly, infinitely interested in their eternal happiness and in faith build this happiness on their faith-bound relation to it, and those who with the opposite passion [offense] . . . reject it—the happy and the unhappy lovers" (PC, 81; CUP, 52). Initially, some of these passages might seem to say that one has to reject the concern for truth when one becomes a Christian. But, taken together, a more plausible interpretation is that a person can and should become so aware of Christ that doubt is no longer a problematic possibility. This interpretation helps to make sense of Kierkegaard's conviction that a person's "eternal salvation is to be decided by" a choice and "a striving in time, in this life" (JP, 3:2551). For the logic of responsibility requires knowledge or understanding, so that being blameworthy for lacking faith in Christ requires being sufficiently aware that one ought to have this faith. Therefore, though Kierkegaard does not think that logic should be used to remove doubts about Christ or to prove that Christ was who he said he was, he nonetheless thinks that nonlogical knowledge of Christ is both possible and required.

Kierkegaard thinks that becoming a Christian requires a revolution in a person, and that an essential part of this conversion is rejecting the basic assumptions by which most people live in order to embrace new foundations for thought and action. A serious problem with apologetics is that it typically begins from premises common to the established order and then attempts to prove that Christianity is probable given these premises. But, Kierkegaard insists, since true Christianity always challenges the lazy, cowardly, and mediocre herd mentality of the estab-

PARADOXICAL RATIONALITY · 67

lished order, it is consequently always improbable in the estimation of that mentality. Therefore, the only way to make Christianity probable is to water it down to accommodate it to politics and society. But to do this, thinks Kierkegaard, is to abolish Christianity, whereas if Christianity were to prevail, it would subvert the establishment.

Finally, Kierkegaard thinks that logic, as Vigilius Haufniensis might say, creates the wrong *mood* for becoming aware of Christ (CA, 14–16, 36). One becomes a Christian by becoming aware of Christ in such a way that one might love and adore him. But the sort of awareness of Christ that results from merely or mainly logical thinking is not loving and adoring awareness. Therefore the logical project of apologetics creates (or more modestly, facilitates) a mood that is inimical both to becoming rightly aware of Christ and to becoming a Christian.

Let us grant, as seems plausible, that Kierkegaard is extreme in his rejection of apologetics, and that he should instead content himself with rejecting some forms of it, or with warning against typical apologetical errors and delusions.[11] Even so, he does not reject apologetics because he rejects reason in matters of faith. Instead, he rejects it *for reasons*. He rejects it because he thinks that reason itself can show that logic cannot serve the function that apologists want it to serve. More generally, he has a rationally worked out idea of faith, reason, and the way to faith according to which reason can and should do some things to promote faith, but not everything. He may be wrong in his rationally worked out idea, but it is all the same intended as a rational idea.

Kierkegaard's indirect communication is to a large degree based on his ideas about the limits of logic, its possible perversions, and its correct use. Kierkegaard writes to promote rational wholeness and integrity in his readers. And since he thinks that logical thinking is only one part of such wholeness and integrity, which also includes imagining, willing, feeling, and acting, his writing does not narrowly focus on logical arguments, but puts together imaginative analogies, lyrical expressions of moods and emotions, polemics against inaction, rhetorical encouragements to action, and dialectic. Moreover, since he thinks that the objective readers whom he wishes to address in his pseudonymous writings are obsessed with logic and pervert it in order to justify their evasion of ethics and religion, he argues with his logic-obsessed readers far less than they might like, so as not to feed their obsession and so as not to invite further perversions. In other words, he thinks that logic is of limited usefulness against the self-deception of others, since self-deceived people, when they are prematurely challenged with logical arguments, often respond by inventing even more lies and sophistries in order to remain in their delusion. Or, as I argued earlier, Kierkegaard thinks that the best way to help deluded people is not to argue with them, but to deceive them into the truth. Finally, since Kierkegaard is convinced that the most important ethical and religious truths are principles to be known directly and not conclusions to be deduced, he does not betray his convictions by logically arguing for what he thinks must be known by means other than logic.

Since Kierkegaard thinks that becoming a Christian requires passing through "the possibility of offense," he sometimes writes so as to provoke offense at Christianity. And since he thinks that most of his readers have been taught a mollycoddling, milksop version of Christianity that obscures the possibility of offense, he emphasizes the offensive aspects of Christianity all the more. This emphasis on the offensive aspects of Christianity is at times extreme and contributes to the impression of readers that Kierkegaard is irrational or uncharitable. But Kierkegaard thinks that the situation confronting him as an author demands a *corrective*, and correctives tend to be extreme and often seem irrational or overly harsh to the people at whom they are aimed (JP, 1:707; cf. PV, 18).

The dialectical character of subjectivity is one of the main reasons that Kierkegaard often communicates subjectivity indirectly. The task of subjectivity is not merely to think, but to be, not merely to theorize the compatibility of opposites, but practically to put them together in one's life and action. Therefore, even in cases in which Kierkegaard thinks that he can explain the reconciliation of a dialectical pair, he sometimes refrains from doing so in order to avoid the theoretical temptation and evasion. Moreover, if people become aware too early that something is only one half of a dialectical pair to be complemented and corrected by its other half, there is a tendency for them not to take the thing seriously, for them to somehow rob the thing of its power, or water it down. For example, Kierkegaard often tries to awaken his readers to an awareness of their sin and to the gravity and seriousness of their sin without so much as mentioning the Christian idea of the forgiveness of sins and grace to heal this disease. He refrains from prematurely mentioning grace and forgiveness, precisely because he wants readers deeply and thoroughly to appreciate the problem of their sin before the solution is offered, so that the solution will also be understood and appreciated, not taken in vain, that is, not used as an excuse to evade taking the problem of sin seriously.

Another reason that Kierkegaard might merely suggest one half of a dialectical pair is that he thinks that the most powerful way to reveal it is indirectly, through its opposite.[12] For example, like Pascal, Kierkegaard thinks that human beings can be deeply wretched precisely because of their potential for grandeur. In other words, humans are often wretched because they sense that they could and ought to be grand. Therefore, Kierkegaard sometimes sets about awakening or developing a sense for the possibility of greatness by the indirect method of starkly emphasizing the actuality of misery.

Owing to the fact that Kierkegaard is a dialectical writer it is necessary to be cautious whenever one encounters a statement in his books that seems extreme, exaggerated, or one-sided. For it is highly likely that this extreme statement is only one half of a dialectical pair of opposites. Sometimes the other half of the pair is obvious and easy to find elsewhere in the same book. Occasionally, however, there is no overt complementary statement, but a suggestion or an implication that comes to light only with careful reading, or only by reading another book in the Kierkegaardian corpus.

The twin facts that subjectivity is dialectical and that Kierkegaard writes dialectically in the service of subjectivity together provide another way of understanding why Kierkegaard pretends to be irrational in order to communicate rationality. Understanding the weakness, limits, and perversion of one's own reason requires that one at least partially transcend these things. In other words, awareness of finitude, temporality, and perversion is an indirect and dialectical awareness of infinitude, eternity, and purity. Thus the power of reason comes to light in the act of becoming aware of its weakness. And this is to say that just as Pascal can reveal the grandeur of human beings by artfully articulating their wretchedness, so Kierkegaard reveals the potential power and purity of reason or of the human mind by artfully expressing its temporality, finitude, and perversion. And since intellectual power comes to light not in Kierkegaard's direct display of it as something to be admired weakly and wistfully, but in the readers' own self-activity or in readers' self-activation of their own dialectical power, the indirect communication of dialectical potency is the fullest and the most effectual communication of it. To put the point simply, Kierkegaard sometimes denigrates reason in an extreme manner in order to provoke his readers to correct him by becoming conscious of reason's potential, and by actualizing it.

System versus *Fragments*

All the idolatries of objectivity converge in its principal idol, the idea of "the system." The most famous, and, Kierkegaard thinks, the most inflated and pretentious system is that of Hegel. Objectivity idolizes logic, and the Hegelian System is one huge chain of arguments putatively created out of nothing by the mediation of mere logic. Objectivity makes an idol of knowledge, and the System claims to be an expression of "absolute knowledge," that is, complete and certain cognition of the *whole*. Objectivity idolizes or *deifies* the "established order," and the Hegelian System sees itself as rooted in and expressing the perfect sociopolitical order. Thus the philosophical idolatry which asserts that the System is logical and perfect public knowledge of the whole corresponds to the sociopolitical idolatry of the established order which announces its own apotheosis.

Although the Hegelian System is now dead and gone, systematizing is still alive and well. For example, scientific naturalists claim to know that all reality is material reality, or that all reality is to be known, to the extent that it can be known, not in diverse ways but exclusively by the public methods of the mathematical and empirical sciences. Even relativism (or some forms of it), whose very purpose might be said to be avoiding the totalizing impulse of system-building, ambitiously claims that all truths, or all truths about controversial matters, are relative and therefore nonuniversal, except of course the putatively absolute and universal truth of relativism itself.

Kierkegaard poses many dialectical objections to the System. We have already considered his arguments against the Hegelian claim to begin the System "without presuppositions." He also argues that systematicians contradict themselves because they claim that the System is complete, but, when pressed, admit that it is "not quite finished," which is especially comical since "a half-finished system is nonsense" (CUP, 107).

Moreover, he argues that although the System claims to represent the culmination of the whole historical development of the world or of the West, it cannot in fact embrace the whole of history, for the simple reason that history is not yet finished (CUP, 149–150). Kierkegaard also argues that in order to construct or to know *the* System, which by definition is complete and perfect, one would need to be an eternal and infinite being. But, he claims, although human beings participate in the eternal and infinite, we are also temporal and finite. Therefore, "existence . . . is a system . . . for God," but not for us, at least this side of eternity (CUP, 118). Finally, his criticisms of the Hegelian claim to reconcile all opposites also apply to the boast of the Hegelians that they have reconciled the grand oppositions between the *whole* of human history with all its many *parts.*

The motive behind the System, according to Kierkegaard, is the desire to evade striving. For if, as the Hegelians claim, the truth has already been accomplished for all of us in the System, then the task of a serious person is just to understand the System, or perhaps to make a scholarly contribution to it, but not to strive, moment by moment, existentially to appropriate the truth. Therefore, Kierkegaard thinks, the System is a surrogate relation to truth whose purpose is to help people evade the struggles and sufferings of individual striving.

Whereas objectivity is systematic, subjectivity is fragmentary. Subjective thinkers strive to know an eternal and infinite ideal and to relate to this ideal in their lives. But, subjective thinkers assert, since human beings are finite, it is questionable whether they can ever grasp or comprehend the infinite and eternal ideal. And since human beings are temporal, they must moment by moment renew their awareness of, and their existential relation to, that ideal. For there is no inertia of the spirit, but all is freedom. And since the ideal eludes our grasp, and our imperfect relation to it fades away whenever it is not actively renewed, our thinking and existing in relation to it are necessarily fragmentary.

To be faithful to the fragmentary character of human relations to the ideal, Kierkegaard writes about the ideal and human relations to it in a fragmentary manner. In other words, he attempts in his writing to express the existential condition of someone striving to appropriate and to imitate the ideal and to encourage such striving in his readers (CUP, 80–83). Moreover, he thinks that the primary truth of subjective writing is not its content, but its form, by which it expresses the human condition and the striving appropriate to it. Therefore, sometimes Kierkegaard might even distort the content of his message and say something that is not literally true in order to redirect the reader to the subjective mode of writing, thinking, and living.

Expressing the truth by the form of one's writing does not consist merely in refraining from making claims to having achieved a system, but in refraining even from expressing *results* in a way that gives the impression that one is finished. Accordingly, Climacus claims that he expresses the *way*, not *results* (CUP, 136–136, 73, 78). This refusal to indulge the desire of objective readers for results that they could carry away from his books sometimes gives the misleading appearance that Kierkegaard is an extreme skeptic. But, as we have seen, Kierkegaard is not such a skeptic; he merely denies that our knowledge of the ideal in this life can be complete or finished once and for all in an eternal comprehension that obviates the need to strive in action.

Incidentally, the need for constant reappropriation of the ideal in time also partly accounts for the repetitive style of the *Postscript,* which is intended to illustrate the process of "artful variation" with which subjective thinkers *renew* their relation to the ideal (CUP, 86, 77).

As putatively complete thinkers, Hegel and the Hegelians have the annoying habit of claiming to appropriate the merely partial truths of other thinkers. Climacus refers to this appropriation as *confiscation* (CUP, 363). Obviously, confiscation does not leave the confiscated ideas in their original form, but alters them, often substantially, so as to fit them into the Procrustean bed of the System. It is not surprising, therefore, that Kierkegaard and his pseudonymous authors take great pains to prevent the Hegelians from co-opting, and thus compromising and corrupting, their subjective message. Part of their strategy for dodging the draft into the system is to hide their meaning in indirection, or to make it seem too irrational to contain anything worth confiscating. When official reason is de facto irrational and insists on co-opting and perverting the authentically rational, then genuine reason must go underground, in the incognito of irrationality.

Professor-Dictation versus Indirect Communication

In this section I will synthesize the remarks about direct and indirect communication scattered throughout this chapter.

Fixated on objects, objective thinkers are under the sway of the logic of objects. For them truth itself is a thing that one person delivers like a parcel into the receptacle of another's mind. The packaging consists of propositions, arguments, theories, systems, or tabulated results of scientific investigation.

Confidence in this direct system of delivery rests partly on the assumption that it is an easy matter for a clever person to understand and apply truths that have been adequately articulated. Reception and application being unproblematic, teachers need not concern themselves with how the learner will receive the teaching. In other words, the objective-thinking, direct-communicating professor naïvely believes that teaching does not require studying either the psychology of learning or the interpersonal dynamics between the student and the teacher.

Because he regards the reception of his teaching as unproblematic, the professor sees himself as a more important agent than the learner in the education of the learner. The professor is the form, the learner the matter to be informed. The teacher gives the truth, and the student passively receives it as the wax receives the imprint of a seal. Having such a picture of himself and of his relation to the learner, the professor tends to think of himself as an authority with the license and duty of imprimatur.

Paradoxically, by setting himself up as an authority over the learners, the professor often ends up granting them authority over himself. For the feeling of one's own authority is intoxicating and addictive. Thus the professor comes to need the approval and ratification of learners, and by needing and seeking their affirmation, he constitutes them as authorities over himself. In order to succeed in winning the approval of his students, it is often necessary for him to pander to them. As Plato argued in the *Gorgias*, easy persuasion of the people that garners praise requires being of the people, accepting and working with their basic assumptions about life and the world instead of challenging them.[13] Typically, these assumptions come from the established order, or, more accurately, from a subsection of the established order. Therefore, despite his pretensions and self-importance, the professor is often not his own person, but essentially a factotum of the state or of this or that political faction.

Thus the objective teacher fails to adapt in the right way, but instead adapts in the wrong way, to the learner. He does not adapt to the true needs of the learner qua learner. But he does adapt to the learner in the way that a salesman adapts to his mark in order to close the deal. This is not to say that teachers are never haughtily aloof from students. Nevertheless, a professor who cares about teaching but does not need the good opinion of at least some of his or her students or readers is a rare creature.

A subjective thinker uses indirect communication to intimate and encourage subjectivity. Knowing that subjectivity is the free self-activity of the single individual, indirect communicators refrain from attempting to do for learners what only they can do for themselves. Instead, he or she aims merely to be an occasion, or a vanishing point, or a Socratic midwife who helps the learner to stand alone, since only when the single individual discovers the truth for himself or herself is it "discovered for" him or her (PF, 14).

Although Socratic midwives do not vainly attempt to give the truth to learners, they nevertheless try to help learners to become more receptive to the truth. They do this by a variety of means: by enticing their readers and winning their attention with poetry and other arts; by suggesting what they wish to communicate rather than by saying it outright, so as to summon learners to exert themselves; by exemplifying the way to the truth in their manner of writing and by showing and encouraging the way of life that supports the discovery of the truth; by gently and indirectly exposing the illusions of learners, which requires pretending to share their illusions and therefore their irrationality too; and, in general, by speaking like "the physician of the soul," that is, by writing therapeutically (SUD, 23).

Since they are aware that subjectivity requires acting for oneself at one's own risk and on one's own responsibility, Socratic midwives do not set themselves up as authorities, and they do not angle for the applause and approval of the learner in a way that gives her authority over them. Instead, they strive to free themselves and to help the learner to free herself from the tyranny that the established order always endeavors to exercise over the hearts and minds of its citizen-subjects. And they seek such freedom so that everyone may become a "single individual alone before God" (SUD, 120, 5).

An Important Qualification

Kierkegaard as presented in this book may seem to be a rather arrogant fellow who regards himself as eminently reasonable and his readers as egregiously unreasonable. Even worse, in pretending to be irrational in order to descend to the low level of existence that he presumes is the milieu of his readers, he seems patronizing and condescending.

This accusation of arrogance attributes to Kierkegaard what he himself would regard as a false dichotomy: that there are rational people, such as, himself, on the one hand, and irrational people, that is, his readers, on the other. Kierkegaard, however, thinks that the truth of the matter is that no one is either perfectly rational or completely irrational, but everyone falls somewhere in a spectrum between these two extremes. Moreover, Kierkegaard thinks, because the human will is free, the rationality of human beings—his own included—is always precarious. Humans are always tempted to pervert ideas intended to guide or to inspire practice into theories to contemplate, or to deceive themselves so as to evade striving, or to set up other people as authorities over themselves so as to shirk personal responsibility. Therefore Kierkegaard does not deem himself fully and stably rational, immune to the temptations of irrationality, nor does he regard his readers as wholly irrational.

Having dissolved this false dichotomy, let us restate the purpose of indirect communication. Kierkegaard does indeed use indirect communication to assist egregiously irrational readers to become less irrational and then more rational, but he also uses it to assist a broad range of readers best described as partly rational and partly irrational to become more fully rational. Thus the idea behind indirect communication is that readers may be irrational enough to need help in undeception, but also be rational enough to do much of the work of undeception for themselves.

Another indication that Kierkegaard is not an exceptionalist who exempts himself from the precariousness of rationality is that he claims that his authorship constitutes and represents his "own upbringing" (PV, 12, 77). In other words, in writing the pseudonymous books he describes his own sins and temptations, and thus works himself through and out of his own objectivity. Therefore it would be misleading merely to say that the pseudonymous books condescend to the reader, and more accurate to say that they describe a path out of objectivity that Kierkegaard himself strives to tread and that he hopes his readers will tread as well.

It is a very important fact that Kierkegaard does not always employ indirect communication in his writings. For in the books that he writes in his own name he uses more or less direct communication, which presupposes *receptivity* and therefore a certain degree of rationality in the reader (PV, 8). This is to say that in his alethonymous books Kierkegaard presupposes that his readers are more or less receptive and rational, and in his pseudonymous books he presupposes that his readers may be unreceptive and therefore irrational. Thus he is so charitable that he attempts to help everyone, both rationally receptive readers and irrationally unreceptive ones, and it would be a bit ungenerous to accuse him of arrogance because he does what he thinks necessary to help even egregiously irrational readers—unless one thinks there are no such people at all.

Curiously, and here's the rub, Kierkegaard's fame as a writer rests mainly on that portion of his authorship that presuppose that readers are irrational. Thus arises the question whether Kierkegaard has written in such a way that readers naturally gravitate toward the books that they need. In other words, are unreceptive, irrational readers naturally attracted to the pseudonymous books, and are receptive, rational readers naturally drawn to the alethonymous books? I myself have spent much more time reading his books for irrational people than his books for rational people—a fact that I would like to think unambiguously indicates the answer to this question.

Still it must be admitted that Kierkegaard thinks that some of his readers are egregiously irrational, and that he thinks of himself as more rational than they are and as descending to their level in order to help them. Does this make him arrogant? Surely it does, *if he is wrong about these things.* But let us suppose that he is right. If so, it seems to me that his lowering himself is an act of charity and humility. Indeed, he does not (often) flaunt his condescension, and does not (often) ask to be thanked, praised, or even noticed for his imitation of Christ. What is more, his humbling of himself has had the result that his rationality has not been sufficiently appreciated, and that he has even been misunderstood as irrational. Therefore, it seems to me, his condescension is not arrogance, but charity and humility.

Ultimately people must discover the truth and relate to it for themselves. Therefore the arrogant or arrogating author is the one who tries to do for his readers what only they can do for themselves. And the humble author is the one who realizes that he or she has a limited role to play in helping others to do what they must do on their own, and who does not attempt to transgress these limits. And since Kierkegaard strives as a writer to respect the freedom, prerogatives, and personal responsibility of his readers, it is arguable that he is not arrogant but commendably humble as an author.

The Rectification of the Name of Reason

One of the main purposes of this chapter has been to argue that in order to understand subjectivity, appreciate its challenge to our ways of thinking, and, if we choose, to imitate it, we must recognize that subjectivity is a conception and practical use of reason. Simply put, we can neither evaluate nor embrace the subjectivity recommended to us by Kierkegaard unless we realize that it is a robust form of rationality. Here is a summary of the evidence for the rationality of subjectivity.

Kierkegaard and his pseudonymous authors claim that subjectivity is more true than objectivity is, and that Christian subjectivity is more reasonable than objectivity. They also claim that subjective thinkers are more honest, more consistent, and less confused than objective thinkers are; that subjective thinkers are more complete in their thinking and acting than objective thinkers are because they strive to do justice to the whole person; that subjective thinkers are less influenced than objective thinkers are by prejudice, custom, tradition, and in general by the opinions of other people, so that they are also more self-reliant, more responsible for their beliefs, and therefore also more free; that subjective thinkers are more aware than objective thinkers are of the dialectic both of learning and of communicating the truth, which truth Kierkegaard considers to be universal, in that it is the same for all people and in that all people can know as much of it as they need to know in order to act as they should now; and, in short, they claim that subjective individuals think, communicate, feel, will, and act in ways that are more in accordance with human nature than are the characteristic activities of objective people. All of these claims are so many ways of asserting that subjectivity is more reasonable than objectivity, and in the *ordinary sense* of the word reason. Therefore it would be a gross distortion of the meaning of *rationality* not to admit that Kierkegaard intends subjectivity as rationality. Surely a good Confucian would insist on this rectification of names.[14]

My Best Arguments for the Claim That Kierkegaard Rejects Reason, and My Responses

Or would a good Confucian perhaps withhold his approval of my terminological proposal? Do grounds perhaps still remain for thinking that Kierkegaard is not ultimately a rational thinker or does not see himself as one?

Perhaps Kierkegaard himself did not realize how committed to reason he was. Perhaps he intended in some ways to reject reason, but unwittingly implied that he was more loyal to reason than he himself understood. This possibility cannot be entirely refuted. But, it seems to me, Kierkegaard is so careful a writer, is so intelligent, thinks so much about reason and faith, is so concerned with honesty and self-knowledge, and, finally, provides so many clues that he pretends to be irrational, that it would be very surprising if he was unaware of (the extent of) his own allegiance to rationality.

Even granting that Kierkegaard thinks that faith perfects reason, perhaps he thinks that faith does this by transcending reason and including reason within itself as a subordinate element. If so, there must be something wrong in stressing that Kierkegaard is a rational thinker. This objection seems to me to be defensible, and, I think, is consistent with virtually everything that I wish to claim in this book. For there is little difference between saying that faith just is reason perfected by grace and revelation, and saying that faith transcends reason but perfects and includes it. For, among other things, in either case it would still be true according to Kierkegaard that one can arrive at faith by a process that comprises the perfecting of reason and the reception of grace and revelation. But perhaps we suspect that reason should refuse to be perfected by something that transcends it, presumably in order to maintain its dignity.

Regardless of what Kierkegaard himself understands or intends, and despite the fact that he is obviously deeply committed to many aspects of reason, perhaps the fact that he is not committed to some aspects of what (almost) always goes by the name of reason entails that we ourselves should judge that he ultimately rejects reason. For example, consider the fact that he rejects most or many aspects of public argumentation as a way of determining what is true. Some readers may deem that such public argumentation is the essence of reason and claim therefore that it cannot be rejected without thereby rejecting reason *tout court*. In response I would say that Kierkegaard has well thought out, rational reasons for not trusting public argumentation as deeply as most or all other rational thinkers do (reasons by the way that can be made public, and that I have attempted to express clearly). More specifically, he rejects public argumentation as the arbiter of truth because he thinks that all public activities are highly susceptible to irrationality, so that any public method of arbitration must be at odds with the Enlightenment and rational ideals of "daring to think" and "judging for oneself." Therefore he does not reject public argumentation in the name of faith or whimsical individuality, but in the name of reason itself. And since this is so, and since he affirms (almost) all other rational goals, norms, and methods, it is a bit of a stretch to think that his relation to reason should be defined primarily as rejection.

Kierkegaard declares his allegiance to Christianity much more clearly than he does his respect for reason—even if it is true that he pretends both not to be a Christian and not to be reasonable. But if he is more committed to Christianity than to reason, then he would presumably deny or betray reason in order to confess Christ, if necessary; and if he is prepared to do that, then perhaps it is a mistake to call him a robustly rational thinker. Perhaps. It is a tricky question. Does being committed to reason mean being more committed to reason than to truth, so that if faced with a choice one would choose reason over truth? Or does being committed to reason above all things mean being committed to truth, so that, if necessary, one would reject reason for love of truth? Incidentally, there is no question at all that Kierkegaard sees himself as loyal to truth. What if reason itself could discover that it was not fit to judge some question of ultimate importance, and what if reason could even discover that some other faculty was more fit for this? In any case,

Kierkegaard does not seem to think that Christ or truth demands the rejection of reason—though he is certainly aware of this possibility. On the contrary, he seems to think that reason is part of God's image in human beings, that affirming God means affirming reason, and that affirming reason means affirming God. But perhaps he leaves it an open question whether reason is to be rejected or affirmed in the ultimate affirmation of God and truth, even as he provisionally affirms reason in order to affirm God. Would such open-mindedness be a betrayal of reason? Does rationality demand a dogmatic and irreversible commitment to reason or perfect certainty that reason is eternally the only competent judge of all important and decidable issues?

An Epilogue on Kierkegaard and the Buddha

One way of confirming that Kierkegaard is neither an irrational individualist nor a narrowly Christian polemicist, but a rational thinker who (partly) transcended his time and his culture, is to point out that even though he and the Buddha belong to very different times, places, and traditions, their teachings are strikingly similar in many respects. With just a few exceptions, which I shall note, the following comparison is drawn specifically between Kierkegaard and the Buddha as he appears in the "Pali Canon."[15]

Like Kierkegaard, the Buddha is an eminently practical thinker. His teaching, or *dhamma,* is not a theory, but a "raft for getting to the other shore."[16] The "other shore" for the Buddha is *nibbana,* which, like Kierkegaard's "eternal happiness," is a state of spiritual perfection. Being practical, the Buddha, like Kierkegaard, often flouts and frustrates the theoretical expectations of his interlocutors. For instance, he frequently refuses to answer *speculative* or impractical questions on the grounds that doing so would *not* be "conducive to the goal" of *nibbana.*[17]

Both the Buddha's and Kierkegaard's practical teachings are roughly medical or psychiatric in structure. The Buddha is a *surgeon* who teaches the "four noble truths," which describe sickness of soul, the causes of this sickness, health of soul, and the therapeutic regimen, called the "noble eightfold path," that leads to spiritual health.[18] Similarly, Kierkegaard writes as a "physician of the soul" (SUD, 22–24) who describes the "sickness unto death," its causes, health of soul, and the *way* to health.

Moreover, the therapeutic disciplines taught by the Buddha and Kierkegaard are roughly similar in that both include dialectical investigation of ideas grounding rival ways of life, ethical discipline, inwardness, psychological/spiritual exercises, self-examination, and *noble, energetic striving* for the *goal.* Finally, both of these spiritual teachers describe in detail "stages on the way" of spiritual growth so as to provide guidance for pilgrims.[19]

The Buddha and Kierkegaard are perhaps most similar to one another in their pedagogical strategies. Both of them refuse to teach as authorities and instead aid learners to discover the truth for themselves; hence both teach dialogically, especially when they communicate with people with whom they deeply disagree. Both of them see self-deception, or *conceit,* as a serious obstacle to learning, and therefore they teach with an eye to helping learners to discern and to overcome their own self-deception. Both of them are also willing to distort and compromise their own teaching to some degree in order to adapt it to the particular needs, limitations, and prejudices of the specific learners whom they wish to assist. This is to say that the Buddha practices something very akin to Kierkegaard's indirect communication. In his own language, he teaches the *dhamma* "by diverse methods."[20] In Mahayan Buddhism the Buddha's tricky and compromising manner of teaching is called *upaya,* or skillful means.[21]

I do not mean to deny that there are great differences between the teaching of the Buddha and that of Kierkegaard. But, even where they disagree most, there is still much agreement. For instance, whereas the Buddha thinks the principal illusion of learners is that they *have* an eternal self,[22] Kierkegaard for his part thinks their principal illusion is that they *do not have* such a self. Obviously this is a great and crucial difference. But, even within this difference, there is nonetheless important and substantial agreement. Specifically, the Buddha and Kierkegaard agree that all imperfect people construct an illusory self, that immense *personal* effort is needed to discover and eradicate this persistent illusion, and that the discovery and actualization of one's true character has infinite worth.

I suspect that Kierkegaard substantially agrees about the nature and use of reason not only with the Buddha, but with many or even most religious thinkers. More specifically, it seems to me that all religious thinkers who claim that a human being is responsible for accepting and appropriating religious truth, even revealed truth, must regard human beings as having a faculty of responsibility—and therefore of knowledge or understanding, since responsibility requires understanding—that must have most or at least many of the properties of reason.

THREE

Reverse Theology

Unknown, and yet well-known. (2 Corinthians 6:9)

No man hath seen God at any time, [but] he that hath
seen me hath seen the Father. (John 1:18; 14:9)

My Father is greater than I, [but] I and
my Father are one. (John 14:28; 10:30)

In his existence-relation to the truth, the existing subjective
thinker is just as negative as positive, has just as much of
the comic as he essentially has of pathos. (CUP, 80)

There are more things in heaven and earth, Horatio, than
are dreamt of in your philosophy. (Shakespeare, *Hamlet*)

In the estimation of Climacus, his contemporaries were uncritical, dogmatic, and altogether too *positive* about such things as worldly wisdom
and the Hegelian System. In order to chasten and correct this foolish
positivity, Climacus wielded the power of the *negative* (CUP, 80–93). As
understood and practiced by Climacus, negative thinking is critical,
iconoclastic, and ironic: it refutes error, exposes the limitations and
incompleteness of the System and other idols of thought, and satirizes
complacency and presumption.

Owing to his spectacular negativity, Climacus often appears to be far more skeptical than he actually is. To see through this appearance and get to the truth about him, one must realize that his negations constitute, not a measured and balanced *normative* theory, but a *corrective* (JP, 1:708, 709). Alternatively, one must come to see that Climacus writes in such a way as to provoke his readers *self-actively* to reaffirm revisions or modifications of the truths that he negates.

When negative thinking plays an important role in religion and spirituality, it goes by such names and employs such formulas as "negative theology," "*via negativa*," and "*apophatic* theology" in Christianity; *neti neti* in Vedanta; and, in Buddhism, *Madhyamaka* and the *Tetralemma*.[1] This negativity is, so to speak, the skepticism of the religious believer, or the antinomianism of the spiritual practitioner.

Although Climacus does not explicitly call himself a negative theologian, he nonetheless suggests his allegiance to the "*via negationis*" (PF, 44). And, more importantly, since much of his thinking is both negative and theological, he is de facto a negative theologian—but with a twist: In the apt phrase of John D. Glenn Jr., Climacus practices an "existential *via negativa*."[2]

Since most negative theology is more or less theoretical in character, Glenn's idea of an "existential *via negativa*," or of a practical apophasis, is somewhat disorienting: It challenges one's theoretical habits and prejudices and artfully issues a summons to a thoroughgoing practicality. This is just the sort of shocking summons that Climacus himself is always issuing. Consequently, Glenn's apt phrase is not just a good interpretation of Climacus, but also an artful imitation of his way of thinking and writing.

In order to bring out the uncompromisingly existential character of the Climacean apophasis, we will compare his practical version of negative theology to theoretical versions of the same. As this comparison unfolds, the reader is asked to bear in mind that by *existential* or *practical* I do not mean a narrow focus on action that ignores or neglects the intellect with its desire to know, but a concern for the whole person that embraces the intellect, imagination, will, emotion, and action.

Our investigation into the practical or subjective character of Climacus's negative theology will enable us to see that he pretends to be far more skeptical about theological issues than he really is, and that he does this precisely to communicate holistic religiousness.

We may draw the distinction between practical and theoretical negative theology by comparing *what* they negate, *why* they negate, and *how* they negate.

What Negative Theology Negates

Theoretical negative theology negates or denies the adequacy of human knowledge of God and of human language about God. More fully, it negates contemplative or theoretical cognition of God regarded as a metaphysical object, and it negates theoretical statements belonging to a metaphysical *science* or *system* in which God enjoys pride of place as the first cause and the highest being. Questions twelve and thirteen of the *Prima Pars* of St. Thomas Aquinas's *Summa Theologica* provide a good example of negative theology theoretically preoccupied with linguistics, epistemology, and metaphysics.

Like theoretical negative theology, the practical negative theology of Climacus also denies the adequacy of human knowledge and language about God regarded as a metaphysical object. But it focuses more on negating the human capacity to describe the *goal* of religious striving, namely, "eternal happiness," than it does on negating cognition and description of God. In the words of Climacus, "nothing else can be said of eternal happiness than that it is the good that is attained by absolutely venturing everything" (CUP, 427). Since Climacus focuses more on negating the goal of religious striving than on negating God as a metaphysical object, his negative theological thinking is more practical or existential than theoretical.

St. Paul provides a model for Climacus's negation of the goal of religious striving when he writes to the Corinthians that "eye hath not seen, nor ear heard, neither have entered into the heart of man, the things which God hath prepared for them that love him."[3] Similarly, the refusal of the Buddha to describe Nirvana, the telos of Buddhist practice, is another apt example of existential apophasis.

The principal negation of Climacus's practical negativity is not, however, his denial that human beings can adequately describe or know eternal happiness. Since the goal of religious striving is not just to describe or to know eternal happiness, but to attain it, the principal negation of practical negative theology is not that human beings cannot know or describe their final end, but that they cannot attain it by their own unaided efforts.

The prototype of the principal negation of Climacus's practical negativity is St. Paul's emphasis on human sin as a practical incapacity to attain salvation without divine assistance.[4] The practical incapacity called sin consists, not just in cognitive limitations, but in a contraction and corruption of the whole person, including the mind, will, emotions, imagination, and actions. Practical negative theology must therefore develop a diagnosis, as Climacus does to some degree, and Kierkegaard his creator does much more thoroughly, of the sinful condition of human beings. Buddhist negativity similarly tends to focus more on the volitional and emotional problem of attachment than on the intellectual problem of ignorance and delusion, at least in the earlier stages of practice.

St. Thomas Aquinas, our main representative of theoretical negative theology, is aware of the Christian teaching that sin is an incapacity of the whole human person to attain its final end. But his awareness of sin is not an official part of his negative theology and does not seem to inform his negative theology to any significant degree. Therefore Climacus might say that the problem with Thomistic negative theology is that it is unnecessarily abstract or partial, in that it is systematically separated from practical thinking and from religious life as a whole. Therefore it is possible to read scores of scholarly articles on Aquinas's negative theology without finding so much as a hint that awareness of the practical problem of sin might be important to the Thomistic *via negativa*.

Thus the *via negationis* of Climacus is less abstract, or more complete, than theoretical negative theology, for it includes negations that theoretical negative theology makes plus negations of the goal of religious striving and of the human capacity to reach this goal without divine assistance. And because it is more complete, it is arguably also more rational, since reason strives for universality and wholeness.

Despite its claim to a sort of completeness, Climacus's practical version of negative theology might nonetheless seem overly skeptical and therefore irrational. For to assert that all one can say about eternal happiness is that it is what you receive by risking or sacrificing everything sounds like a severely skeptical negation. What is worse, to encourage readers to risk everything and to be ready to sacrifice everything for an undefined and undescribed goal called eternal happiness seems like a recommendation not only of irrationalism, but even of fanaticism.

Why Negative Theology Negates

Climacus's existential negative theology makes its negations as a means to attaining the goal of eternal happiness, conceived as a vital relation of the whole person to God. In other words, practical negative theology conceives its goal as the perfection of practice.

Theoretical negative theology also makes its negations as a means to its goal, which it defines as the beatific "vision of the divine essence," in the case of Thomas Aquinas, and "knowledge beyond knowledge," in the case of Dionysius the Areopagite.[5] Thus for theoretical negative theology the goal is the perfection of theory.

To be fair to St. Thomas and Dionysius, they do not conceive of salvation merely as knowledge of God. Instead, like Climacus, they think that salvation involves the whole person. But they differ from Climacus in that they think knowledge is somehow dominant or at least highly prominent in salvation, whereas Climacus thinks that if anything has priority or dominance in salvation it is or would be love and not knowledge. Thus one might perhaps say that Climacus, Thomas, and Dionysius agree that salvation embraces the whole person and differ only in that they emphasize and lionize different parts of this whole.

How Negative Theology Negates

For Climacus, the question of how one does something is almost always of decisive importance (CUP, 202–203). Are one's means artfully adapted to one's ideas or ideals, or does one contradict one's ideas or ideals by the way one goes about expressing or pursuing them, thus revealing oneself as either confused or hypocritical (CUP, 75, 153)?

The principal means by which theoretical negative theology makes its negations is *stating and arguing for them.* Climacus might admit that in principle there is nothing wrong either with asserting negations or with supporting them with arguments. But, he would probably add, means have an insidious way of transmuting into ends, especially such means as philosophical inquiry. Thus a negative theologian might begin with eminently practical motives but end up preoccupied with elaborating a theory of the limits of all theological theories. Consequently it is necessary for the religious person to beware of transforming negative theology into a theoretical project.

It is hard not to suspect that Thomas Aquinas sometimes makes idols of his own ideas and arguments, even his ideas and arguments about the limits of ideas and arguments. Conversely, one might suspect that, in avoiding the error of Thomas, Climacus goes to the opposite extreme in that he argues too little for his negations and takes too little care in formulating them. I think that Climacus would probably admit that his negative theology is unbalanced in this way—at any rate I agree with this criticism of him—and then point out that he writes as a *corrective* to theoretical negative theology, and that correctives are (almost) by nature unbalanced in order to be effective (JP, 1:709).

Practical negative theologians make negations not just in their thinking and communicating, but in the whole range of their activities as human persons. Thus practical negative theology denies the whole person, for the sake of the whole person, and with the whole person. More expansively, it denies the adequacy of the natural relation of the whole person to the goal of religious striving, for the sake of helping the whole person to relate rightly to that goal and with or through the whole person. Climacus describes several practical or holistic acts of negation: *resignation, suffering, guilt-consciousness, sin-consciousness,* and acknowledgment that one is "capable of nothing at all" "before God" or without God (CUP, 430, 461; cf. 383, 486).

Resignation means renouncing, or being ready to renounce, any or even all finite goods for the sake of the infinite good (CUP, 393–396, 385, 391, 404; and in general 387–431). As such, resignation involves not just thinking, but also feeling, willing, and acting. Resigned people choose and emotionally accept their renunciation, and act in the world as beings who have what they have only as a precarious gift.

The effort to extricate oneself from attachment to finite goods brings on religious *suffering,* which despite its etymology is an action in that it is chosen or voluntary (CUP, 433–440; cf. PC, 109). Like resignation, suffering voluntarily for eternal happiness also involves the whole person: an understanding of the requirement of suffering, painful feelings, and a steadfast will in actions that risk or incur tribulations.

Two other acts occasioned by resignation are *guilt-consciousness*, or *total guilt*, and *consciousness of sin*. The former arises when one honestly admits to oneself one's failure to achieve perfect resignation (CUP, 525–555), while the latter is the Christian intensification of *guilt-consciousness* (CUP, 532, 583–585; cf. PF, 47). Guilt- and sin-consciousness also involve the whole person, in that they are self-awareness, modulated by feelings of shame and remorse, and activated by resolute attempts at resignation, repentance, and endurance of suffering.

To become conscious of one's guilt or sin is to become aware of one's insufficiency in the most important tasks of life, and therefore of one's *need* for God, to become aware that "without God's help" "a person is capable of nothing . . . at all," or that "to need God is a human being's highest perfection" (EUD, 322, 297, 307). Thus a natural development of consciousness of guilt or sin is to become aware of one's weakness and then to strive to rely on God in all things. Reliance on God is holistic in that it integrates consciousness of one's need, a feeling of dependence, reaching out with one's will for divine aid, and striving in one's actions to cooperate with grace.

The feeling of dependence alluded to is closely connected to an act of the existential *via negativa* that goes by such names as reverence, awe, adoration, worship, or as Johannes de Silentio calls it, "fear and trembling." Reverence consists in an intense emotional awareness of God's transcendence, a volitional disposition to submit to and to obey God and therefore also acts of submission and of obedience.

If the purpose of the *via negativa* is not scholarly accuracy but the salvation of the whole person, then it is arguable that the integrated acts described have a greater claim to belonging to the *via negativa* than all the merely abstract theorizing that more often goes under this name, and that the omission of these acts from many accounts of negative theology reveals an allegiance to theory in a realm where practice ought to reign.

Since the existential *via negativa* is not partial but holistic, it does not neglect but includes negative thinking. Climacus describes many types of negative thinking, such as *irony, humor, the comic,* the *pathos-*

filled, and *dialectic.* Their common basic activity is to become conscious of the *misrelation* between the *finite* and the *infinite,* or between the *temporal* and the *eternal,* or between the "daily everyday" and the *ideal* (CUP, 86, 87, 89, 92, 502, 505). Climacus carefully elaborates and distinguishes the character of these different types of negative thinking. For instance: "The interpretation of the misrelation, viewed with the idea ahead, is pathos; the interpretation of the misrelation, viewed with the idea behind, is the comic" (CUP, 89). This is to say that pathos focuses on the absent greatness of the infinite, and the comic focuses on the present inadequacy of the finite.

Kierkegaard's indirect communication is also a deployment of negative thinking. One mode of indirect communication consists in ironically, humorously, or comically artful negations of the lives and ideas of oneself or others. Another consists in the self-restraint that says less than one could—even to the point of being silent—about important things such as God and eternal happiness. Yet another consists in exaggerated, misleading, or even outright false denials about these same things. Finally, another might consist in dialectically accurate denials of the adequacy of human knowledge and language.

Climacus seems to think that it is crucial for an ethical or religious writer to take into account that there are people who are not ready for dialectically accurate denials in that they would misunderstand or misuse them to their own harm. For example, someone might use dialectically nuanced negations as an occasion to philosophize in an abstract, and therefore unhealthy, mode. To prevent such misuse, indirect communicators such as Climacus hide or conceal as much as possible anything that could become an object of contemplation or cogitation for its own sake and thus indirectly encourage subjective appropriation of their message. But in order to help those who are ready to understand and rightly use dialectically accurate denials, indirect communicators may additionally provide hints and clues of their nuanced negations. Thus indirect communicators have the task of saying enough to assist those who are ready and receptive, but also of saying little so as not to harm those who would misuse their message. For like all finite goods, dialectic is medicine in moderation, but poison if used wrongly or to excess. Therefore indirect communicators think the universal to themselves, but partly conceal and partly reveal their universal idea by their elusive manner of communicating it (CUP, 73). As Heraclitus the Obscure, that famous indirect communicator, put the point, "the lord whose oracle is in Delphi neither declares nor conceals, but gives a sign."[6] Thus indirect communication sacrifices dialectical accuracy for the sake of pedagogical adequacy.

In practicing restraint in his spiritual teaching, Climacus is in the company of many great spiritual teachers. In the Gospels, Jesus frequently explains to his disciples that he does not speak plainly to the *multitude* because they do not "have ears to hear."[7] Similarly, St. Paul tells the Corinthians that "I could not speak unto you as unto spiritual, but as unto carnal, even as unto babes in Christ. I have fed you with milk, and not with meat: for hitherto ye were not able to bear it."[8] And the Buddha of the Pali Canon frequently refuses to answer *speculative,* or metaphysical-theoretical questions about nirvana, the ultimate goal of Buddhist practice, not on the grounds that he does not know the answers, and not even because his interlocutors could not understand his reply, but because answering such questions would not be "useful in attaining the goal."[9]

When one discovers something for oneself by one's own efforts instead of passively receiving instruction about it, one turns toward it more enthusiastically, understands it more thoroughly, and appreciates it more deeply. Therefore, one reason for teachers to say less than they might, or even to be silent, about important things is to give learners the opportunity to discover the truth for themselves, perhaps with the aid of a few apt hints or artful suggestions.

For the purpose of encouraging learners to discover the truth for themselves, exaggerated, misleading, and even outright false negations can sometimes be even more useful than reticence or silence. In other words, by denying the truth or arguing against it in the right way, the artful teacher can encourage learners to discover the right affirmation of the truth or the right argument for it for themselves. Such artfully false denials are a philosophical species of irony, or a dialectical analogue of reverse psychology. But whereas reverse psychology tends to provoke an unthinking, contrarian rejection of authority, reverse philosophy tends to provoke a reasoned or responsible affirmation of the truth. Thus we have found yet another way that Kierkegaard pretends to deny reason in order to provoke his readers to affirm it in the right way.

Here is one way of understanding how negation in the deft hand of Climacus suggests something positive and thus provokes a reasoned reaffirmation in his readers. To rationally or responsibly deny the actuality and especially the possibility of knowing or describing something, one must know something about what one denies, something about one's own capacities in relation to that thing, and something about the world as the ultimate context of one's relation to the unknown thing. Therefore, correctly reflecting on the process of negation should reveal the positive basis of the negation, and therefore something positive about the thing negated. Chapter 6 will investigate at length how Climacus's artfully revealing negations form a ladder to an awareness of transcendence.

Revealing by negating is one way of achieving a balance between the positive and the negative. Thus we arrive at another aspect of how Climacus thinks negations must be performed if they are to serve their function: *"In his existence-relation to the truth, the existing subjective thinker is just as negative as positive, has just as much of the comic as he essentially has of pathos"* (CUP, 80; original emphasis). This balance shows up in many ways and in many modes in the thinking and writing of Climacus and Kierkegaard. In his dissertation Kierkegaard writes that "irony is a healthiness insofar as it rescues the soul from the snares of relativity," but it is a "sickness insofar as it cannot bear the absolute except in the form of nothing" (CI, 77). This is to say that mere irony is an imbalance and an exaggeration. Typically the ironist or iconoclast thinks of himself as being as far removed from idolatry as possible. But, as Kierkegaard suggests, to be purely ironic or merely iconoclastic in fact makes an idol of negation, or of one's own power of negation, and is therefore in the end that idolatry of oneself better known as pride. In Buddhist thinking the analogue to Kierkegaard's warning about irony is the recognition of the fact that one can become nihilistically attached to detachment.

Another aspect of balancing the positive and the negative according to Kierkegaard is balancing trust and doubt. On the one hand, and as we have already seen, Kierkegaard is skeptical, critical, iconoclastic, and therefore negative in that he frequently argues against unthinking or dogmatic adherence to various opinions. But, on the other hand, Kierkegaard is a critic of the "poisonous spirit of distrust" and an advocate of faith or trust in Christ (WL, 7). In *Works of Love* he argues that distrust or unbelief in love is based on *fear* of being *deceived,* or on a "flattering conceit that considers itself absolutely secure against being deceived," or on a "morbid, anxious, niggardly narrow-mindedness that in petty, miserable mistrust insists on seeing the fruits" of love before it will believe in love, or on the foolish notion that the only way we can "be deceived" is "by believing what is untrue," when "we certainly are also deceived by not believing what is true," so that to doubt love is "to defraud oneself of love" and therefore also a *self-deception* (WL, 5, 6, 16). Thus Kierkegaard argues that doubting love is irrational.

He also argues that belief in love is rational: "we must believe in love—otherwise we simply will not notice that it exists" (WL, 16). Similarly, he explicates—and to some extent argues for—the proposition that "love believes all things—and yet is never deceived" (WL, 225–245). Obviously these last two quotations are echoes of Anselm's famous formulas for uniting faith and reason: namely, "faith seeking understanding," and "I believe in order that I may understand."[10] Therefore, although Kierkegaard is frequently skeptical, he is also critical of excesses and misuses of skepticism, so that his position is a balancing of doubt and trust. Indeed, according to Climacus, faith in itself is just such a balance, since it is essentially trust in something whose dubitability the believer sees very clearly (CUP, 203–204).

Louis Mackey points to a theological aspect of the balance between the positive and the negative in Kierkegaard's thinking when he refers to the "apparent contradiction between Kierkegaard's negative theology and his habit of thinking in images, similes, and analogies."[11] This balance has always been important in Christian thinking. In the words of St. Paul, God is "unknown, and yet well-known."[12] And in the iconoclast controversy of the seventh century, the church declared that just as the affirmation of images carried to excess was the error of idolatry, so the negation of images carried to excess was the error of iconoclasm. Similarly, in the Middle Ages, Thomas Aquinas powerfully critiqued the extremism of the negative theology of Maimonides and explained how the way of the negation of images must be complemented by the way of the affirmation of images.[13] And in a postmodern context, Merold Westphal has also argued for the importance of "how to speak nevertheless about God."[14] For a nontheological, personalist account of this balance, it is worth looking at Martin Buber's "Distance and Relation."[15] The most famous nontheological, but nonetheless spiritual version of the balance of the positive and the negative is the "Middle Way" of Buddhism between essentialism and nihilism.

However important it may be to achieve an equilibrium between the positive and the negative in thinking, the most important equilibrium according to Kierkegaard is existential. The fact that there are relatively few famous theological writings about this existential balance is an apt commentary on the theoretical tendency of theology. This is not to say that religious people in general neglect to strive for this balance. The alternation of fasts and feasts in the liturgical calendars of the Orthodox and Catholic Churches is obviously meant to promote a kind of existential equilibrium. But liturgical calendars are not generally reckoned among theological writings.

Climacus describes this existential balance of the positive and the negative in a highly compressed form: "simultaneously relating . . . absolutely to the absolute *telos* and relatively to the relative ends" (CUP, 431). *Fear and Trembling* develops this same idea much more expansively and poetically in its account of the "double movement" that involves *resignation* and *receiving* back the good that one has renounced (FT, 36–37). The clearest account of the double movement in Kierkegaard's authorship is in *Sickness unto Death,* in the sections that describe the synthesis of the poles of the self (SUD, 29–42). Essentially and briefly, the double movement consists, on the one hand, in existentially denying finite, created goods by being resigned to their possible loss and ready to renounce them if necessary for the sake of the infinite and eternal God, and, on the other hand, in existentially reaffirming these goods by enjoying and loving them gratefully as the gifts of a good and generous God.

As I have already indicated, the surface of Climacus's writings is unbalanced in that it focuses more on the negative than on the positive—not, however, because Climacus himself is in fact more negative than positive, but because he strategically leaves it up to readers to achieve equilibrium for themselves. It will be useful for us to examine at length some clues that he lays in his writings about how to correct for his exaggerated or hyperbolic negations of eternal happiness.

Climacus strongly suggests that very little can be said or known about eternal happiness. For instance, he writes, "nothing else can be said of eternal happiness than that it is the good that is attained by absolutely venturing everything" (CUP, 427). Similarly, he insists that eternal happiness is *abstract*, and *esthetically* the "poorest idea" and the "meagerest of conceptions" (CUP, 393–394). The dullness and darkness enveloping eternal happiness, however, is not discouraging for the person who "wills the absolute *telos*," since such a person "does not want to know anything about this telos except that it exists, because as soon as he finds out something about it, he already begins to be slowed down in his pace" (CUP, 394). Therefore, it seems, orderly and well-behaved strivers after eternal happiness never feel that they have the right or the leisure to look up from their strenuous work and gaze heavenward at that goal for which they labor with the utmost dedication and exertion.

Climacus corrects his claim that very little can or should be said or known about eternal happiness in many ways. But his corrections are less conspicuous than his negations. To begin with, *eternal happiness* is rich in meaning for readers whose imagination is strong and healthy. Moreover, Climacus clearly implies that eternal happiness consists in a right relation to the personal God of the Christian scriptures, which is already to say more than that eternal happiness is "the good that is attained by absolutely venturing everything." The Danish word *salighed* can be translated not only as *happiness*, but also as *bliss, blessedness,* or *salvation,* and is thus an allusion to the New Testament. Furthermore, Climacus connects eternal happiness with such words and phrases as the *hereafter,* "eternity in the next world," *immortality,* "eternal life," and a *reward* following a *judgment* that could just as well result in "eternal unhappiness" as in eternal happiness (CUP, 400, 347, 367, 154, 403, 231, 94). Most of these suggestive descriptions are obviously derived from the New Testament and thus point to Christianity. Finally, Climacus professes to be deeply interested in Christianity's promise of an eternal happiness, and explains that one of his main questions is "how [he] may enter into relation to this [Christian] doctrine" about "eternal happiness" (CUP, 15–16). By connecting eternal happiness with Christianity in so many ways, Climacus indirectly indicates to his readers that they can learn about eternal happiness by reading the New Testament. This is not to say that the Christian scriptures give a complete or unproblematic account of the spiritual end of believers, but they certainly say a lot more than that it is the good you obtain by risking the loss of everything. For instance, Jesus indicates that paradise means loving friendship and communion with God, and *The Revelation of St. John the Divine* positively abounds in symbolic representations of heaven.

The very passages from the *Postscript* that seem most severe in their negations of eternal happiness also strongly suggest the intelligibility of this highest good. For example, Climacus does not write that nothing else can be *known,* but that "nothing else can be *said* of eternal happiness than that it is the good that is attained by absolutely venturing everything" (cup, 427; emphasis added). Presumably one cannot *say* anything more, because anything more is likely to be misunderstood by those who are not themselves venturing. But this does not mean that venturers themselves do not *know* more of eternal happiness than what they can or will *say* of it to nonventurers.

If we take Climacus at his word, venturers who will the absolute telos want "*to know . . .* that it exists" (cup, 394). But to want to know that something exists is also to want to know, at least in part, what it is; for one cannot know *that* something exists without also knowing in part *what* it is. Even more surprisingly, it appears that it is possible to *demonstrate* the existence of eternal happiness! Surely it would be strange to demonstrate the existence of what one does not know (cup, 174, 201, 204, 424).

Finally, Climacus calls eternal happiness a *good.* To be sure, Climacus has a lot to say against regarding the good of eternal happiness as univocal with such goods as "wealth, good fortune, the most beautiful girl," for example, but he nonetheless chooses to call it "*the good* that is attained" by venturing, and not *the result* that is attained (cup, 391–392, 427; emphasis added). Consequently this good has some analogy with other goods that are more easily known and may therefore be partly known and partly described by its analogy with those other more intelligible goods. According to Climacus, eternal happiness has the strongest analogy with the ethical good, of which everyone has some innate knowledge and which everyone can come to know better through ethical striving (cup, 424, 155, 392–393).

However revealing the implications of the language of Climacus may be, in his own estimation, the best corrective to the exaggerated negations of his *via negativa* is subjectivity or practice. Climacus writes that "eternal happiness, as the absolute good, has the remarkable quality that it can be defined only by the mode in which it is acquired, whereas other goods, just because the mode of acquisition is accidental . . . must be defined by the good itself" (CUP, 426–427). And because the mode of acquiring eternal happiness, variously named by Climacus and Kierkegaard as *practice, subjectivity, striving, existing,* and *appropriation,* has a *nonaccidental* and therefore an *essential relation* to eternal happiness, subjectivity reveals the essential character of this telos. But it reveals this, not to *observers* and bystanders, but only to those who actually strive for it, since understanding such existential goals as eternal happiness requires striving for them in action (CUP, 52, 53, 56, 57, 79, 87). Consequently the best corrective to negative theology is not a high-powered, theological-epistemological investigation resulting in subtly nuanced formulae, nor a careful interpretation of the implications of the language of Climacus, but subjectivity or practice.

Appropriation reveals eternal happiness by making it *present.* When Climacus insists that eternal happiness "cannot be *totally present* in this way even for the existing person who has ventured everything," he implies that it can be *partially present* for such a person (CUP, 425; emphasis added). And if eternal happiness is partially present to strivers, presumably this partial presence enables them to know it partially. Moreover, since partial presence is a matter of degree, strivers may hope to know eternal happiness more deeply by making it more present through their progress in striving. As we have already seen, Climacus thinks that it is possible to make eternal happiness present to so high a degree that one can demonstrate it in some sense, not for others, but for oneself.

As I noted earlier, Climacus thinks that of all things the ethical good has the strongest analogy with eternal happiness. Just as Climacus says very little about eternal happiness, so also he says very little about the ethical good. It is obvious that Climacus's silence about the ethical is grounded, not in skepticism, but in his belief that everyone already knows the ethical to some degree and in his conviction that the best or only way to learn more about it is to strive to live it. Similarly his silence concerning the highest good, of which the ethical good is the aptest image, is based not on his skepticism about the human capacity to know it, but on his confidence in that capacity. Presumably it is because the ethical good is analogous to eternal happiness, and because ethical knowledge is "co-knowledge with God," that striving to be good can demonstrate the existence of eternal happiness (CUP, 155, 152). Incidentally, we must understand Climacus's claim that eternal happiness can be demonstrated as qualified by his claim that eternal happiness is essentially *uncertain* (CUP, 426).

Thus Climacus's negations of eternal happiness initially seem quite stark and severe, but in fact they are complemented by many positive correctives. These correctives, however, are implicit, inconspicuous, and incomplete—deliberately so. For Climacus wants to avoid being an occasion of his readers' idolizing mere ideas of eternal happiness, and he wants them to discover and complete the correctives for themselves, by their own self-activity in subjective thinking and subjective striving.

One question concerning eternal happiness that I personally wish Climacus had addressed explicitly is the question of the relation of happiness to the ethical and religious good: Do right-minded strivers will the good for the sake of happiness, or do they will the good for its own sake and in doing so ignore their desire for happiness, or are the good and happiness so intimately related that in desiring true happiness strivers will the true ethical good, and in willing the true ethical good they desire true happiness?

In *Purity of Heart Is To Will One Thing*, Kierkegaard addresses these questions more explicitly than Climacus does, but not so clearly as to settle the matter. For example, he writes in that book: "there is nothing so certain" as that "the good is its own reward" (UDVS, 39). My hunch is that Kierkegaard here implies that the subjective striver ultimately must give the good some sort of priority over happiness, but that the good and happiness are bound so tightly to one another that for the most part aiming at the one is aiming at the other. At any rate, Kierkegaard and Climacus appeal to their readers' desire for eternal happiness—something Kant with emphasis on duty and his rejection of inclination as morally irrelevant would consider problematic or objectionable.

In *Christian Discourses*, Kierkegaard clearly claims that the best thing a person can do is to desire his or her own good, welfare, or salvation, when he writes that "the simple and humble way" to "love God" is not "'because God is the highest, the holiest, the most perfect being,'" but "because one needs him"; and "you are humbly to understand that your own welfare depends upon this need, and therefore you are to love him" (CD, 188). Therefore it follows that Kierkegaard thinks that in an obvious sense a person is to love his or her own good, his or her own happiness, more than or in preference to, the good as such. Or better, Kierkegaard thinks that one most truly loves the good by loving one's own good in the right way.

FOUR

The Subtle Power
of Simplicity

To give subtlety to the simple. (Proverbs 1:4)

The traversed path is: to reach, to arrive at simplicity. (PV, 6–7)

He now followed the method he was in the habit of following—
namely, to make everything as simple as possible. (JC, 165)

Do you not come your tardy son to chide,
That, lapsed in time and passion, lets go by
The important acting of your dread command?
(Shakespeare, *Hamlet*)

Just as one would not expect to hear a panegyric on meekness and modesty from Nietzsche, the author of the doctrines of the *superman* and of the "will-to-power," so one does not expect to hear high praise for *simplicity* from Kierkegaard, the subtle and sophisticated "indirect communicator." But, if we listen attentively to Kierkegaard, this is exactly what we hear.

Writing under the Climacus pseudonym, he praises Lessing for writing *simply*, invites his readers to "talk quite simply about" "great tasks" "as neighbor speaks with neighbor in the evening twilight," and claims that "the simple" is both *essential* and the "most difficult" thing "for the wise person to understand" (CUP, 99, 145, 160). We also learn from the philosophical biography of Climacus that his *method* and *habit* is "to make everything as simple as possible" (JC, 165). Similarly, Kierkegaard himself speaks highly of *simplicity*, often refers to his hero Socrates as that "simple wise man of old," and claims that both the "traversed path" of his authorship and the "**Christian** *movement*" are "to *reach*, to *arrive at* simplicity" (JFY, 116, 119; PV, 7; original emphasis).

As Kierkegaard uses the word, *simplicity* means *translating* "one's understanding" "immediately into action" (JFY, 116, 119). As such, simplicity is the heart of the means to both ethical perfection and eternal happiness. Indeed, "the rule" for the development of ethical and religious "capability is: begin immediately to do it. If the learner says: I can't, the teacher replies: Nonsense, do it as well as you can" (JP, 1:653, 4). Although Climacus does not, like Kierkegaard, explicitly endorse the rule *to do one's ethical or religious duty as well as one can without delay*, he indicates his acceptance of this rule with his warnings against *delay* and the *parenthesis* of inquiry, and his assertion that a person is ethically responsible for time spent on deliberation (CUP, 547, 24, 29, 526). Therefore, like Kierkegaard, his creator, Climacus recommends trying really hard without delay to become good.

As the means to such lofty goals as ethical perfection and eternal happiness, *trying really hard now* seems, not elegantly simple, but simplistic, unrealistic, and artless. For there is something in the human soul that obdurately resists even the most serious efforts not only to reform oneself ethically but even to attain peace of mind. As St. Paul testifies in Romans, one cannot always do "the good" that one *would* by sheer strength of will, owing to some mysterious power *dwelling* within the soul that is far stronger than good intentions.[i] This is not to say that we can never improve ourselves or our condition by commonsense thinking and plain hard work. It is undeniable that there are many cases in which even a modicum of prudence and a little exertion suffice for modest self-improvement. But the twin goals of ethical perfection and eternal happiness are more ambitious and more difficult than ceasing to bite one's nails or sticking to an exercise routine. It is therefore surprising to find someone as subtle as Kierkegaard recommending something so crude as *exerting oneself maximally and immediately* as the means of spiritual regeneration. When intelligent people have the task of lifting a heavy load they use a lever, pulleys, or some other contrivance so as to gain a mechanical advantage. Similarly, one might suppose, when intelligent people have the weighty task of spiritual transformation, they should not simply try as hard as they can, but use a spiritual method that gives them ethical leverage or a religious advantage. As we shall see, however, Kierkegaard thinks that there is profound power and a subtle psychology concealed within the simple rule to try hard now to become good and happy.

The Definition of Simplicity

In order to bring to light the hidden power of simplicity, we require a more complete conception of this spiritual virtue.

Sometimes Kierkegaard refers to uneducated people, or humble, salt-of-the-earth folk, as simple, so that one aspect of simplicity is to be like such folk, or to be in solidarity with them over against the rich, the educated, and the politically powerful. Thus simplicity has what might be called a democratic dimension. Ultimately, however, to be simple does not mean to identify oneself with any subclass of humanity, but to strive to achieve a greatness which is accessible to all people, but which few people earnestly attempt to achieve. Thus, in addition to its democratic dimension, the ideal of simplicity also has an elitist or aristocratic axis. One might say that this ideal is egalitarian elitist, or democratically aristocratic.

To achieve the greatness available to all human beings requires that one understand and put into practice simple and *essential ethical* and *religious* truths (CUP, 243, 247). Being simple, these essential truths can be understood by everyone, even a *child* (CUP, 391). But, and also because they are simple, they are also hard to understand for clever and sophisticated people in the habit of complicating things: *"is it not precisely the simple that is most difficult for the wise man to understand?"* (CUP, 160; original emphasis). Furthermore, "the difference between the wise person and the simplest person is this little evanescent difference *that the simple person knows the essential* and the wise person little by little *comes to know* that he knows it or *comes to know* that he does not know it, but what they know is the same" (CUP, 160; cf. 181; original emphasis).

Another important aspect of simplicity is an honesty with oneself by which a person acknowledges ethical and religious truths that are inconveniently demanding or that put one's life in an unflattering light. In other words, to be simple is the opposite of being self-deceived (JP, 1:650, 1:654). According to Climacus, honesty with oneself enables one to distinguish what one *understands* from what one "does not understand" (CUP, 558; JP, 1:650, 2). This distinction is vitally important for avoiding proud pretension and fatuous complacency with ill-considered *life-views*. Climacus is clear that every human being, from the most uneducated person to the most brilliant epistemologist, is capable of making this distinction. Honesty is also closely connected to what Kierkegaard calls *primitivity*, which is "honesty in the deepest sense" (JP, 1:657). More fully, primitivity means accepting one's *responsibility* to *reexamine* for oneself "fundamental questions" of ethics and religion, and not evading this responsibility by *thoughtlessly* accepting conventional beliefs (JP, 1:657). Thus *primitivity* means being true to oneself in order to discover the "universally human": "The issue pertains to me alone, partly because, properly presented, it will belong to everyone in the same way" (CUP, 17).

Simplicity's most important characteristic is "acting immediately" on what one has understood. The qualifier "on what one has understood" is important here. Simplicity does not mean rashness or blind haste. The simple person must deliberate and seek understanding so as to act responsibly. But, as Climacus puts it, one is ethically responsible for the time one spends on deliberation (CUP, 526). Therefore *simplicity* means to deliberate or inquire in good faith and until one understands well enough to act responsibly, and then to enact one's understanding immediately.

The various aspects of simplicity that we have examined form a unified whole. All people can act immediately on what they have understood, though few people in fact do this. Therefore prompt enactment of understanding is both accessible to all people and a criterion of greatness. Furthermore, unhesitatingly converting conviction into action is a form of honesty. For, just as not translating one's understanding immediately into action is to dissimulate one's convictions with one's actions, or to behave as if one did not understand what one does in fact understand, so, conversely, unhesitatingly to enact one's convictions is to be true to them and thus honest. Finally, honesty requires investigating fundamental questions for oneself and not accepting other people's beliefs about these things in an unquestioning manner.

An important consequence of the requirement to enact one's understanding without delay is that, as much as possible, the means that a person employs to become good must themselves be good. As Kierkegaard puts it, "the means and the end are one and the same," namely, that which is "the good in truth" (UDVS, 141). The reason for this rule is that not to do the best act of which one is now capable is to delay doing the good. Alternatively, when division of means and ends is minimized, simplicity or wholeness is maximized.

One way to delay doing the good is to do a lesser good, or a partial good, or even something neutral, when one could and should have done a greater good. For instance, a Christian might fast—a lesser good in the Christian hierarchy of values—but not attempt to fulfill his duty to love his neighbor—a greater good in that same hierarchy. What is worse, he might even use the fact that he is fasting as an excuse not to exert himself in neighbor-love.

Another form of delay is that one can do the good with only part of oneself. For instance, one might inquire into the good without forming a resolution to enact what one learns. Or one might cultivate noble feelings by reading inspiring accounts of heroic deeds, but with no intention of imitating those deeds, or without attempting accurately to understand those deeds, or without comparing one's own actions to them. One might also do the good that one should, but in a perfunctory and routine manner, that is, thoughtlessly, without feeling, and with no attempt to deeply engage one's will.

Thus to employ means to the good other than doing the best act of which one is currently capable is (or often is, or can be) to delay doing the good. Such delay is doubly divisive, doubly inimical to integrity. For delay divides the human person into parts, with only some of which the delayer tries to conform to the good, and it divides the good in parts, only some of which the delayer attempts to do.

The Subtle Power of Simplicity

A critic of Kierkegaard might object: I grant that means other than the good are problematic. But simplicity is even more problematic, since it is naïve and foolish to attempt to overcome the soul's titanic resistance to spiritual transformation with a "method" so artless and unscientific as trying really hard without delay to become good and happy.

Kierkegaard perhaps would reply: Trying really hard without delay to become good and happy would be artless and unreasonable if one expected immediate success from the effort. But good results other than immediate success might come out of prompt and maximum effort. For example, such striving might slowly break one of bad habits or slowly strengthen one's spiritual muscles. Moreover, if there is a providential God who commands such striving, assists it, and eventually rewards it, prompt and maximum effort will be the best of methods.

Once one sees that trying really hard could have benefits other than immediate success, it is no longer so clear that simplicity is artless and simplistic. Let us therefore examine Climacus's and Kierkegaard's descriptions of what happens when one exerts oneself fully and unhesitatingly in spiritual matters.

One important consequence of trying really hard without delay to become good and happy is that it removes the need to deceive oneself about why one is procrastinating. According to Anti-Climacus, to postpone acting on one's awareness of the good is an evasive maneuver whose ulterior purpose is to wait for one's awareness of duty to "simmer down" or even to vanish (SUD, 94). Thus the purpose and actual effect of delay is self-deception. Conversely, the effect of acting immediately is to remove a major source of self-deception and, by removing it, to lead to an increase in self-knowledge. As the Gospel of John puts it, he who "does the truth comes to the light in order that his deeds may be revealed," but he who "does evil hates the light and does not come to it, lest his deeds be reproved."[2] Incidentally, one might suspect that Kierkegaard's striking phrase, "subjective truth," which means the close conformity of conscience and action, has its origin in the Johannine phrase "to do [or to make] the truth."

The self-knowledge gained by acting immediately in turn leads to a clarification of conscience and thus to a better understanding of the good that one is to do. And if one acts promptly on one's better understanding, then such action will lead to yet deeper knowledge of oneself and of the good, and to action informed by this knowledge, and so on. Thus prompt performance of the good leads to a sort of virtuous cycle of spiritual growth. Kierkegaard sums up this growing process when he writes that the "rule is to do it [the ethical or the religious] as well as one can at every moment, and then again to do it as well as one can the next moment, and so on further, *in order continually to get to know it better and better*" (JP, 1:650; emphasis added).

Kierkegaard's "theory of the stages" is precisely a description of how one gets to know the ethical and the religious better and better by doing one's ethical or religious duty as well as one can at every moment. In other words, the theory of the stages is a report of what happens when one tries as hard as one can to become good and happy.

The ethical stage, which is the first stage of striving, commences when, having become aware of the ideal through conscience or imagination, a person attempts to conform as a whole person to the ideal. Climacus explains that this stage is marked by "struggle and victory," because beginning strivers struggle for ethical perfection in the confident expectation of attaining the ideal through their efforts (CUP, 288; cf. 294–295). In other words, ethical strivers see their struggles as the short first chapter of a glorious success story.

Their struggles lead ethical strivers to an awareness of a new task called *resignation* (CUP, 394–396). *Resignation* means "relating absolutely to the absolute *telos* and relatively to the relative" (CUP, 407). In other words, it means being ready to renounce (or actually renouncing, as the case may be) anything or everything for the sake of ethical perfection and eternal happiness even as one gratefully uses, loves, and enjoys various finite, temporal goods. Striving leads to awareness of the task of resignation, because by striving one learns that one has strong attachments to partial or relative goods that stand in the way of ethical perfection and eternal happiness. With the effort to be resigned strivers enter into the stage of spiritual development that Climacus calls "the religious," or "Religiousness A" (CUP, 307, 555).

The effort to be resigned in turn leads to an awareness of a new task: to suffer for the sake of eternal happiness. Resignation leads to suffering because the self-denial required to extricate oneself from the snares of finitude and temporality is strenuous and painful, and because one must never (or perhaps rarely) relax from the rigors of self-denial. Thus arises the task of "suffering continuously" as the expression of one's relation to eternal happiness (CUP, 443, 445, 452, 483, 499).

Striving to relate to eternal happiness through resignation leads to awareness of yet another task: "guilt-consciousness," or consciousness of "total guilt" (CUP, 526, 532). As one strives to be resigned and experiences failure in this striving over and over, one becomes more and more aware of the distance between one's current condition and one's ideal goal. Similarly, as one stops making excuses and stops delaying and deceiving oneself with excuses for delaying, one develops a more sensitive conscience, and with this deepened conscience one becomes more aware both of the loftiness of the ideal and of one's lowliness in relation to it. Through this growing awareness both of the ideal and of one's own imperfection, one eventually reaches, according to Climacus, the point at which one realizes that even a single failure to conform to the ideal is of decisive significance in relation to eternal happiness (CUP, 529, 533). For when the reward of striving is a perfect prize, the striving ought to be perfect too. Thus, when one decisively puts together the idea of eternal happiness with even one instance of guilt, however minor, one achieves *guilt-consciousness,* or total guilt. Obviously, guilt-consciousness with its sorrows is another major source of the suffering that a striver undergoes for the sake of eternal happiness.

Incidentally, total guilt is not the same thing as total depravity. Indeed, totally depraved beings would be incapable of the self-transcendence involved in knowing the discrepancy between the ideal and eternal happiness, on the one hand, and their own spiritual condition, on the other.

According to Climacus, striving leads to yet another, vitally important deepening of one's awareness of one's relation to the goal of striving. As one becomes more aware by striving of the difficulty of one's tasks and of new and more difficult tasks, one has the opportunity to become more aware of one's weakness. Moreover, as one experiences setbacks, or as one learns that just because one could succeed at a task on one occasion does not mean that one can always succeed at it, one becomes more and more aware of the precariousness of one's hold on virtue. Perhaps one even begins to get a sense that one's occasional successes are the result, not of one's own power, but of assistance that comes from outside—which Pure Land Buddhism calls "other power." The culmination of this growing awareness of one's total guilt, of one's weakness, of one's precarious link with virtue, and of the mysterious power that comes to one's assistance is the realization that "before God" "the individual is capable of doing nothing" (CUP, 461). As Kierkegaard titles one of his *Upbuilding Discourses,* "To Need God Is a Human Being's Highest Perfection" (EUD, 297). Thus strivers become aware by their striving that they must always humbly admit their absolute need for God and rely totally on God in everything.

Incidentally, Climacus thinks that the combination of resignation toward worldly goods, suffering, guilt-consciousness, and total reliance on God prepares the way for a deep and decisive awareness of Christianity. With the move to Christianity, guilt-consciousness intensifies as *sin-consciousness,* and the person who becomes aware of his sin learns to ask for, to accept, and to take joy in the forgiveness of sins (CUP, 524, 534). As the crime is aggravated, mercy is multiplied.

Let us sum up our account of Kierkegaard's theory of the stages. The beginning of striving is to try as hard as one can to become good and happy with bold confidence and eager expectation. By doing this one discovers the tasks of resignation, suffering, guilt-consciousness, and total reliance on God. The process of discovery works by a sort of feedback loop: by striving, one learns a new task; by trying to do this new task, one discovers yet another task; and so on. Thus striving is a process of discovery that deepens and elaborates one's awareness of oneself, of one's task, and of one's goal. Therefore, although simple striving initially seems crude, irrational, and simplistic, in fact it conceals a hidden and subtle power. Thus we find yet another example of how Kierkegaard's apparent irrationality is based on hidden reasonableness.

Some Complexities in the Means to Simplicity

At this point an important qualification is in order. I do not mean to say that Kierkegaard and Climacus are absolutely opposed to spiritual means that involve only part of a person or part of the good. Such opposition, it seems to me, would be extreme and irrational. The passage in the *Postscript* that describes an anguished investigation into the question of whether one may rest from striving and relax in "Deer Park" clearly indicates that one is not required to maintain full-tilt, maximum exertion at all times (CUP, 472, 485–487).

Kierkegaard and Climacus would be quick to insist, however, that partial means must not be employed with the intention to evade doing the best act that one can do, but with the intention to return to doing one's best as quickly as possible, armed with new strength. Thus the rule of Climacus to "make everything as simple *as possible*" is compatible with some complexity in the means, as long as one honestly believes that a departure from simplicity is necessary or efficacious (JC, 165; emphasis added).

Furthermore, even as one employs partial means, one should try to involve one's whole self in them as much as possible. For instance, one might deliberate about how to act with a firm intention to put the results of one's deliberation into practice. It might even be argued that the crucial distinction is not between partial and complete means (partial or complete with respect to the good that one does), but between ethico-religious activity that one does reservedly, and ethico-religious activity that one does as enthusiastically and vigorously as possible. Keeping this qualification in mind, let us examine various partial means that are recommended by Kierkegaard, Climacus, and other pseudonymous authors.

One partial means recommended by Climacus is reading, inquiry, or deliberation about life and practice. The very fact that Kierkegaard writes books indicates that he thinks such inquiry is permissible and useful. But, he would add, it is also dangerous, since one can use it as a means of evading action. It is with this danger in mind that Climacus explains that one is ethically responsible for the time one spends on deliberation.

One of the chief fruits of Kierkegaard's existential inquiry is his theory of the stages of ethical and religious growth that we examined. Optimally, one learns about the stages of spiritual growth by existential striving, so that one is not tempted to turn a practical knowledge of them into a theory of action that one merely contemplates. But one can also learn about the stages in a more or less theoretical manner. Climacus even has names for people who have used dialectic instead of striving to learn about stages beyond their current spiritual development: namely, the ironist and the humorist (CUP, 500–505). Even though Kierkegaard thinks that one learns about the stages best by existentially working one's way through them, he nonetheless risks the danger that his readers may turn his written account of the stages into an impractical theory to think or write about. And he does this presumably because he thinks a road map of the stages will be useful to at least some aspirants and travelers on life's way, so as to make them aware of *possibility* and so as to give them guidance as they strive.

Another important partial spiritual means is self-examination. Many of Kierkegaard's books are intended as aids to self-examination, especially *For Self-Examination* and *Judge for Yourself!* Kierkegaard thinks that of all forms of inquiry, self-examination is the least corruptible in that it is the least likely to be engaged in theoretically. For it is not especially interesting or enjoyable to examine oneself in the light of an ideal that one takes seriously and to see how far short one falls of it. But, Kierkegaard would add, it is very hard to attain self-knowledge without acting, or without at least acknowledging that the absolute requirements of ethics and religion are binding upon oneself as a single individual. Thus the best way to attain self-knowledge is a combination of striving in action with reflection in repose. But there may be some exceptional individuals who achieve deep self-knowledge with relatively little striving.

Anti-Climacus describes a spiritual method whose chief component is imagination. According to him, imagination is the "capacity for all capacities," by which one becomes "aware of oneself," of the *ideal,* and of *God* (SUD, 31, 41; PC, 186). He describes a *youth* who with his imagination "perceives some image of perfection (ideal)," which might be either "handed down by history" or "formed by the imagination itself" (PC, 186). Because this "young man" *loves* his image of perfection and constantly imagines it, he is "transformed in likeness to this image, which impresses itself on all his thought and on every utterance by him" (PC, 189). Indeed, "his whole deepest inner being is transformed little by little, and seems to be beginning to resemble, however imperfectly, this image" (PC, 193). Thus Anti-Climacus describes a sort of *imaginative meditation* on the ideal that transforms the feelings, thoughts, and will of a person into an image of that ideal. St. Paul is evidently recommending such meditation when he writes: "Finally, brethren, whatsoever things are true, whatsoever things are honest, whatsoever things are just, whatsoever things are pure, whatsoever things are lovely, whatsoever things are of good report; if there be any virtue, and if there be any praise, think on these things."[3]

Despite the power of this method, Anti-Climacus is nonetheless wary of imaginative activity, since it can be used for *fantasy,* or for "poeticizing instead of being," or as a substitute for subjectivity (SUD,

30–33, 77). Thus he thinks that imaginative meditation, which is a partial means, has great power to support subjectivity, but is nonetheless liable to perversion.

Since subjectivity is striving at the same task day after day and year after year, there is a danger that over time it may decline into a dull and lifeless routine. Therefore another important partial means is using the powers of poetry and of thought to reformulate the idea of subjectivity with artful variations so as to *renew* and rejuvenate oneself in one's striving (CUP, 259–260). One fruit of Kierkegaard's efforts at renewal is the concept of simplicity, which, as a nonprocrastinating unity of thinking and action, is consistency, wholeness, and integrity, and therefore a synonym of subjectivity. The pseudonymous author Constantine Constantius calls this renewal in the same *repetition*.

A partial spiritual means that is especially important to Climacus is "hidden inwardness." According to Climacus, hidden inwardness is at the heart of subjectivity, and consists in a full acceptance of the consequences of the fact that striving is an "essential secret"—an interiority incommensurate with external, public action (CUP, 73, 382, 410, 414, 492). One reason that hidden inwardness is at the heart of subjectivity is that, as Kierkegaard indicates, it is a means of transforming oneself, since preserving silence about one's passion for the ideal intensifies that passion.[4] Climacus, however, goes further than Kierkegaard does by making hidden inwardness, not just one tactic among many in the repertoire of the striver, but almost the principal rule of spiritual life (CUP, 490).

Much of what Climacus says in favor of hidden inwardness is clearly correct. For instance, Climacus is surely right that there are no sure external signs of striving, since the motive of any public action could always be deeply at odds with the appearance that the action presents to others. This is to say that the Hegelian idea that the inner is the outer is a reductive exaggeration. Moreover, Climacus is also correct in asserting that there are questionable ways of attempting to reveal one's striving. For instance, one may do the good so as to be recognized or praised for one's efforts and thus pervert one's service of the good. Climacus also seems right in his claim that one might need to hide certain aspects of one's passionate subjectivity so as to honor it, nourish it, and not debase it by exposing it to the scorn or chattering gossip of others. "Cast not your pearls before swine, lest they trample them under their feet."[5]

Even if we grant that hidden inwardness is ever so important and ever so powerful, it is clearly going too far to make an absolute rule of it. For hidden inwardness itself is not without dangers and defects.

Inasmuch as hidden inwardness exists only or almost entirely in the soul of the striver, it appears to be a total rejection of the body and of public life. It is as if Climacus were saying that what one does with one's body in public has nothing to do with what one is doing in one's soul, or that one cannot train one's soul by the use of one's body and public persona. This neglect of the body's effect on the soul seems to me obviously bad psychology and at odds with the cultivation of the crucial virtue of simplicity. For radically to separate body and soul, or private and public life, is doubleness and divisiveness, not simplicity.

Hidden inwardness means going out of one's way to "[look] just like everyone else," but being very different from most people in one's heart (CUP, 410, 414). To use an image that is a favorite with Climacus, to be qualified by hidden inwardness is to be a *spy* (CUP, 466–480). This is to say that hidden inwardness is duplicity, and therefore also duplexity, which is clearly contrary to simplicity. Therefore, one might well doubt whether a simple, spiritually healthy person can always be playing the spy. At any rate Kierkegaard, as he developed, became convinced that at some point one must take a stand and declare oneself, by witnessing to the truth and thus risking suffering and persecution. Kierkegaard's change of mind about hidden inwardness is obviously in line with many sayings of Christ, for instance: "Let your light so shine before men, that they may see your good works, and glorify your Father which is in heaven."[6] Therefore, from Kierkegaard's point of view, Climacus's unbalanced and one-sided endorsement of hidden inwardness is untruth. This is not to say that hidden inwardness is always or utterly wrongheaded, but only that it cannot be made into an absolute rule. "But when you pray enter into your closet, and when you have shut the door, pray to your Father who is in secret; and your Father who is in secret will reward you openly."[7]

A further, related objection to hidden inwardness is that when one confines action just to the soul, or to thinking, willing, and feeling, it is all too easy to deceive oneself about what one is really doing. For instance, if someone tries to love another person, but confines his efforts at love to the private theater of his own soul, he might easily convince himself that his performance is successful, when a serious attempt to love the other in deed would quickly reveal the shallowness of his love. Thus love at a distance is just as problematic for Christians as action at a distance was for early modern materialists. And since the world is a touchstone which very effectively reveals that our efforts to transform ourselves are not nearly as successful as we might like to think they are, avoiding the test of public action seems tantamount to courting the unhealthy complexity of self-deception.

Curiously, although Climacus has harsh words for speculation and for contemplation, because they are thinking for its own sake and divorced from practice, his endorsement of hidden inwardness could be interpreted as approval of a kind of contemplation. As a mode of subjectivity, hidden inwardness is a striving to unify oneself as a whole person in conformity to the ideal. And insofar as this striving includes willing and feeling in addition to thinking, it is different from mere contemplation, or what often goes by that name. But since the striving of hidden inwardness does not include external actions and can be done alone in an armchair, it nonetheless resembles contemplation. Thus hidden inwardness is a sort of existential contemplation, whose purpose or activity is an intense integration of thinking, feeling, and willing.

The combination of Climacus's endorsement of hidden inwardness with his condemnation of contemplation reveals his inconsistency and irrationality. More generally, his seeming lack of awareness of the problems with hidden inwardness, his one-sided recommendation of clandestine spirituality, and (so far as it is possible to say this of a pseudonymous author) his one-sided practice of this secrecy, all reveal the irrationality of Climacus. Thus we find yet another instance of Kierkegaard's pretending to be irrational in an effort to communicate rationality (or perhaps we are here looking at an instance of Kierkegaard's growth).

Hidden inwardness and indirect communication form a natural pair: when a person qualified by hidden inwardness attempts to communicate his subjectivity to others, he will do so indirectly. And since hidden inwardness has serious flaws, it would not be surprising to discover that indirect communication is similarly flawed. The purpose of the next chapter is to examine indirect communication to reveal its defects, but also to defend it as much as possible from some imperfect criticisms of it.

FIVE

A Critique of
Indirect Communication

I send you forth as sheep in the midst of wolves; be ye therefore wise as serpents, and harmless as doves. (Matthew 10:16)

By indirections find directions out. (Shakespeare, *Hamlet*)

More matter, with less art. (*Hamlet*)

The track of writing is straight and crooked. (Heraclitus)

In many ways Climacus creates a false dichotomy between indirect and direct communication: He gives the false impression that there is a neat and tidy distinction between these two modes of writing, when in fact they shade into one another, interpenetrate one another, and differ from one another as much in degree as they do in kind; he idolizes indirect communication by exaggerating its strengths and ignoring its weaknesses, and demonizes direct communication by exaggerating its vices and ignoring its virtues, when it would be more just of him to admit that each mode of writing has both advantages and disadvantages for the communication of subjectivity; and, finally, he employs and recommends a strategy of writing that relies too much on indirect communication and too little on direct communication, when a wiser policy would be to use both of them in tandem as complements and correctives of one another.

The purpose of this present chapter is to expose and to break down this false dichotomy. More broadly, its function is to criticize Climacean rationality by posing objections to its conception and practice of communication.

The criticisms of and objections to indirect communication expressed in this chapter are aimed primarily at the pseudonym Climacus, not at Kierkegaard himself. Indeed, I learned many of them from Kierkegaard. But since Kierkegaard never explicitly addresses some of the vices or weaknesses of indirect communication that I attempt to expose, it is possible that even he is vulnerable to some of the following criticisms.

Since I have already analyzed indirect communication at some length in earlier chapters, a summary of those previous analyses should serve our present purposes. Indirect communication is not plain, simple, clear, or easy, but complicated, obscure, elusive, and difficult. Where direct communication is dogmatic, didactic, and assertive, indirect is tentative, hypothetical, and questioning. Indirect communication is often ironic, that is, it often says something importantly different from what it really means, or it says something serious in the form of a jest. It makes concessions to its intended readers without announcing that what it says is a concession. Alternatively, it says things that are merely provisional as if they were absolute and final. It emphasizes less important points and makes important points in footnotes, parentheses, subordinate clauses, and seeming digressions. It is often shocking, disorienting, and confusing or rude, offensive, and provoking. It exaggerates in one direction in order to correct against one-sided extremes in the opposite direction. It is poetic and makes use of the subtlety, suggestiveness, and elusiveness of poetry. And finally, it employs pseudonymous authors, who do not always speak for Kierkegaard himself, as Polonius does not always speak for Shakespeare.

Just as indirect communication takes many forms, so also it has many purposes: to provoke the free self-activity of readers and thus respect their need to discover the truth for themselves; to avoid being an authority for readers or going partners with them so as to encourage them to accept their responsibility for themselves; to remove the delusions of readers by deceiving them into the truth; to avoid implying that results are more important than the way; to renew appreciation for ideals to which readers have become jaded; to avoid having one's message conscripted and corrupted by objective systematizers; and to avoid suggesting, or tacitly consenting to, the objective delusion that the most important task of a person is simply to think the truth, and not mainly to appropriate it by willing, living, and even being it.

A Continuum of Communication

By stressing the differences between indirect and direct communication and downplaying their similarities, Climacus gives the false impression that they are sheer opposites, when in fact they are part of a spectrum or continuum. He does the same thing with subjectivity and objectivity (CUP, 75), which correspond respectively (and roughly) to indirect and to direct communication.

Climacus starkly and without qualification claims that "direct communication is a fraud towards God," *oneself* as the communicator, and "another human being" who receives the communication (CUP, 75). This extreme condemnation implies that direct communication has no place in the economy of subjectivity and subjective writing, that direction and indirection differ only in kind, not in degree, and that direct communication cannot or should not be part of indirect communication.

Climacus exaggerates the role of the *how,* the *way,* and *style* in indirect communication and subjectivity, and he misleadingly downplays the role in them of the *what, results,* and content (CUP, 69, 73, 78, 85–86, 357). For example, Climacus suggests that he has no *opinions,* but in fact he expresses many convictions, or *theses,* though he *attributes* them to "Lessing"; or prefaces them with *if, perhaps,* or *suppose;* or expresses them in the form of (seemingly rhetorical) questions; and then at the end of the *Postscript* ostentatiously *revokes* them all (CUP, 72, 619; cf. PF, 7).

Climacus is at odds with himself about the role of direct communication in indirect communication, since he himself admits that within his indirect communication of subjectivity there is a hidden but *universal* meaning, namely, "old-fashioned orthodoxy" (CUP, 275). But old-fashioned orthodoxy rigorously distinguishes its own dogmatic content from the errors of heterodoxy, so that in communicating orthodoxy Climacus must carefully attend to *what* he is saying. Furthermore, a major function of indirect communication is to confront readers with *either/or,* that is, with clearly demarcated alternatives between which they must choose (CUP, 304–307; WL, 45; M, 94). For example, the function of *Fragments* is to distinguish between the "A" and "B" *hypotheses* and thus bring readers to a decision between them; while the function of the *Postscript* is to pose a choice between subjectivity and objectivity. And since clearly demarcated alternatives must have clearly articulated contents, accurately expressing the content of their message is often of immense concern to indirect communicators of subjectivity. Therefore Climacus falsifies indirect communication by implying that it does not include direct communication.

Climacus sometimes gives the false impression that direct communication is almost all content with scarcely any form. This impression is false for several reasons. Effective direct communicators typically care a great deal about such formal features of their writings as clarity, logical consistency, and organization. Moreover, as Climacus himself admits, direct communicators do in fact communicate indirectly with their diction, syntax, idiom, and turns of phrase, even if they are not artfully in control of what they obliquely express (CUP, 254). Consequently there is indirect communication in all direct communication.

It is quite likely that Climacus himself is perfectly aware that all indirect communication includes direct communication and vice versa, and that for rhetorical or pedagogical purposes, he exaggerates their differences and downplays their similarities. Therefore in this section I may not be criticizing the opinions Climacus holds, but only the false impression(s) that he gives. But in the next section, it seems to me, I will be criticizing his opinions.

The Imperfections of Indirect Communication

Indirect communication has numerous weaknesses and limitations and is liable to many dangers and possible perversions. Climacus seems virtually oblivious to these. And, judging by the way that Kierkegaard himself writes about indirect communication, it may be that even he is not adequately aware of its pitfalls and shortcomings.

According to Kierkegaard, the most serious problem with Climacus's one-sided use of indirect communication is that it is at odds with the Gospel injunction to *witness* to the *truth* (PC, 288). Witnessing to the truth, as Kierkegaard sees it, means stating unwelcome spiritual truths in such a way that one risks being *persecuted* (JFY, 129; JP, 4:4964, 4973; and in general 4958–4986). Therefore witnessing must be direct in order to ensure that the audience understands clearly that the witness intends to say something that seriously challenges or severely criticizes them.

Obviously, Kierkegaard's criticism of indirect communication for its failure to risk persecution is similar to his objections to hidden inwardness that we examined in the last chapter. This is not surprising, since the mode of subjectivity that Climacus calls hidden inwardness characteristically employs indirect communication, and indirect communication is often an expression of hidden inwardness.

There is a way in which Climacus's (and Kierkegaard's) attempt to communicate subjectivity by means of indirect communication is guilty of a sort of contradiction. For Climacus thinks that there must be consistency between what a communicator says and how he says it, or between the form and the content of a message (CUP, 75, 153). But subjectivity, as we saw in the last chapter, is honest and simple, while indirect communication is cunning, devious, super-subtle, and immensely complicated. Thus there seems to be a contradiction between what Climacus says and how he says it. If this contradiction is real and not merely apparent, it strikes at the heart of the whole Climacean project to communicate subjectivity by means of indirect communication.

Climacus claims that a person is "ethically responsible" for time spent on *deliberation* (CUP, 526). This is to say that one must beware of using deliberation as a way of evading action. One form of deliberation is reading such indirectly written books as the *Postscript*. And since the indirect *Postscript* is confusing and difficult, its readers can spend a great deal of time studying it—surely too much time in some cases—because they lack the intellectual or academic qualifications it requires, or because they could have learned and taken to heart what it has to teach from an easier, more direct book. Some readers of the *Postscript* may more or less innocently squander their time reading it. In such cases, Kierkegaard himself bears some responsibility for having occasioned this excessive deliberation. Other, less innocent readers may intentionally use the task of interpreting the *Postscript* with its (to them) welcome complications and difficulties as an occasion or an excuse to delay serious existential efforts, or even as a substitute for them.

Paradoxically, Climacus himself seems to use his writing of the *Postscript* as a means of delay and evasion of the subjective tasks that he describes in that book. For Climacus is a self-professed humorist, and a *humorist* is someone who is aware of and artfully describes existential possibilities and duties that he himself does not strive to actualize or to fulfill (CUP, 451). Thus Climacus is similar to Johannes de Silentio, the "lyrical-dialectician" (see chapter 1), who claims that his task is only to describe and to praise the hero of faith, not to imitate him. By using dialectical lyric to describe subjectivity and faith, both Climacus and Silentio provide seductive models of evasion that their readers might imitate.

The humorist evasion of the religious and the ironic evasion of ethics amount to something that strongly resembles what is sometimes called art for art's sake. In his eagerness to wean objective readers from their unhealthy attachment to theories, results, and the objects or the what of thinking, and to lead them to an understanding of the importance of the how and the way of thinking, Kierkegaard pours the power of subjectivity into the style of his pseudonymous (and therefore mostly indirect) publications. The stylistic verve that issues from this outpouring is so fascinating that readers can come to love it for its own sake and then enjoy or imitate it detached from its content and its deeper purpose. More fully, readers of Kierkegaard might come to love his style, secrecy, and masks for their own sakes, without concerning themselves with the ethical and religious message with which Kierkegaard wishes to confront them. Thus in working against idolatry of content, Kierkegaard ends up inviting or tempting his readers to idolatry of style.

Indirect communication is very well suited to another sort of evasion. By writing indirectly (perhaps on the pretext that one is imitating Kierkegaard), a writer can express his ideas so elusively that it is difficult or even impossible for anyone to criticize them rationally. Thus Kierkegaard teaches readers who may stand in dire need of rational criticism how to avoid the inconvenience of dealing with serious and helpful critics.

The difficulty and deviousness of Kierkegaard's indirect communication can lead to dangerous misinterpretations and abuses of his ideas that are utterly contrary to his intent. As we saw in chapters 1 and 2, Kierkegaard often gives the impression that he is an irrational and relativistic individualist—things which he in fact is not and of which he strongly disapproves. And since he lends poetic verve and vigor to his apparent irrationalism, relativism, and individualism, it is likely that he will seduce some readers to these three *isms* and confirm others in them.

It is not just a remote possibility that Kierkegaard's indirect communication might lead to or confirm dangerous misinterpretations, abuses, or errors; it has in fact happened. It is unquestionable that Kierkegaard has contributed to the rise of atheistic existentialism and individualistic relativism, on the one hand, and to (irresponsibly) fideistic Christianity, on the other. Thus Kierkegaard's efforts to prevent his message from being misappropriated and misused by objectivity open him up to being misappropriated and misused by perversions of subjectivity that he himself would consider gravely erroneous. Presumably he would not take his responsibility for occasioning these misappropriations lightly.

Indirect communication as practiced by Kierkegaard involves perilous compromises. One tactic of indirect communication is to find or meet readers where they are, provisionally accepting their delusions at face value, thus validating these delusions, at least initially (see chapter 2). Moreover, Kierkegaard not only meets his readers where they are, he also uses his poetic gifts to make the place of that encounter more exciting and more interesting than it was before his arrival. You might even say that he invests the way of thinking (and of life) of his targeted readers with the power of the ideal. On the one hand, this idealizing of error provides a path from error to sublime possibilities. On the other hand, it also makes error more interesting, more exciting, and therefore more attractive. Thus in meeting his readers where they are Kierkegaard can make staying there an attractive option. For example, Kierkegaard's "The Diary of a Seducer" succeeded so well in meeting the erotic in its own milieu that it was sold, separated from its context in Kierkegaard's authorship, as pornography in Italy (or at least as prurient and titillating literature). By the way, the Diary is still available, all by itself, in many editions, and is frequently cited in the popular "how to" book, *The Art of Seduction*.

Kierkegaard might defend his practice of communicative compromise by appealing to the example of the *prototype*, Jesus Christ. He could urge that the whole mission of the incarnation was compromisingly to meet humanity where it was (or is). He could also point out that Christ offended religious prudes by eating, drinking, and associating with sinners. But, I would reply, surely there must be limits to the compromises of evangelism. If Christ went to parties with prostitutes in order to win them to truth, virtue, and salvation, may an evangelist in good conscience patronize their services in order to woo them as the future brides of the eternal bridegroom? Surely one cannot justify any and every compromise of communication by the example of the prototype. And if this is right, by what criterion or process does Kierkegaard determine the proper bounds of evangelical compromise?

Kierkegaard might also attempt to justify his pedagogical compromises by appealing to "the parable of the lost sheep."[1] In this parable the shepherd leaves ninety-nine of his flock untended, and therefore in danger, in order to go out and search for just one lost sheep. This parable seems to give dominical authority to the practice of risking the welfare of the many in order to promote the welfare of a single individual. But, even assuming that the parable establishes Kierkegaard's right to risk harming some readers in his efforts to help others, what is the calculus of injuries and benefits that justifies the particular way that Kierkegaard goes about this?

Applying the parable in question to Kierkegaard's project more fully, the lost sheep is bewildered in a complicated maze of self-deception that he himself has constructed (our sheep is a deviously artful sheep). The shepherd Kierkegaard enters this maze, maps it, and drops clues as to how to escape from it so that the lost sheep may find its way to freedom and security. But—and "here's the rub"—some readers who were only on the margins of the labyrinth may be seduced by Kierkegaard's fascinating and seductive description of its interior and then decide to their harm that they would like to do a little exploring. Just so a moderately sane person might listen sympathetically to the horrible rantings of a madman only to find the formerly congenial theater of his own mind troubled by disastrous and monstrous visions. Thus arises the question whether it is clear that the road from moderate sanity to perfect health requires a detour through madness.

Perhaps Kierkegaard would admit that he does indeed tempt readers to become worse than they are in some respects, but he would boldly add that it is better for them on the whole to become worse—in order that they might then become better. More specifically, he might say that the readers whom he makes worse already have a spiritual sickness of which they will (spiritually) die if they do not confront it and strive to be healed of it. Furthermore, he might continue, people need to become aware of their sickness before they will strive to be healed; but most people will become aware of it only if its symptoms are aggravated or intensified. Therefore, Kierkegaard might conclude, in "[taking] measures to disclose" the "sickness unto death" of readers, he follows the standard therapeutic procedure of the "physician of souls" (SUD, 23). To develop this self-defense further, perhaps Kierkegaard would appeal to Revelation, in which Christ expresses a preference for *cold* rejection of the Gospel over *lukewarm* indifference to it.[2] Using this passage, Kierkegaard might claim that all (or many of) the perverse subjectivities to which he tempts his readers are movements away from "bourgeois-philistinism" to greater strength and intensity—even if that intensity is sometimes demonic—and thus preferable in Christ's judgment to a mediocre appearance of health.

There are many ways of objecting to the imagined self-defense of Kierkegaard. For example, one might claim that it is not clear that the only way to help a spiritually terminal disease is first to make it worse, or to risk making it worse. One might also wonder whether some people who are actually on the mend might take a turn for the worse under the influence of Kierkegaard's experimental methods of treatment. Therefore, to say the least, Kierkegaard must consider carefully the dangers that his therapies pose to the patient if he is to be responsible in his medical practice. And we for our part must wonder whether Kierkegaard did in fact adequately consider the risks involved in his methods.

To sum up the main point of this section, many of the risks and dangers of Kierkegaard's indirect communication are a result of his decision to offer assistance not only to those who welcome it and who try to help themselves, but also to those who need help but do not seem to be helping themselves, and who may even resist overtures of assistance. The chief questions of this section, therefore, are: What justification does Kierkegaard have for this decision to help the few at the risk of harming many others? How well aware is he of the risks involved in his choice? What measures does he take to avoid the worst dangers and to mitigate the rest?

The Power of Direct Communication and Its Correct Use

Kierkegaard differs from Climacus in stressing that subjectivity sometimes requires direct communication. When subjective thinkers address people who are *receptive* to the truth, Kierkegaard recommends the use of direct communication. But "when an illusion is involved," so that the subjective thinker's targeted audience is unreceptive to the truth, Kierkegaard recommends indirect communication (PV, 8). This is to say that direct communication is helpful for people whom Climacus calls *simple* (CUP, 160, 170, 181–182). For simple people listen with open hearts and minds to plain, straightforward advice, and, if they judge the counsel to be sound, do their utmost to apply it to their lives. Such people obviously have no need of being deceived into the truth by indirect communication. Used on such simple folk, indirect communication is at best a confusing distraction and at worst a seduction.

One form of direct communication, witnessing to the truth by risking persecution, is according to Kierkegaard often appropriate even when the audience is not friendly to truth. For a person who is willing to suffer and die for the truth often has the power to penetrate through deaf ears into stubborn souls. Thus direct communication, according to Kierkegaard, is not just a regrettably necessary corrective to the weaknesses and limitations of indirect communication, but a crucial and powerful means of spreading the Gospel.

Combining Indirect and Direct Communication

Given that both indirect and direct communication have strengths and weaknesses, it is reasonable to suppose that the optimal strategy for communicating subjectivity must employ both of these modes in such a way that they complement and correct one another. Alternatively, since indirect communication of subjectivity always has elements of direct communication, and vice versa, it seems that an adequate plan for the communication of subjectivity must think through the question of the best way of blending these two modes.

Although Kierkegaard thought profoundly and extensively about direct and indirect communication, he does not seem to have considered with equal care the question of the best way to combine them. At any rate, his published thoughts on the question seem inadequate, and his actual communicative practice is also problematic and questionable.

By combing through Kierkegaard's writings we get only glimpses of a strategy for combining direct and indirect communication. For example, we learn that for communicating the way that subjective individuals think and feel, indirect communication is in some respects more effective than direct communication is (though in other ways less effective, since subjectivity is simplicity), and that for communicating the Christian willingness to suffer for the truth, the direct form of communication called witnessing is more apt, since witnessing is more likely to offend people and thus provoke a persecution that demonstrates the communicator's willingness to suffer for the truth.

Incidentally, witnessing all by itself is according to Kierkegaard a synthesis of direct and indirect communication, or as he says, "direct-indirect" (JP, 1:657). It is direct in order to pose a clear condemnation of the way of life of its audience and a clear challenge to reform; it is indirect in that the witness shows, by standing up to and opposing the established order, his or her willingness to suffer for the truth that he or she proclaims.

Kierkegaard explains that with all of his pseudonymous esthetic (and therefore indirect) publications, he simultaneously published ethical or religious books written directly and in his own name (PV, 29–37). One might have supposed that the purpose of this simultaneous publication was an efficacious blending of the two modes of communication. When Kierkegaard comments on this simultaneous publication, however, the only purpose or function that he mentions is that he wanted to make it clear from the beginning of his authorship that he was an ethical and religious writer (PV, 23, 29–37). Since his earliest pseudonymous works were esthetic in character, Kierkegaard deemed it necessary to prevent history from judging that he began as an esthetic writer who only later became religious. Surprisingly, he also published esthetic writings late in his authorship (just?) to show that he had not lost the esthetic. There is perhaps reason to doubt that an authorship not carefully designed to establish a harmony of direct and indirect communication will succeed in this delicate task.

Kierkegaard explains that all direct communication of subjectivity must "end finally in 'witnessing,'" which Kierkegaard understands as a form of direct communication, or direct-indirect (JP, 2:1957; JP, 1:657). Moreover, his authorship as a whole exemplifies this pedagogical trajectory, in that he grew suspicious of indirect communication as he matured as an author and consequently came to write more and more directly. The finale of this process was that he eventually embarked on a direct, polemical attack on both church and state that resulted in his suffering a sort of persecution.[3] Therefore, we might consider whether the trajectory in his authorship toward the simple constitutes an artful intermingling of the two modes of communication.

In at least two ways it seems prudent for a subjective writer to begin with indirect communication and to end with direct communication. Indirect communication should usually come first because it is apt for addressing readers who are not or may not be receptive to subjectivity or to Christianity, so as to develop in them an adequate awareness of the possibility of subjectivity. Direct communication should come second in order to make the choice between objectivity and subjectivity (or Christianity) perfectly clear, or in order to provide those who choose subjectivity or Christianity with counsel, consolation, and encouragement. Moreover, it is also fitting for authors to use indirect communication for as long as they lack the strength to confront the established order and thereby risk persecution at its hands, and to use direct communication when they have grown into the wisdom and courage required for the trial of witnessing. Thus the progression from indirect to direct communication matches the spiritual development both of the recipients of an "existence communication" and of its senders.

One obvious weakness in Kierkegaard's plan to use directly written books to complement and correct books that he wrote indirectly is that there is no guarantee that readers of his indirectly written works will read the corresponding, complementary, and directly written works, especially since the latter books are not nearly as interesting as the former ones. Indeed, many misinterpretations of Kierkegaard are precisely a result of the fact that his readers tend to focus on his fascinating pseudonymous production and to neglect his more stark and severe alethonymous writings. Moreover, there is also no guarantee that readers who read widely in his authorship will read Kierkegaard's books in the right order, which is to say that there is reason to doubt that they will naturally find and read the books that they need when they need them. Or does Kierkegaard think that readers inevitably gravitate toward the books that are appropriate to their stage of development, like sick people who instinctively prefer the color and taste of the medicines that can cure them? Kierkegaard has indeed skillfully flavored his medicine, but flavoring surely has its limits as a selector of patients.

The Quixotic Mission of Finding
All People Where They Are

In the *Phaedrus*, Socrates claims that the rhetorician must know the many types and varieties of souls and adjust his speech at any given time to the kind of soul that he is actually addressing.[4] If Socrates is right that there are many types of souls, then it becomes doubtful that Kierkegaard (or any author) could in a single book find all the readers where they are. The sort of book that helps readers with one type of temperament might not help others and might even hurt the others. Kierkegaard does not seem to have seriously considered the question of how temperament or type would affect his attempt to find readers where they are, and his (apparent) failure to consider this casts doubt on the ability that he claims to be able to tailor his writing to his reader's mentality. To be sure, he distinguishes between wise and simple people, and among esthetes, ethicists, religious people, and Christians, but it is perhaps doubtful whether these distinctions are adequate to all the varieties of humanity.

Kierkegaard claims that his authorship constituted his own education and *upbringing* (PV, 12, 77). In other words, there is something deeply autobiographical in the sequence of his writings—they form a sort of record of his own struggle to work his way "through and out of objectivity" so as to move toward and into subjectivity and Christianity. But, if this is so, then we must ask whether it is likely that the pedagogical-developmental course of his writings will benefit all or most of his readers, or whether it might even harm some people who are sufficiently different from him in temperament, ability, situation, and level of development. In his first book, *From the Papers of One Still Living*, Kierkegaard explains that art requires a "transubstantiation of experience" and of the author's "finite character" into a "total survey (a life view)"—an admirable ideal, but also a questionable one in the case of spiritual growth, if universal human nature can be drastically modified by individual peculiarities (FPOSL, 76, 82–83).

Thus we might call into question not only whether Kierkegaard in fact succeeds in his finding his readers where they are, but also whether this goal is even possible in principle. Meeting one interlocutor where he is in a Socratic conversation seems both possible and highly advisable, assuming that one has the dialectical ability and psychological insight of a Socrates. But, given that encountering a reader where he or she is requires entering fully into their assumptions and into their way of thinking and feeling, doing this for all or even most of a wide readership with just one book seems implausible, if not impossible.

Let us step back and note that the purpose of finding readers where they are is to help people who may be widely different from the author. Perhaps there are ways of adjusting to one's readers other than fully entering their mentality. The Christian Patristic writers and the Scholastics interpreted scripture as consisting of three or four levels of meaning. In their view, scripture had something to offer readers at every stage of spiritual development: It helps the simple with simple advice, and the subtle with subtle suggestions, all the while concealing subtleties from the simple so as not to confuse or scandalize them. But, and here is the key point, scripture on this view does not go so far as to accommodate itself to its readers, by, say, taking their delusions at face value, as Kierkegaard claims to do. At any rate, there seems to be little evidence that Kierkegaard wrote his books the way the Scholastics say scripture was written, or that he attempted to write this way, or that he even considered it. But, it seems to me, given the magnitude and importance of the task that he set himself as a writer, he should at least have considered the scriptural strategy of writing. To sum up, Kierkegaard might have imitated scripture and tried to help many readers of many sorts without going so far as to try to meet all readers where they are.

It might seem that I am holding Kierkegaard and his writing to unreasonably high standards. But, I reply, Kierkegaard invites severe criticism by the immodest claims that he makes about his own writing. For example, he does not say cautiously that he finds some readers where they are, but implies that he does this for all his readers. Similarly, he claims that he can compel the reader to become aware of the religious, a questionable claim, as I shall argue in the next section. Were Kierkegaard more modest, he would deserve more generous and more lenient criticism.

Could it be that Kierkegaard's claims are more modest than what I represent them to be? Maybe his claim to "find readers where they are and begin there" means something humble and limited. Maybe his claim means only that he takes a single delusion of his readers at face value, say, that they are Christians, or that they know what Christianity is, not that he perfectly addresses them as the unique individuals they are. My response to this way of defending Kierkegaard is to say that if he means something very modest, he should speak in a manner that is more in tune with his modesty, and not claim to be able to compel readers, presumably in opposition to their freedom, to become aware of the religious or of Christianity. Moreover, if his claim is humble and cautious, he should explicitly admit, as Socrates his hero did, that the best way of finding readers where they are is a one-on-one dialogue with them. And, having admitted this, he should have proceeded to reflect on what it means to find his readers in a less than optimal fashion.

Perilous Freedom

Powerful things are dangerous. For example, strong medicines are typically potent poisons. Similarly, profound spiritual teachings can work great harm in the world, and not only because their ideas are corruptible, but also because they develop powerful desires and great capacities in people that can be used for good or for evil. The Buddha witnessed to the corruptibility of his teaching, or *dhamma*, when he said that it was like a *snake* that can *twist* around and *bite* you if you do not take hold of it in the right way.[5] Thus the Buddha did not merely blame his followers for their injurious misuses of his teaching, but he admitted that he himself had set loose a mordant snake in the midst of suffering humanity. Jesus likewise warned that his teaching might lead to the "last state of a man" being "worse than the first," or that it might lead to a condition in which a person is possessed by *seven* "unclean spirits" instead of only one.[6]

Although Kierkegaard is well aware that a profound spiritual teaching is a perilous thing, *he nonetheless says very little about the dangers of his indirect way of communicating subjectivity and Christianity.* And most of what he does say about these dangers concerns the sender of the message, not its recipient. The following is almost the only danger for the hearer of his message that he mentions explicitly: Having claimed that an "illusion can be removed only indirectly," and having boasted that through indirection he can "compel a person to become aware" of the *religious,* Kierkegaard then admits that the people whom he has made aware might use their awareness to choose "the very opposite of what [he] desire[s]" them to choose (PC, 50). Thus Kierkegaard does not exactly blame himself, or his indirect communication, for the harm that might result from his own writing; instead he seems to put the blame on the people who are harmed for misusing their freedom. Furthermore, he thinks that Christianity essentially requires that people be tempted by the "possibility of offense," and he describes *offense* as an *unhappy* and tortured condition of soul (CUP, 585; cf. PC, 81, 139; PF, 49). This is to say that his interpretation of Christianity posits that proclaiming the Gospel must risk putting people into a miserable and tormented condition. Perhaps he is correct in this interpretation, perhaps not; in any case, his interpretation of Christianity has the result that he knowingly risks great harm to his readers, and that he (probably) places the responsibility for this risk (mostly) on Christianity, not on himself.

Given that Kierkegaard thinks his readers' misuse of freedom is the most important cause of any harm that they might incur from his writing, let us examine freedom in relation to his indirect communication.

On the assumption of human freedom, Kierkegaard's claim that "an illusion can . . . be removed . . . only indirectly" seems highly dubious (PV, 43). For human freedom entails that a willfully self-deceived person might succeed in undeceiving himself by his own unaided efforts. If a person may undeceive himself, then surely he may also do this upon the occasion of someone's else's speaking to him in a direct manner about his delusion—unless one person could destroy another's freedom and prevent him from being undeceived simply by speaking directly to him. Moreover, I imagine that many of us have witnessed an undeception achieved by means of direct communication—at any rate, I would say that I have. Consequently, it seems that Kierkegaard has exaggerated the need for indirect communication in the removal of a delusion.

Kierkegaard's claim that he can compel a person to become aware of the religious seems similarly exaggerated. Human freedom, especially a freedom as robust as that posited by the semi-Pelagian Kierkegaard, precludes that one person can compel another person to do anything.

As Kierkegaard himself is well aware, the freedom and power of human beings to deceive themselves is very great, but if this is so, then attempts to compel awareness might fail in the face of this powerful and potentially perverse freedom. What is worse, and again as Kierkegaard himself is well aware, if a seriously threatening attempt to undeceive a person should fail, then it may also have provoked the deluded person to dig himself deeper into delusion. And the devious complexity of indirect communication that Kierkegaard employs in his attempt to undeceive his readers might even be seized on by them as digging tools. Thus it is not so hard to see how indirect communication could harm readers in ways other than bringing them to a clearly understood decision in which they make the wrong choice. And if so, then Kierkegaard should have mentioned these other dangers and explained what measures he took to counteract them.

Kierkegaard often explains indirect communication as the appropriate response to human freedom, as a way of leaving it up to his readers to do for themselves what only they in their freedom can do. But he also explains that indirect communication presupposes the unreceptivity of the learner, presupposes, that is, that the learner's freedom is perverted or not in working order. Thus indirect communication as described by Kierkegaard both respects and does not respect the freedom of the learner, treats the learner as both potentially very rational but as actually very irrational. Kierkegaard alludes to this paradox when he speaks of *helping* another person to "stand alone" (WL, 274). Given the difficulty of balancing respect for and distrust of the reader's freedom, it should not be surprising that Kierkegaard will, in the case of some readers, fail to strike the right balance. Thus we arrive again at the difficulty that although Kierkegaard dedicates much of his writing to "that single individual," his encounter with his readers is not in fact a one-on-one conversation, but a text that keeps "a solemn silence" "if you ask" it "about something" that it does not address.[7] It seems to me that Kierkegaard should have admitted this difficulty, its consequences for his readers, and his partial responsibility for these consequences more forthrightly than he did.

So far all of my criticisms of Kierkegaard's indirect communication have assumed that what he communicated indirectly was true. But what if it was false? If Kierkegaard is wrong about the truth, but recommends a way of life that borders on the fanatical, and does not argue directly for this way of life, but instead attempts to manipulate his readers and deceive them into taking this nearly fanatical and therefore dangerous way of life seriously—if all this is true, then Kierkegaard bears the responsibility for risking the ruination of many lives. Or, to put the point in another way, if Kierkegaard wishes to recommend a dangerous, lonely, and painful life to his readers, and if he is not totally certain that this way of life is the best or required life, perhaps he should communicate his recommendation as directly and straightforwardly as he can, and leave it up to his readers to decide how they will approach his writings in order to choose a life for themselves. Thus it is arguable that the seemingly skeptical Kierkegaard acts in a way that is justifiable only if he really knows the truth that he attempts to communicate indirectly.

When it comes to helping and harming others to find or to live the best life, or the divinely required life, all courses are perilous for those who lack perfect wisdom, and maybe even for God. To say this or that, or to be silent, to act this way or that, or to refrain from acting—all these may prove either beneficial or harmful to the person whom one attempts to help or refrains from helping, depending on an infinity of conditions, so that there is no escape from risk. Given that this is so, there may be something ungenerous in my criticisms of Kierkegaard's indirect communication. But Kierkegaard does talk big about his abilities as a communicator, and his brashness invites criticism. Moreover, as far as I can tell, his writings do not explain how he thought to navigate through all the perils of helping others that I have attempted to express here, and yet these perils are serious and worth considering. It is just possible that Kierkegaard was silently aware of all the dangers (and more) of indirect communication that I have here described, and that he adjusted his writing intelligently so as to be as harmless and as helpful as possible to as many readers as possible. For, as the saying goes, "know ten, but say nine." Or, as Kierkegaard himself put it, but without explaining what exactly he had in mind: "What responsibility I bear [in my attempt to introduce Christianity into Christendom] no one understands as I do" (PC, 139).

A defender of Kierkegaard might say that Kierkegaard simply did his best to help others and left the result to God. But did Kierkegaard know that he in fact had done his best to be helpful to his readers? Did he know that there was a God to whom it was fitting to entrust the product of his labors as a writer? And is it true that a benevolent deity would never allow one human being truly to harm another? "For it is necessary that temptations come, but woe to the man by whom they come."[8]

SIX

The Figure of Socrates and
the Climacean Capacity of
Paradoxical Reason

I have said that ye are gods; and all of you are children
of the most high. But ye shall die like men, and
fall like one of the princes. (Psalms 82:6)

That . . . ye might be partakers of the divine nature, having
escaped the corruption that is in the world. (2 Peter 1:4)

Work out your own salvation with fear and trembling.
For it is God which worketh in you both to will and to
do of his good pleasure. (2 Philippians 2:12–13)

A human being is a synthesis of the finite and the infinite,
and of the temporal and the eternal. (CUP, 56, 92)

What a piece of work is man, how noble in reason, how
infinite in faculties . . . in action how like an angel, in
apprehension how like a god . . . and yet to me, what is
this quintessence of dust? (Shakespeare, *Hamlet*)

Philosophical Fragments officially confines human beings within seemingly rigid limits,[1] but it also suggests that the man Socrates transcends
these limits. For example, *Fragments* claims that all non-Christians
"move away" from the *truth* of Christianity, but it also intimates that

Socrates longs for and prepares himself for the mystery of Christ. Bearing in mind that a *climacus* is a *ladder*,[2] we might say that *Fragments* dramatically depicts Socrates as a climacean figure, or as a climber over boundaries and a transgressor of limits, and that the function of this depiction is to provoke readers to become aware of their own climacean capacity and to inspire them to use it. This present chapter is an explication of Kierkegaard's artful use of the climacean figure of Socrates in *Philosophical Fragments*.

What *Fragments* merely suggests about Socrates, other works of Kierkegaard say more or less explicitly. Therefore, to make it easier to detect and decipher the suggestions about Socrates in *Fragments*, we will briefly consider some more overt claims that Kierkegaard makes about him in other portions of his authorship.

The Figure of Socrates in Kierkegaard's Authorship as a Whole

Kierkegaard is "definitely . . . convinced that [Socrates] has become" "a Christian" (pv, 54). In other words, he believes that the historical Socrates was a pilgrim on a path of spiritual growth that led him, postmortem, to faith in Christ, or that Socrates developed in himself wisdom, virtues, and desires that prepared him to understand, appreciate, and joyfully embrace Christian faith as the miraculous fulfillment of his existential striving. The remainder of this section elaborates the story that Kierkegaard tells of Socrates' heroic quest for Christ.

Socrates is for Kierkegaard a great exemplar of subjectivity, as he indicates by way of various paraphrases of subjectivity. That is to say, he calls Socrates *simple*, or a "single individual," or describes him as practicing *inwardness* and *primitivity*, or as "continually express[ing] the existential," or as "an existing individual who understood existing as the essential" (pv, 123; cup, 206). Furthermore, Kierkegaard frequently attributes virtues of subjectivity to Socrates, as he does, for example, when he calls him wise, noble, or righteous.

The subjectivity of Socrates and his journey toward Christian faith are not unrelated facts, but one and the same thing. The *Postscript* describes in great detail how subjectivity progresses by stages toward Christianity and situates Socrates within these stages as an "ethicist . . . bordering on the religious" (cup, 503). Thus the *Postscript* places

Socrates on the margins of "Religiousness A," which is the last sphere of human development before Christian faith. Similarly, Kierkegaard claims that Socrates was a virtuoso of "infinite resignation" (which Silentio in *Fear and Trembling* calls the "last stage before faith") when he writes that Socrates "is the only person who . . . took everything with him to the grave" (FT, 46; JP, 4:4303).

In *Sickness unto Death*, Anti-Climacus writes the following about Socrates:

> Let us never forget that Socrates' ignorance was a kind of fear and worship of God, that his ignorance was the Greek version of the Jewish saying: The fear of the Lord is the beginning of wisdom. Let us never forget that it was out of veneration for God that he was ignorant, that as far as it was possible for a pagan he was on guard duty as a *judge* on the frontier between God and man keeping watch so that the deep gulf of qualitative difference between them was maintained . . . between God and man. (SUD, 99)

By discovering and practicing a Greek version of the "beginning of wisdom," Socrates set himself on a course that culminates in the Christian end of wisdom. In other words, Socrates is for Greeks what the law and the prophets were to early Jewish converts to Christianity, a *preparatio Evangelii*.

The wisdom, virtues, and heroic actions of Socrates do not merely prepare for faith and lead to faith; they are also to be incorporated within the life and communication of faith. Let us consider several examples of Socratic elements of Christianity.

"Christianity teaches that everything essentially Christian depends solely upon faith; therefore it wants to be precisely a Socratic God-fearing ignorance, which . . . keep[s] watch so that the gulf of qualitative difference between God and man may be maintained" (SUD, 99). Thus Socratic ignorance is an essential component of faith and Christianity. It is also crucial for rightly reading the New Testament, since "one man alone with God's word" is "secured by Socratic ignorance" (JP, 4:4296). Similarly, Climacus claims that the "simple wise person" knows that Christianity is the paradox, knows that he does not understand it, and is thus prepared to approach Christianity in the right frame of mind (CUP, 227–228). And since Socrates is that "simple wise man of old" who was aware of his ignorance, Socrates has the prerequisites for rightly approaching Christianity (PC, 12; FSE, 9).

"*The single individual*—this category has been used only once, its first time, in a decisively dialectical way, by Socrates, in order to disintegrate paganism. In Christendom it will be used a second time in the opposite way, to make people (the Christians) Christians" (PV, 120; original emphasis). This is to say that the idea and practice of single individuality was discovered by Socrates, but it is to be appropriated, perfected, and fulfilled by Christianity.

In the belief that the true definition of Christianity has been lost, Kierkegaard writes that the "only analogy I have before me is Socrates; my task is a Socratic task, to audit the definition of what it is to be a Christian," that is, to *revise*[3] it, to restore the correct definition of it (M, 341). Similarly, the Christian "catechetical art is patterned on" Socrates and his pedagogy (CD, 218). Thus lost Christianity is to be recovered by Socratic methods, and converts are to be taught what Christianity is by way of Socratic midwifery. Similarly, Kierkegaard writes that Christian *preaching* should be "just as earnest" as the pagan apology of Socrates (FSE, 10).[4]

Kierkegaard goes even further than saying that Socrates prepares the way for Christianity and must be incorporated within the body of Christ; he also claims or suggests that Socrates is the equal of great Christians, and in some cases even their superior. For example, "outside of Christianity Socrates is the only man of whom it may be said: he explodes existence, which is seen quite simply in his elimination of the separation between poetry and actuality" (JP, 4:4301). This is to say that Socrates imitates and instantiates ideals as well as Christians, who are specially aided by grace and revelation. Furthermore, even though "Socrates is a pagan" and "Bernard of Clairvaux" is a *Christian* and a saint, "there is more Christianity in the Socratic approach" to converting people to a better way of thinking and living "than in St. Bernard's" (JP, 4:4295). Similarly, Socrates is a greater *reformer* than Luther, the greatest figure of the Protestant Reformation and Kierkegaard's greatest Christian hero (JP, 3:2514). Again, Christian *catechism* requires an "art of questioning" "modeled after" Socrates, but "no catechist has ever been able to ask questions as [Socrates] did" (CD, 218).[5] Thus Socrates is a greater teacher than any Christian.

As noted, the act of "infinite resignation" is an essential part of faith, and yet the pagan Socrates performs this act more perfectly than any

SOCRATES & CLIMACEAN CAPACITY OF PARADOXICAL REASON · 137

Christian does, since "Socrates is the only person who . . . took every-thing, everything with him to the grave" (JP, 4:4303). Finally, in a con-text in which Kierkegaard is discussing Christianity and Christians, he says that "of all men old Socrates is the greatest" (JP, 3:2514). Thus, to repeat, Kierkegaard presents Socrates as equal to and even greater than Christians.

As the church fathers saw types, figures, and analogues to Christ and Christianity in the Hebrew scriptures, likewise Kierkegaard sees Socrates as a prophetic figure who "prepared the way of the lord" and "made straight his paths" by way of his similarity or analogy with Chris-tianity, and even with Christ himself. For example, Socrates is a *martyr,* not for Christ to be sure, but for an *ethical skepticism* (JP, 4:4285). This is to say that he is a "witness to the truth," which for Kierkegaard is a crucial Christian category (see JP, 4:4962, 4968, in which Kierkegaard uses Socrates to illustrate what a Christian martyr—literally, a witness—should be). More provocatively, the "Socratic inwardness in existing is an analogue to faith," and "Socratic ignorance is an analogue to the category of the absurd," which is an essential element of Christian truth when it is proclaimed to the world (CUP, 205). Even though "Christianity was the first to discover the paradoxes," and paradox is essential to Christianity, Socrates is paradoxical before Christianity, and the "Socratic paradox consisted in this, that the eternal truth was related to an existing person" (SUD, 100; CUP, 207). Similarly, Kierkegaard claims that when Socrates talks about his death sentence "as if he were an entirely separate third party," he provides an "infinitely faint analogy to how God is infinite sub-jectivity" (JP, 4:4571). Finally, Socrates was analogous not just to Chris-tian ideas and practices, but even to Christ himself: "The difficulty with Socrates is not to understand his teaching but to understand himself; how much more so with regard to Christ" (JP, 4:4270). As with Christ, so with Socrates, the wonder is not the teaching but the man. Thus Socrates showed that human reason and human nature anticipate the Incarnation.

Sometimes Socrates even goes so far as to intimate and anticipate Christian things that Kierkegaard usually claims are totally new—so new that no human being could have an inkling of them without revela-tion, or without being *reborn* by the gift of the *condition.* For example, after denying that the *pagan* could have the "true conception of sin," Anti-Climacus writes that "the pagan must be eulogized who reached the point of despairing, not over the world, not over himself in general, but over his sin" (SUD, 116). Presumably this pagan was Socrates, since Socrates was the "greatest hero" of Greece (CUP, 368). And since Socrates despaired over his sin, it follows that he must have had some awareness of it, however confused and imperfect that consciousness may have been.

Works of Love describes Socrates' anticipation of Christian love in great detail. "See, that simple wise man of old," in addition to speaking of love of "the beautiful," where the beautiful is the "beloved and the friend" and the "choice of inclination and of passion," also "spoke about loving the ugly." But his saying this was only a "kind of jest." For the ugly is "the neighbor, whom one shall love." But "that simple wise man knew nothing at all about this. He did not know that the neighbor existed and that one should love him; when he spoke about loving the ugly, it was only teasing" (WL, 373; original emphasis).

It seems that Kierkegaard is "only teasing" when he says that Socrates "knew nothing at all" of the neighbor and of loving the neighbor. For surely part of Kierkegaard's reason for alluding to the Socratic love of the ugly is precisely to show how prophetic Socrates was in relation to Christian love (or, maybe, how marvelously Providence used Socrates). At any rate, there is a journal entry of Kierkegaard that leaves out the proviso that Socrates was only a tease: "What Socrates says about loving the ugly is really the Christian doctrine of love for the neighbor" (JP, 1:942; cf. CA, 70). Perhaps the teasing of Socrates consisted not in his saying something he thought was obviously ridiculous, namely, that one could or should love the ugly, but in his ironically hiding the beauty of his thought behind a jest.[6]

Since Socrates lived before Christ, he could not have Christian faith. Nonetheless he came pretty close:

> Venerable Father Abraham! Second Father of the Race! You who were the first to feel and to bear witness to that prodigious passion [faith] that disdains the terrifying battle with the raging elements and the forces of creation in order to contend with God, you who were the first to know that supreme passion [surely faith is the supreme passion], the holy, pure, and humble expression for the divine madness that was admired by the pagans. (FT, 23)

The "divine madness that was admired by the pagans" is a patent reference to the account of Socratic eros in the Phaedrus. By calling faith an *expression* of Socratic eros, this passage clearly implies that faith is a version or variation of Socratic eros, or that the eros of Socrates was a prophetic prefiguring of faith. We might even suspect the passage of suggesting that Socrates erotically longed for Christ.[7]

Inasmuch as Kierkegaard presents Socrates as anticipating mysteries that remained hidden from the foundation of the world until the revelation of Christ, we might say that Kierkegaard regards Socrates as a sort of pagan prophet of Christianity. In *Christian Discourses* he comes pretty near to saying exactly this when he ascribes to Socrates the prophetic function of "fetch[ing] wisdom down from heaven" (CD, 219).

Thus in many ways Kierkegaard portrays Socrates as a heroic figure on a quest for Christian faith—a quest in which, as we have seen, Kierkegaard thinks Socrates succeeded, postmortem.[8]

The Figure of Socrates in *Philosophical Fragments*

Having examined Kierkegaard's overt claims about Socrates in his authorship as a whole, we are ready to investigate his suggestions about Socrates in *Fragments*.

Climacus claims that in order to "to elucidate the difference between . . . the pagan philosophical position" and Christianity with as little *confusion* as possible, *Fragments* misrepresents Socrates as a "speculative philosopher instead of what he was, an existing [i.e., subjective] thinker who understood existing as the essential" (CUP, 206). In other words, Climacus claims that he sets out deliberately to distort Socrates in *Fragments* by portraying him as an objective philosopher, and he does this in order to make a clear distinction between objective (or speculative) philosophy and Christianity.

The main way that Climacus gives Socrates a *speculative* appearance in *Fragments* is by using him to represent a theory of knowledge. According to the *Postscript*, Socrates must "part with" his epistemological *thesis* that "all knowing is recollecting" in order to *exist* subjectively (CUP, 206). Therefore, as Climacus sees things, to present Socrates as an epistemologist in *Fragments* is to cast him in the role of a speculative philosopher. Moreover, Climacus's readers are likely to see things as he does. From the time of Descartes at least, epistemology has typically been conducted in a theoretical or speculative mode. Therefore speculative readers of *Fragments* will naturally suppose that if Socrates is interested in epistemology, he must be speculative like them. By not overtly and unambiguously correcting the false impression that he gives of Socrates, Climacus allows and even encourages his readers erroneously to suppose that Socrates is a speculative philosopher.

Fragments suggests in many ways that beneath Socrates' speculative appearance there is a subjective reality. To begin humbly, Climacus criticizes some contemporaries of his who claim to "go beyond Socrates," but "nevertheless say essentially the same as he, only not nearly so well" (PF, 111). The mere fact that Socrates is presented in *Fragments* as the best speculative philosopher already mildly suggests that Socrates is subjective, or moving toward subjectivity. For presumably the superiority of Socrates consists in his having the courage to seek the truth and the humility, honesty, and self-knowledge not to exaggerate how much truth he has found. And since courage, humility, honesty, and self-knowledge are essential to subjectivity, by implicitly attributing these virtues to Socrates, Climacus intimates his subjectivity.

Socrates is that "simple wise man" (PF, 19). As we saw in chapter 4, *simple* is a Kierkegaardian synonym for *subjective*. As a simple man, Socrates "artistically exemplifies what he has understood" with "wonderful consistency" (PF, 10). For instance, he penetratingly *perceives* that the *relation* of *midwifery* "is the highest relation a human being can have to another" and practices the art of midwifery with "rare integrity" (PF, 10, 24). But practicing what one has understood with wonderful consistency and with rare integrity is the very definition of subjectivity. Socrates possesses "noble, thoroughgoing humanity" (PF, 11). But Climacus thinks that objectivity is *impersonal* and *inhuman* (CUP, 196), and that subjectivity is *personal* and human, so that by ascribing "thoroughgoing humanity" to Socrates, Climacus thereby attributes subjectivity to him as well. Socrates *loves* the *learner,* whom he addresses as a "single individual" (PF, 30, 11). But, since a single individual is another Kierkegaardian variation on the idea of a subjectivity, when Socrates addresses the learner as a single individual he must be doing this in order to promote subjectivity in both himself and the learner. Socrates holds to the thesis that human beings have the *condition,* which is a condition, according to Climacus, not only for the *truth,* but for "eternal happiness" (PF, 58). And since an interest in eternal happiness is characteristic of subjectivity, by presenting Socrates as concerned about eternal happiness, Climacus presents him as a subjective thinker. Again, Climacus claims that Socrates was "zealous for what is human" and practiced a "disciplining of himself with" a "divine jealousy . . . in which he loved the divine" (PF, 23–24). But to have zeal for the human and to discipline oneself out of love for the divine are very good descriptions of subjectivity. Yet again, Climacus writes that the *work* that Socrates "carried out was a divine commission," and working for the god is yet another apt expression of subjectivity (PF, 10). Finally, Socrates has many other virtues that Kierkegaard often associates with subjectivity: Socrates possesses "rare magnanimity"; is *unbribable;* is *uncompromising;* has the *courage* to reject *half-measures,* "empty talk," and "vague words"; practices *self-denial;* and exhibits *profundity* in his thinking (PF, 10–12, 19, 23). Thus there are many pieces of evidence in *Fragments* that individually point quite clearly to the subjectivity of Socrates and that collectively point uncontrovertibly to it.

In its eagerness to distinguish Christianity from merely human things, *Fragments* distorts not only Socrates but also the limits of human capacity. *Fragments* corrects its distortion of human limits similarly to the way that it corrects its distortion of Socrates—by suggesting that Socrates surpasses the limits that it has misdrawn of human nature.

According to *Fragments,* all virtues outside of Christianity are merely "glittering vices" (PF, 53). This is to say that genuine virtue is not possible for Greeks like Socrates. And yet, Climacus attributes many virtues to Socrates—self-denial, magnanimity, nobility, courage, and so on—with evident admiration, and with little or no hint that these virtues are sham or counterfeit. Thus Climacus suggests that Socrates has virtues that are not merely *vitia splendida.*

Climacus claims in *Fragments* that every non-Christian is "not even a seeker" but is "going away from" the *truth* (PF, 13). Indeed, the non-Christian is so far outside the truth that he cannot even "ask about" it (PF, 14). Nor would he want to inquire into it even if he could, since he is "polemical against the truth," that is, "untruth" (PF, 15). Thus Climacus claims that all non-Christians both flee and fight the truth. But Climacus also suggests that Socrates seeks the truth. For in chapter 3 of *Fragments* he suggests an interpretation of Socrates' philosophical eros as the "passion of thought" whose proper object is Jesus Christ, who is the *truth* (PF, 37).

There are many indications that Climacus intends his idea of the passion of thought as an interpretation of Socratic eros. First, he introduces this idea in a context in which he makes many references to the *Phaedrus* and to the *Symposium*, the two Platonic dialogues whose themes are philosophical eros. Second, the phrase *the passion of thought* functions quite nicely as a synonym for philosophical eros, since philosophical eros is passionate in that it is erotic and of thought in that it is philosophical. Third, in the *Phaedrus*, Socrates claims that the hidden meaning of erotic desire is a longing for a happiness that is rooted in contemplation and imitation of the divine, and he argues that authentic philosophy is the highest expression of eros. Climacus echoes the *Phaedrus* doctrine of eros when he says that the "passion of thought" "wants to discover something that thought itself cannot think," that is to say, something transcendent or divine (PF, 37). Consequently, both the passion of thought and philosophical eros are tropisms toward divine transcendence. Fourth, and finally, Climacus constructs two analogies in chapter 3 of *Fragments* that compare "erotic love" and "the understanding's paradoxical passion," thereby linking the passion of thought tightly with eros (PF, 38–39, 47–48). Therefore, I conclude, *Fragments* presents the passion of thought as an interpretation of Socratic eros.

Climacus not only offers the passion of thought as an explication of Socratic eros, he also suggests that this eros is an incipient longing for Christ. Climacus claims that the passion of thought desires "to discover something that thought itself cannot think." He also presents the "absolute paradox" (which is his thinly veiled redescription of the God-man, Jesus Christ) as the prime example of the unthinkable (PF, 37–48). Putting these two ideas together, we arrive at the conclusion that Climacus presents the passion of thought as a desire to discover Jesus Christ. This conclusion is also suggested, but much less clearly and forcefully, by two analogies in *Fragments* that compare faith and erotic love (PF, 38–39, 47–48, 49). I leave it to readers to examine these analogies for themselves. That Climacus presents Socratic eros as a desire for Christ also seems to be confirmed in the *Postscript*, which describes a *maiden* who *reads* in the *Gospel* "of the joyousness of her erotic love" (CUP, 35). Presumably the object of the maiden's erotic love is Christ. Furthermore, the *Postscript* claims that "erotic love" in the *Symposium* "manifestly means existence," or subjectivity (CUP, 92). Since the *Postscript* presents faith as the culmination and perfection of subjectivity, and since it interprets Socratic eros as subjectivity, it clearly posits *Christos* as the telos of eros. Therefore, as Socrates claims that the deepest desire of sexuality is for something divine, so Climacus suggests that the divine object of eros is Jesus Christ.

Here is another example of *Fragments*'s positing a human limit and implying that Socrates surpasses that limit. According to Climacus, the infidel pagan is "absolutely different" from the *truth* and therefore cannot have any glimpse of the truth unless he is *reborn* (PF 47, 19–22). Consequently, a pagan like Socrates cannot share any essential truth with Christianity, much less contribute anything essential to it. And yet Climacus explicitly says that Socrates correctly *perceived* that being a *midwife* is the "highest relation that a human being can have to another"; that Socrates is "forever right" about midwifery; and that Socrates not only correctly conceived midwifery, but practiced it with "wonderful consistency" (PF, 10). One might have suspected that for Climacus the love of neighbor commanded in the Gospel would utterly supersede Socratic midwifery as the way for human beings to relate to and communicate with one another. Instead Climacus presents Socrates as at least sharing, perhaps as contributing, truth essential to Christianity and to the loving communication of Christianity.[9]

Although *Fragments* claims that all pagans are "absolutely different" from God, or that there is "no analogy" in paganism to Christ, it also suggests that Socrates is an analogue to Christ (PF, 47). *Fragments* says that out of *love*, God establishes *unity* between himself and humanity by a *descent* (PF, 31–32). This loving, unifying descent is commonly called the *incarnation*, or Jesus Christ. *Fragments* also claims that the *ignorance* of Socrates was "the unitive expression of love for the learner" (PF, 30). This seems to mean that Socrates loved the learner, and sometimes achieved unity with learners by pretending to be as ignorant as they in order to achieve unity with them. In any case, *Fragments* presents Socratic ignorance as loving and unifying, and admitting one's ignorance requires the descent called humility. It follows that *Fragments* describes Socratic ignorance as an analogue to the *incarnation*, in that it presents both Socratic ignorance and the incarnation as loving, unifying, and self-humbling descents. Nor does the analogy end here. For just as Christ came for everyone and consorted with the poor, the outcast, and even notorious sinners, likewise "Socrates did not keep company solely with brilliant minds," but conversed with ordinary men "in workshops and in the market-place" (PF, 31, 11). Furthermore, in Climacus's analogy between a fairy-tale king and Christ he calls the king a "connoisseur of human nature," and later in the book he also describes Socrates in exactly the same terms (PF, 29, 37). Thus *Fragments* presents Socrates in many ways as analogous to Christ.[10]

Fragments claims that the non-Christian is so far outside the truth that he cannot even ask about it, or that the non-Christian needs revelation and mental faculties regenerated by grace in order to achieve even an inkling or an intimation of Christian truth. For example, Climacus claims that Socrates *lacks* "the consciousness of sin," which is to say that Socrates lacks the truth about himself (PF, 47). And yet, as I shall argue at length in the next chapter, Climacus hints that Socrates is vaguely aware of his sin.

Thus *Fragments* suggests that Socrates (at least partly) surpasses the limits of human capacity that it officially declares. And this is to say that *Fragments* presents Socrates as a Climacean figure who climbs over boundaries and transcends the limits of human capacity as he anticipates and even prophesies Christianity, or as a dauntless frontiersman on the border regions between humanity and divinity, or as a Greek John the Baptist, greater than anyone born of woman, but still lesser than the least in the Kingdom of Heaven.

The Universality of the Climacean Capacity

Socrates heroically transcends human limits, not by being an exceptional *genius*, but by achieving "virtuosity in the universally human," or by "being great in that which everyone could be" (JP, 4:4271). This implies that Climacus uses the figure of Socrates to provoke readers to become aware of their own climacean capacity for heroic greatness and to challenge them to use it as Socrates did. In other words, Kierkegaard uses the figure of Socrates not as an image to contemplate, but as an exemplar to imitate. *Fragments* intimates the universality of the climacean capacity by means of numerous paradoxes.

Near the beginning of *Fragments*, Climacus refers to the famous problem that Meno poses to Socrates, and to its Socratic solution:

a person cannot possibly seek what he knows, and, just as impossibly, he cannot seek what he does not know, for what he knows he cannot seek, since he knows it, and what he does not know he cannot even seek, because, after all, he does not even know what he is supposed to seek. Socrates thinks through the difficulty by means [of the principle] that all learning and seeking are but recollecting. Thus the ignorant person merely needs to be reminded in order, by himself, to call to mind what he knows. (PF, 9)

Thus Socrates suggests that human beings are both limited by ignorance and at the same time somehow surpass their ignorance with an obscured or latent knowledge that belongs to them eternally. By referring, at the beginning of *Fragments*, to this Socratic claim that humans in their usual condition are both limited and transcend their limits, Climacus intimates his paradoxical theme of the climacean capacity of human beings.

According to Climacus, human *understanding* is so impotent and corrupt that the best thing for it is to "will its own downfall." Curiously, this weak and perverse understanding can discover its need for a downfall and then will this disconcerting event (PF, 37). How is it that the understanding can be so blind and yet so discerning, so perverse and yet so nobly self-denying?

Thought "wants to discover something that thought itself cannot think" and can (PF, 37; CUP, 558). But how can thought discover what it cannot think? If Climacus had written that thought wants to discover and can discover what it cannot *know, grasp,* or *comprehend,* we could perhaps go along with him. But how can *thought* discover what it cannot even *think*? In what exactly does thought's finding something unthinkable consist if not in thinking it? In other words, how can thought transcend the boundaries of the unthinkable enough to know or even to sense that it has encountered something unthinkable, but come away from the encounter with so little that it has not thought the unthinkable and cannot say anything about it even with the aid of "negative theology" (PF, 44)?

Although the *understanding* "cannot think" the *paradox,* it can "detect that the paradox will likely be its downfall" (PF, 47). What a prophetic understanding to detect so much in what it cannot think! For surely the understanding would be more likely to label a paradox that it cannot think as gobbledygook than to detect some great mystery in it that would spell its own downfall. And yet, according to the *Postscript*, the understanding is supposed to be able to "penetratingly perceive" the difference between mere *nonsense* and genuinely paradoxical transcendence (CUP, 568; cf. 558). But how does the understanding penetratingly perceive this in a manner consistent with its limits?

Human understanding can discern "that this [i.e., the incarnation of God as an individual human being] is the paradox" (PF, 59). To understand that the incarnation is the paradox seems to mean understanding that it is the greatest possible paradox. But how does one understand so much about the unthinkable paradox and its status?

In the Interlude of *Philosophical Fragments*, Climacus writes at length about the "absolutely different"—clearly a reformulation of the unthinkable paradox—which in no way can be thought except on the false assumption that the person thinking the absolutely different is similar to the absolutely different. And he seems to expect this meditation on absolute difference to mean something to readers who are (presumably) absolutely different from the paradox (PF, 44–47).

Climacus writes that *rebirth* can be *understood* only by the *reborn;* yet he writes this for the once born and asks them to understand rebirth, or at least to understand that only the reborn can understand rebirth (PF, 47, 20–21). But how can the merely earth-born understand any of this?

Although Climacus describes the *god* as the *unknown*, as the "absolutely different," and as so loftily transcendent that even the "*via negationis*" is inadequate for speaking about it, he also attempts to evoke in his readers an intimation of the god's "unfathomable sorrow" over the difficulties presented by his goal of loving communion with humans (PF, 28). In other words, Climacus attempts to assist his readers to glimpse what it is like to be the utterly transcendent God and to see human beings as God sees them. He claims, moreover, that only a "lumpish soul" could lack "an intimation" of the sorrow of the god (PF, 28). But how is it possible for human beings to attain an intimation of what it is like to be the absolutely different and unknown God? How can we even so much as glimpse the ineffable and unfathomable life of divine love? And how is it possible for Climacus to evince sympathy for the divine *sorrow* in language, when "all human language has no intimation" of such sorrow (PF, 28)?

According to Climacus, every "single individual's thought" contains the "passion of thought" to discover the unthinkable "insofar as he, thinking, is not merely himself" (PF, 37). But in what sense is a single individual not merely himself? It seems that the individual as such has limits that the individual as such naturally exceeds. In other words, the human appears to be a kind of thing that in its very being naturally climbs over its own limits. This ontological paradox that a human being can somehow exceed the limits of his or her own being is presumably connected to the epistemological paradox that a human being can somehow exceed the limits of human knowledge.

Faith is "just as paradoxical as the paradox" (PF, 65). And yet the paradox is that the eternal and infinite God has become an individual human being. How can an ordinary human being be or become as paradoxical as the divine paradox by any efforts, human or divine?

Kierkegaard sets limits to human capacity and then implies their transcendence in virtually all his books. Consider this example from the *Postscript*:

> There is no contradiction in a person's being capable of nothing at all before God except that he becomes aware of this, since this is only another expression for the absoluteness of God, and that a person would not even . . . potentially be capable of this would be an expression for his not existing at all. (CUP, 461)

Presumably Climacus uses *existing* in this passage in its technical sense to mean *subjective*. If so, Climacus is claiming that if one could not discover one's incapacity before God, then neither could one exist as a being who attempts to live in time according to an eternal ideal. But how can one be both capable of nothing at all and at the same time capable of knowing the eternal and one's incapacity in relation to it? Perhaps knowing matters so little to Climacus that it counts as nothing for him.

Let us consider one last paradox, which pervades Kierkegaard's whole authorship. On the one hand, "there is nothing at all that can be 'known' about" Christ (PC, 23), and "one cannot *know* anything at all about *Christ*," who "exists only for faith" (PC, 25; cf. 35). On the other hand, as discussed in chapter 1, Kierkegaard and his pseudonymous authors say or imply over and over and in many ways that they and others do or can achieve "knowledge of Christ"—at least in part (SUD, 113).[11]

Distinguishing between Socrates and Christianity

A critic of Kierkegaard might make the following accusation: The reason Kierkegaard draws limits to human nature and then suggests that Socrates and other human beings do or can surpass these limits is that he is in a hopeless muddle about the relation between Socrates and Christianity, or about the relation between reason and faith. Nor is it surprising that Kierkegaard has contradictory ideas about the relation of reason and faith, since he numbers both Socrates and Luther among his heroes, and therefore attempts to synthesize them. But such a synthesis is simply not viable. For Socrates said that he was "the kind of person who did only what seemed best to him upon rational reflection," while Luther described reason as a *whore*, "this pestilent beast," "the fountain and headspring of all mischiefs," and "the enemy of God."[12] Thus it is plain as day that Kierkegaard's ill-advised effort to marry Lutheran fideism and Socratic rationalism was predestined to issue only in monstrous contradiction and enormous confusion.

In what follows I aim to show that Kierkegaard is not confused, but supremely and artfully in control of his paradoxes. But first I will briefly suggest how Kierkegaard might draw the distinction between Socrates and Christianity without contradiction and confusion.

The non-negotiable core of the distinction between Socratic subjectivity and Christian faith is that neither Socrates nor any other human being could, without grace and revelation, fully discover Christianity so as to become a Christian and save his own soul. More specifically, without grace and revelation one cannot have faith in the incarnate deity who died for the atonement and forgiveness of human sin. Even though Climacus suggests that Socrates and others can unwittingly prepare themselves for Christianity; obscurely long for it; and have virtues, wisdom, and practices that are analogues, or anticipations, or intimations, or even prophecies of Christ and Christianity, he never goes further than this to suggest that Socrates can simply dispense with grace and revelation.[13]

The Function of the Climacean Figure of Socrates

In this section I will elaborate on the claim that Climacus deliberately and artfully uses Socrates as an image of the climacean capacity in order to awaken and develop this capacity in readers and in order to encourage them to use it subjectively and Christianly.

As we have seen, Climacus admits that he distorted Socrates in *Fragments* by presenting him as a pagan "speculative philosopher," when in fact Climacus thinks that Socrates is a subjective individual on a quest for Christian faith (CUP, 206). In misrepresenting Socrates as a speculative epistemologist Climacus also distorts Christianity, by presenting it as the epistemological alternative to the Socratic epistemology; he also distorts himself, by writing as an objective epistemologist whose purpose is to distinguish between alternative epistemologies;[14] and finally, he distorts the distinction between Christianity and Socrates by expressing it primarily in epistemological terms. And yet his reason for distorting Socrates in the first place was to facilitate making the distinction between Socrates and Christianity. How then are we to understand Climacus's drawing this distinction by deeply and deliberately distorting its terms?

Climacus distorts the very distinction he wishes to draw as part of the two-stage strategy of writing that we have already seen Kierkegaard and his pseudonyms employ several times. The first stage is *finding* or meeting readers "where they are" (PV, 45). Since Climacus writes *Fragments* for speculative readers, he meets them by giving his message a seemingly speculative content. Presumably he thinks that if he were to present the distinction accurately, speculative readers would themselves distort it, or ignore it, or not read it, or remain existentially unaffected by it—even if they did read it. Therefore he preemptively concedes to his speculative readers their speculative misunderstanding of his message in order to set them at ease, put them off their guard, capture their attention, and thus win a hearing from them.

The second stage of Climacus's double strategy for dealing with speculative readers is to *suggest* or *hint* that the seemingly speculative Socrates is in fact a subjective striver on a journey to Christian faith. Readers who pick up on this suggestion, even subliminally, are nudged to follow Socrates in this movement, by sympathizing with him, or inclining toward him, or imitating him—at least in their thought. And if they follow Socrates in this movement, they may reach the point at which they can understand and appreciate subjectivity and faith well enough to make a genuine decision about them. In other words, *Fragments* induces readers to become actively involved (at least in thought) in a quest for subjectivity or for Christianity before they know what they are doing, so that when they finally realize that they are being summoned to subjectivity or Christianity they have already begun to appreciate it and to imitate it or participate in its movements. This existential induction is the supreme art of *Fragments.*

In part 1 of *Either/Or* the Kierkegaardian pseudonym named "A" indicates another way of understanding the strategy of suggestion in *Fragments,* when he writes that "the dramatic sacred coin" is "action and situation" (E/O, 1:117). Drama reveals human beings not by overt description, but by setting them in various situations and having them act. Instead of straightforwardly *saying* something about a character, or about human nature, drama *shows* us characters in action, and thereby suggests something about them and human nature. Applying these remarks about drama to our current investigation, we might say that in *Fragments* Socrates is not merely the spokesman for a philosophical position, but a dramatic character who performs heroic deeds (just barely offstage, in the tradition of Greek tragedy) so as to point out human possibilities for the audience to imagine, appreciate, and perhaps imitate.

Dramatic suggestion is superior to direct communication in many ways for the purpose of inviting readers to become subjective. Being incomplete, it requires readers to become self-active in completing its meaning. And since self-activity is essential to subjectivity, drama can be used to invite or encourage incipient subjectivity. Moreover, inasmuch as drama is more interesting and more personal than direct communication is, it engages its audience more deeply and more fully than direct communication does, in that it engages not just their intellects, but their emotions and imaginations as well. Finally, since observers of drama tend to sympathize and even identify with the dramatic hero, they also tend to imitate the hero, at least in their imagining, thinking, and feeling, if not yet in their choosing, living, and acting. Thus dramatic suggestion is an effective means of inviting observers to emulate heroes and their subjectivity.

Climacus is concerned not just to invite his readers to subjectivity, but also to train them for it by developing and exercising in them a mode of consciousness capable of appreciating it. Alternatively, Climacus does not write with the purpose of logically proving the truth or worth of subjectivity or Christianity, nor again with the aim of rhetorically per-suading people to become subjective, but in order to evoke and encourage in his readers a way of thinking that can understand subjectivity well enough to make a decision for or against it. Without this attempt to evoke and encourage the mode of consciousness needed for understanding subjectivity and Christianity, arguing for these two things is like trying pick up and read a digital signal with an analog antenna.

"A," the pseudonymous author of *Either/Or,* describes a form of "lyrical thought" that is "so ecstatic that it goes beyond thought" (EO, 1:59). Similarly, Climacus writes that "in lyrically seeking to surpass itself, thinking wills to discover the paradoxical" (CUP, 104). "A" further claims that lyrical thought is an instance of the "paradox that . . . in presentiment and ignorance one can have a kind of experience" of that of which one is ignorant (EO, 1:66). Presumably this idea of a paradoxical presentiment within ignorance is an interpretation of Socratic ignorance and points toward the possibility that an intimation of Christianity might fall within the purview of the ignorance of Socrates. Climacus himself also indicates the possibility that truth might be "possessed . . . in the form of ignorance"—though he denies that the truth of Christianity can be possessed in this way (PF, 13). Similarly, he writes in the *Postscript* that the *god* is "present just as soon as the uncertainty of everything is thought infinitely" (CUP, 87). In any case, returning to *Either/Or,* "A" goes on to indicate that one way to evoke lyrical thought is to deny that which transcends thought. For it is "evident upon reflection that in the positing of something the other that is excluded is indirectly posited. . . . That which is to be negated . . . really comes to light, is really posited, first by the act that excluded it through a positing of the opposite positive" (EO, 1:61). This is to say that the most effective way to reveal something sometimes is to negate it.[15] Applying this maxim to *Fragments,* we might conclude that its repeated denials of the natural or Socratic sympathy or capacity for Christianity are precisely a way of revealing this capacity. More generally, many of the assertions in *Fragments* of human limits seem to be indirect assertions of a capacity to transcend those limits.

The book *Johannes Climacus* seems to confirm that Climacus aims to evoke a higher mode of awareness in his readers. We read in this book that "consciousness . . . is the relation . . . whose form is contradiction," and that consciousness "emerges precisely through the collision" be-

tween "ideality and reality" (JC, 171). Part of the meaning of this quotation is that *consciousness*—which "A" calls "lyrical thought"—emerges
through awareness of the collision, contradiction, or opposition between
such opposites as the ideal and the actual, or the eternal and the temporal, or the infinite and the finite. With this idea of consciousness in
mind, we might say that the function of the Socratic paradoxes in *Philosophical Fragments,* which are *collisions* or apparent contradictions between human finitude and infinite ideals, is to provoke the emergence
of *consciousness.* These paradoxes are thus the *torment* and *incentive* of
the *passion* or passionate thinking which can "correctly [perceive] the
unknown as frontier," or which can perceive a new world of possibility
beyond the ordinary, workaday world (PF, 44). When Climacus denies
that this kind of thinking can "absolutely transcend itself," he implies
that it *can* do so partially (PF, 45). Thus *partially transcending oneself in
thinking* is yet another description of the mode of consciousness that
Climacus aims to elicit in his readers with his puzzles, paradoxes, and
antics with limits.

In *Fragments,* Climacus says that he *suggests* a certain *analogy* "in
order to awaken the mind to an understanding of the divine" (PF, 26).
Presumably, by awakening the mind Climacus does not mean merely
providing new information, or offering a clever new argument, but alter-
ing and elevating the mind's mode of awareness.

Similarly, in a reply to a critic of *Fear and Trembling,* Kierkegaard
writes that Johannes de Silentio thinks that when it comes to the *decision*
of faith, "everything . . . depends upon passionate concentration," which
seems to be an intense and heightened mode of awareness (FT, 377, 259).

Kierkegaard again shows his concern for assisting readers to transform their consciousness when he defines a *deliberation* as a form of
writing that "does not presuppose the definitions as given and understood," but aims to "*awaken* and provoke people and sharpen thought"
(WL, 469).

Kierkegaard seeks to evoke lyrical thought in his readers so that they
can become aware of subjectivity not only as an enticing possibility, or
gift, but also as a task. In *The Concept of Anxiety,* the pseudonymous
author, Vigilius Haufniensis, writes the following: "At every moment, the
individual is both himself and the race. This is man's perfection viewed
as a state. It is also a *contradiction,* but a contradiction is always the

expression of a *task,* and a *task* is movement" (CA, 28; emphasis added). This passage indicates that correctly perceiving certain contradictions, or paradoxes, makes one aware of subjectivity as the task of synthesizing or somehow doing justice to such opposites as the individual and the universal. Thus the function of the paradoxes in *Fragments* is to evoke a form of consciousness that is aware of both the gift and the task of subjectivity.

By now it should be very clear that Kierkegaard attempts not just to describe subjectivity and Christianity well, but to evoke in his readers a mode or modes of awareness capable of understanding and appreciating his descriptions. It should also be quite clear that his efforts at evocation make frequent use of certain contradictions, paradoxes, and artful negations of what he wishes to posit.

The mode of consciousness that Kierkegaard seeks to evoke in his readers might be described as *intermediate,* in more than one sense of the word. Climacus claims that a human is an "intermediate being," a "synthesis of the temporal and the eternal," and of the "infinite and the finite," and that *existing,* or subjectivity, "is a somewhat intermediate state" that is "suitable for an intermediate being such as a human being is" (CUP, 56, 92, 221, 329). Since human nature and subjectivity are intermediate things, and since human beings need to reflect their condition not only in what they think but also in how they think, they have much need of an intermediate mode of consciousness. Moreover, it is fitting that a transition from one mode of existence to another as great as that from objectivity to subjectivity (and then on to Christianity) will require transitional or intermediate modes of thinking. Therefore Kierkegaard needs to evoke intermediate thinking not only because subjectivity itself requires it, but also in order to support the transition from objectivity to subjectivity.

Climacus sees himself as learning about the intermediate character of subjectivity from Socrates. He writes that "erotic love manifestly means existence" in the *Symposium,* a dialogue which describes eros as a spiritual intermediary that links the human and the divine (CUP, 92). Furthermore, he writes that "as existing the human being must indeed participate in the idea but is not himself the idea," thus using the Socratic idea of participation (which is clearly an intermediate condition between pure ideality and utter materiality) as a gloss or interpretation of *existing,* or subjectivity (CUP, 331). Finally, Climacus sees "Socratic ignorance" as "the expression, firmly maintained with all the passion of inwardness, of the relation of the eternal truth to an existing person," and he thinks that this ignorance is a *paradox* because it bridges the gap between a temporal person and eternal truth (CUP, 202). Thus Climacus sees the eros, participation, and ignorance of Socrates as manifestations of the intermediate character of subjectivity.

Climacus artfully unites intermediate consciousness and intermediate existence in his conception of "infinite *interestedness* in eternal happiness" by calling our attention to the etymological root of *interest,* namely, *interesse,* which means "to be in between" (CUP, 314). Thus to be conscious of eternal happiness in one's care and concern for it is "to be in between" a merely human condition and an eternal, divine state. This is to say that Kierkegaard aims to provoke not only intermediate thinking, but intermediate feeling and being in unity with intermediate thinking, or that thinking can be rightly transitional only when it is rightly modulated by spiritual emotion.

To sum up, the climacean capacity is a power of synthesizing an eternal, infinite, universal, and absolute ideal with or in the temporal, finite, particular, and relative aspects of oneself and one's everyday life, which is to say that the climacean capacity is a capacity for subjectivity. And the function of the Socratic paradoxes in *Fragments* is to awaken and develop this capacity in readers.

Intermediate Thinking in the *Postscript*

In the *Postscript,* the subtitle of the chapter titled "Becoming Subjective" includes the following words: "examples of thinking oriented to becoming subjective" (CUP, 129). Thus Climacus explicitly announces his interest in thinking oriented to becoming subjective, or in thinking that is intermediate between mere objectivity and pure subjectivity. In what follows we will consider many examples from the *Postscript* of thinking that is intermediate between objectivity and subjectivity, both to confirm Climacus's interest in intermediate thinking and to show more fully how he conceives its character and function.

C. Stephen Evans points out that Climacus uses *subjectivity* in the *Postscript* ambiguously. Sometimes by *subjectivity* Climacus means passionate striving to appropriate an eternal and infinite ideal within temporality and finitude. And sometimes he merely means passionate thinking about whether, or how, to appropriate such an ideal.[16] Obviously, this second sort of subjectivity, which consists in thinking about striving without yet striving, is an intermediary or transitional mode of thinking between objectivity and subjectivity in the eminent sense.

Climacus describes the "skeptical *ataraxia*" of some ancient Greek philosophers as "an existence-attempt to abstract from existing" (CUP, 318; cf. 309, 399). Whatever this paradoxical existence attempt may be, insofar as it is an "attempt to abstract from existing," it is objective, but insofar as it is an "existence-attempt," it is subjective. It is therefore intermediate between objectivity and subjectivity, and as such could lead from the former to the latter.

Don Quixote, whom Climacus calls a *zealot* and a *lunatic,* represents a mode of thinking *and acting* intermediate between objectivity and subjectivity (CUP, 35–36, 195). A zealot like the Knight of the Sad Countenance is objective in that his goal is *finite* or worldly, and subjective in that he strives with "infinite passion" for his finite goal (CUP, 35, 195). By striving with infinite passion for a finite goal the zealot puts himself in a position to learn that only an infinite ideal is worthy of infinite passion. Thus zealotry or lunacy is a transitional mode of thinking and living that might lead from immature to mature subjectivity.

Climacus suggests that Lessing practiced a "continued striving for a system" (CUP, 108). Lessing's goal, namely, "a system," marks him as speculative and objective. But his "continued striving for" that goal marks him as subjective, so that in Lessing we find yet another mode of thinking that could be transitional between objectivity and subjectivity. Presumably striving for a system is an example of *working* oneself "through and out of . . . objectivity," which work Climacus claims is necessary for the passage from objectivity to subjectivity (CUP, 66–67). In any case, working oneself through and out of objectivity is yet another apt description of thinking that is between mere objectivity and subjectivity.

Climacus claims that *poetry borders* on the religious (CUP, 443; cf. SUD, 77–78). Poetic thinking "verges on" the religious because it can appreciate it, admire it, long for it, and in general be deeply and passionately aware of it. This is to say that poetic thinking is the means of becoming aware of a religious ideal for which a person might live and die. But mere appreciation is not yet imitation, and appreciation without imitation is much easier and more pleasant than appreciative imitation with its suffering and strenuousness. Therefore poetic thinkers are tempted to admire and appreciate the religious ideal without imitating it. When they succumb to this temptation, they practice a poetic mode of awareness of the ideal that is in between objective obliviousness of the ideal and subjective imitation of it. Anti-Climacus seems to agree with this analysis of the possibilities of poetry when he describes a "poet-existence verging on the religious," which he says is "the most dialectical frontier" between merely human and strictly Christian categories (SUD, 77). The reader here may also recall the account (see chapter 1) of Johannes de Silentio, which described him as intermediary between Kierkegaard's own understanding and practice of faith, on the one hand, and the presumptuous ignorance of faith of Kierkegaard's targeted readership, on the other.

In the *Accounting,* Kierkegaard describes yet another aspect of the way that he uses poetry in his maieutic mode of writing:

> The maieutic lies in the relation between the esthetic [and therefore poetic] writing as the beginning and the religious as the telos [goal]. It begins with the esthetic, in which most people have their lives, and now the religious is introduced so quickly that those who, moved by the esthetic, decide to follow along are suddenly standing right in the middle of the decisive qualifications of the essentially Christian, are at least prompted to become aware. (PV, 7)

Thus Kierkegaard uses poetry to appeal to and to evoke esthetic passion and esthetically passionate thinking; then he attempts to direct this esthetically passionate thinking toward subjectivity and Christianity so as to make people aware of a summons to these things.

In the *Postscript,* Climacus describes two "border territories" of thinking besides poetry, namely, *irony* and *humor* (CUP, 451, 500–502). Irony is a way of thinking and existing that is between esthetic objectivity and ethical subjectivity. And humor lies on the border between different modes of subjectivity—in one case between the ethical and the religious, and in the other, between Religiousness A and Christianity. Irony and humor are like poetry in that they are ways of thinking that deeply and passionately appreciate an ideal for which the ironist or humorist has not yet begun striving. And since Climacus is professedly a humorist, the *Postscript* not only describes and praises intermediate thinking, it constantly exemplifies it in the character of its humorist-author.

The "total thought" of Kierkegaard's "entire work as an author," as he himself describes it, is "*becoming* a Christian" (PV, 41; emphasis added). According to Kierkegaard, becoming a Christian means going through various transitional or intermediate modes of existing *and thinking*. And though he insists that he cannot force his readers against their will to become Christians, Kierkegaard employs all his great genius and sublime art as a writer to induce them to think in a way that is intermediate between being utterly non-Christian and being a Christian, and he does this precisely in order to invite them to faith.

An Intimation of the Climacean Capacity

Although it is not possible to demonstrate the existence of the climacean capacity, nor indeed would Climacus welcome attempts at such a demonstration, it is possible even through direct logical argumentation to get an intimation of its existence and perhaps to refute attempts to demonstrate its nonexistence.

Human beings seem to be finite, temporal, particular, and conditioned animals. And yet they also seem to be able to conceive, however inadequately, the infinite, the eternal, the universal, and the unconditioned. Nor can they merely conceive these things, but they can seek to relate to them, by studiously theorizing about metaphysical principles, or by longing and questing for a haven beyond the dangerous seas of this world, or by unconditionally obeying an absolute ethical or religious duty. In the words of Climacus, lowly human beings are both tormented and incited by the thought or poetic intimation of a tremendous unknown something. Thus human beings by nature act as if they have a climacean capacity.

In accordance with the idea that sometimes the best way to reveal something is to deny it, the best means of intimating the climacean capacity may be to argue against attempts to negate it. One way of denying the climacean capacity is a form of relativism that claims we cannot know universal or absolute truths. As is often said, such a relativist claim that we cannot know universal or absolute truths is itself a claim to a knowledge of universal or absolute truth. Thus (this version of) relativism is self-contradictory. This kind of contradiction arises over and over in attempts to establish once and for all the limits of knowledge. Similarly, some forms of skepticism deny the possibility of the human mind's knowing the essences of things as they really are, thereby implicitly claiming to know the essence of the human mind as it really is so as to establish its necessary and essential limits.

More generally, claims to know the limits of human knowledge are often based on implicit claims to know the relation between the mind and some unknowable entity, and hence to know both the mind and that unknowable entity. In other words, attempts to set limits to human knowing presuppose a knowledge of that which putatively cannot be known so as to know that it is the kind of thing that cannot be known. For example, consider the skeptic who denies the possibility of human knowledge of an infinite and eternal being. The climacean thinker might reply that the skeptic is implicitly claiming to know that an infinite and eternal being could not know itself in and through a human mind. And this is to say that the skeptic is claiming to know the infinite and eternal being. In other words, the skeptic who denies knowledge of the infinite implicitly claims to know that human beings are hermetically sealed against the immanence of the infinite and therefore to know a limit to the infinite's power of immanence. Thus the attempt to deny the possibility of human knowledge of an infinite and eternal being (often, typically, maybe necessarily) implies a claim to a knowledge of that being.

A qualification is in order here. It must be acknowledged that I am probably more confident than both Climacus and Kierkegaard are that human beings can discover contradictions in all attempts to set absolute limits to human understanding. They both almost certainly think that we can come to know our limits *with God's help*. But they also think that even as divine aid reveals people's limits, it also enables them partly to transcend them. In any case, it is telling that Kierkegaard and Climacus do not carefully argue for limits to human knowing, and that the only reason Climacus gives in *Fragments* for human beings' lacking the *condition* is *sin*.[17] The fact that they do not argue (extensively) for fixed bounds of human cognition seems to imply that Kierkegaard and Climacus are well aware of the difficulties involved in making a solid, philosophical determination of such bounds. Finally, Climacus sets or suggests limits to human capacity in *Fragments* with the tacit understanding that the means of transcending those limits by non-natural means are present to readers in the form of Christian revelation.

SEVEN

The Figure of Socrates and the Downfall of Paradoxical Reason

Unless a grain of wheat fall into the ground and die,
it abideth alone; but if it die, it bringeth forth much fruit.
He that loveth his life shall lose it; and he that hateth his life
in this world shall keep it unto life eternal. (John 12:24–25)

Christ . . . *willed his own downfall.* (PC, 246)

It is . . . the ultimate passion of the understanding to will
the collision . . . that must become its downfall. (PF, 37)

An eternal happiness is specifically rooted in the subjective individual's
diminishing self-esteem acquired through the utmost exertion. (CUP, 55)

He who is by art a tragic poet is also a comic poet.
(Socrates in *Symposium*, 223d)

Virtue cannot so inoculate our old stock but we shall relish of
it. . . . What should such fellows as I do crawling between earth
and heaven? We are arrant knaves all. (Shakespeare, *Hamlet*)

In the drama of *Philosophical Fragments* Socrates not only climbs the
ladder of paradoxical reason, he also falls. We might suspect that his fall
is a tragic climbing accident resulting from ill-advised overconfidence in
his climacean capacity, or a divine punishment for impious and immod-

erate ambition. In fact, it is a voluntary self-humbling: Socrates himself wills the downfall of his own understanding.

Socrates wills this downfall because the synthesis of the infinite and the finite within human nature requires that a person embrace both climbing and falling. Being infinite, human beings are equipped to climb. But being finite, they are also destined to fall. Therefore, without aspiration and ascent, lowliness is cowardice, laziness, or complacent mediocrity masquerading as meekness; without humble acceptance of finitude, transcending is titanic and transgressive pride. Thus climbing and falling complement and correct one another.

They are also components of one another. Socrates climbs and wills to fall by one and the same erotic "passion of thought," or by "paradoxical and humble courage" (PF, 37; FT, 49). According to an analogy suggested by Climacus, just as one makes progress in *walking* by "a continuous falling" and rising, so one advances through the stages of subjectivity by energetic aspiration and dejected desperation (PF, 37). As the "angels of God" "ascend and descend" Christ, or on Jacob's Ladder, so Socrates climbs up and down the ladder of paradoxical reason.[1] Climacus himself hints at the balance in question when he writes the following: "In his existence-relation to the truth the existing person is just as negative as positive" (CUP, 80). Or, in the language of theology, to humble oneself before God in need and petition is to acknowledge one's limits in order to transcend them.

By his double movement Socrates both prophetically anticipates the unique Incarnation and represents a universal human possibility. In willing his own downfall, Socrates is a type or symbol of Christ's passion and crucifixion; in climbing over and transcending human limits, he figures forth the resurrection and the ascension into heaven. And in doing these things, he shows what all human beings can do if only they will to do it.

Socrates Wills the Downfall of His Understanding

Climacus does not explicitly assert that Socrates wills the downfall of his own understanding. But he repeatedly suggests this in the third chapter of *Philosophical Fragments,* "The Absolute Paradox (A Metaphysical Caprice)" (PF, 37–48).

Climacus says that if one makes the assumption that one knows "what man is" and seeks to make "this wisdom . . . richer and more meaningful," something curious happens: "But then the understanding stands still, as did Socrates, for now the understanding's paradoxical passion that wills the collision awakens and, without really understanding itself, wills its own downfall" (PF, 38). By comparing Socrates' coming to a standstill to the understanding's willing its own downfall, Climacus suggests that Socrates is among those who will the demise of their own intellects. And by alluding to the famous episode of Socrates' standing still from the *Symposium*,[2] which is about eros, he suggests that it is Socrates' eros that leads him to will the downfall (a curious thing, since it is also eros that motivates the climacean capacity).

Climacus writes that it "seems to be a paradox" that "although Socrates did his very best . . . to know himself" and "has been eulogized for centuries as the person who certainly knew man best . . . he was still not quite clear . . . whether he . . . was a more curious monster than Typhon or a friendlier and simpler being, by nature sharing something divine" (PF, 37; cf. *Phaedrus*, 229e). Climacus then links the paradox that Socrates, the heroic seeker of self-knowledge, is in such perplexity about himself with the paradox that under the influence of its highest *passion*, the *understanding* "wills the collision" that inevitably spells its "own downfall" (PF, 37). By linking the paradox that Socrates, who "knew man best," was so perplexed about himself with the paradox that the erotically impassioned understanding wills its own downfall, Climacus suggests that Socrates wills this downfall, and that his willing it consists in or essentially comprises his profound perplexity about himself.

Climacus goes on to set forth an analogy between the downfall of self-love and the downfall of the understanding. In the conclusion to this analogy he writes:

> Just as the lover is changed by this paradox of love so that he almost does not recognize himself anymore . . . so also that intimated paradox of the understanding reacts upon a person and upon his self-knowledge in such a way that he who believed that he knew himself now no longer is sure whether he perhaps is a more curiously complex animal than Typhon or whether he has in his being a gentler and diviner part. (PF, 39)

According to this analogy, just as the downfall of self-love consists in a change so deep that the lover "almost does not recognize himself anymore," the downfall of the understanding consists in so deep a change that "he who believed that he knew himself" becomes so perplexed that he cannot decide between utterly opposite self-interpretations. Thus we arrive again at the conclusion that the downfall of the understanding results in or comprises a profound perplexity about oneself. And by illustrating this perplexed condition of the downfall with words said by Socrates about himself in the *Phaedrus,* Climacus clearly implies that Socrates wills the downfall of his own understanding.

The Character of the Downfall of the Understanding in *Philosophical Fragments*

When Climacus claims that faith demands that reason "will its own downfall," or that it "step aside," or that it be *discharged, surrendered, or crucified,* he gives the impression that he thinks faith denies or destroys reason, so that the downfall of reason is its destruction (PF, 37–39, 59, 54; CUP, 559). But in fact, as I shall argue, he thinks that to will the downfall of reason is to transform and perfect reason.

Kierkegaard asserts that "Christ . . . *willed his own downfall*" (PC, 246; original emphasis). Presumably Kierkegaard does not mean by these words that Christ chose to be utterly destroyed or everlastingly defeated. Instead he means that Christ submitted to crucifixion in order to be resurrected. Therefore, analogously, when Climacus indicates that reason must will its own downfall, he means that reason must submit to crucifixion so as to be resurrected, transfigured, and perfected.

According to a striking analogy in chapter 3 of *Fragments, self-love* becomes "erotic love" by willing its own downfall (PF, 48). Climacus explains that in its downfall self-love "is not annihilated but is taken captive and is erotic love's spoils of war" (PF, 48). Therefore, to will the downfall of self-love is not utterly to reject self-love, but to will its integration within a greater love, and therefore to will its perfection. Similarly, according to the analogy, to will the downfall of reason (or of the understanding) is not utterly to reject reason, but to will its integration within something greater that perfects it, namely faith.

Climacus claims that an important part of faith is receiving the truth and the condition for the truth, that is, the Christian truth, from the god. By receiving this condition, the understanding is reborn, that is, perfected, or at least radically corrected. Therefore faith as understood by Climacus includes becoming aware of the truth with a perfected or corrected understanding.

Most commentators of *Fragments* interpret the downfall of the understanding as a recognition and acceptance of the limits of the understanding's capacity for knowledge.[3] The most important result of the downfall of the understanding, according to this standard interpretation, is an openness or receptivity to a divine revelation of truths that exceed the capacity of natural reason. This receptivity to revelation is the human contribution to the perfection of reason.

At first sight, *Fragments* appears to support the standard interpretation of the downfall. The "thought-project" that Climacus sets for himself in *Fragments* is to discover and to elaborate an alternative to the *Socratic* position that human beings have the *condition* for the *truth* (PF, 14–19, 31, 56, 62). The most obvious way to parse the condition for the truth is as a capacity for knowing the truth. If this parsing is correct, then willing the downfall of the understanding would mean denying or doubting that one has the condition for knowing the truth, or discerning that one lacks it. Moreover, given that the downfall can be occasioned by something that thought itself cannot think—that is, by something that the understanding cannot know, understand, or even conceive—it is plausible that willing the downfall of the understanding means denying or doubting that one has the condition for cognizing transcendent truth.

Climacus also indicates, however, that the condition is (primarily, I think) a capacity for "eternal happiness" (PF, 58; cf. 1, 12, 24). Being a capacity for eternal happiness, the condition is not primarily a capacity for theoretical knowledge, but a capacity for achieving a practical or holistic goal. But if the condition is a condition for eternal happiness, which is a practical goal, it does not make sense to think of the truth in the phrase "the condition for the truth" as a theoretical object of contemplation. Instead, it is more fitting to think of the truth as what the *Postscript* calls *subjective truth*, which may be defined as a conforming to what is real with one's whole person, including one's mind, will, passions, and actions. Therefore, if, as seems plausible, willing the downfall of one's understanding means denying or doubting that one has the condition, it means denying or doubting that one has the capacity for that subjective truth which is called eternal happiness.

In the remainder of this section, I shall argue that the downfall of the understanding is primarily a denial of this capacity for eternal happiness. In arguing this I do not mean to deny that the downfall is secondarily or inclusively a negation of a capacity for theoretical knowledge. For the standard interpretation is not so much wrong as incomplete. Denying or doubting the adequacy of theoretical reason for achieving its goals is a partial downfall of the understanding that can lead to or be part of a more complete downfall that includes both a theoretical and a practical dimension.

It will be useful for me to state my interpretation of the downfall more fully before I argue further for it. The thing that falls in the downfall of the understanding is the whole human capacity to achieve the highest human end—an eternal happiness, which includes not only joy, but wisdom and goodness as well. Consequently, the downfall is a disavowal of the pretension that one can become good, wise, and joyful on one's own, a rejection of the determination to rely only on oneself in striving for one's highest end. The downfall comes about, not simply as a result of frustration in inquiry, but also and mainly as a result of a failure, despite one's bests efforts, to become good, wise, and joyful. In the language of the *Postscript,* the downfall of the understanding is an event within subjectivity that leads a person deeper into subjectivity, not an event that terminates objectivity and inaugurates subjectivity.

That the downfall is an event within subjectivity, not an event preceding it, is indicated by the following considerations. According to *Fragments,* objectivity is extinguished not when reason falls down but when reason flares up in passionate intensity. But, according to Climacus, passionate intensity must already be actual before there can be any question of a downfall, since it is at its peak of passion that the understanding wills its own downfall. Therefore, it is an already subjective and impassioned understanding that wills its own downfall, not an objective understanding. And this is to say that the downfall occurs within subjectivity and its quest for eternal happiness, not within a disinterested objective inquiry.

Since the downfall, as Climacus understands it, is meant to lead a person to accept revelation, and since one accepts revelation not in order to become a better philosopher but in order to become a perfect *person*— good, wise, and joyful—it makes sense that the downfall should result mainly from one's suspicion that one cannot become good, wise, and joyful on one's own, and not primarily from an abstract cognition of the limits of theoretical reason. Alternatively, since Climacus thinks that the deepest human desire is not for knowledge, but for happiness grounded in goodness and wisdom, he thinks that the downfall is deepest, most humbling, and most fruitful when it consists in despair of achieving this happiness without divine assistance.

Let us re-examine a key passage concerning the downfall of the understanding willed by Socrates.

> Although Socrates did his very best to gain knowledge of human nature and to know himself—yes, even though he has been eulogized for centuries as the person who certainly knew man best—he nevertheless admitted that the reason he was disinclined to ponder the nature of such creatures as Pegasus and the Gorgons was that he was still not quite clear about himself, whether he (a connoisseur of human nature) was a more curious monster than Typhon or a friendlier and simpler being, by nature sharing something divine. (PF, 37; cf. *Phaedrus*, 229e)

In this passage, Climacus suggests that Socrates wills the downfall, and that the downfall consists in his failure to know himself despite his best efforts.

It is highly suggestive that Climacus presents Socrates' downfall as the result of an attempt to "know himself." For Kierkegaard and his pseudonymous authors see a serious effort to know oneself as part of and indicative of ethical and religious striving. For instance, in the *Sickness unto Death,* Anti-Climacus writes that the "law for the development of the self with respect to knowing . . . is that the increase of knowledge corresponds to the increase of self-knowledge" (SUD, 31). By "the development of the self," Anti-Climacus means the ethical and religious growth of the human person. Therefore a serious attempt to know oneself is a sign of ethical and religious striving, and when Climacus suggests that Socrates willed the downfall after doing "his very best to gain knowledge of human nature and to know himself," he implies that Socrates willed the downfall as a result of ethical or religious striving.

The inference that the Socratic search for self-knowledge that leads to his willing the downfall is part of an ethical and religious project is confirmed by the fact that the knowledge he seeks is itself ethical and religious. Consider the questions that Socrates asks about himself.

He wonders whether he is a "more curious monster than Typhon or a friendlier and simpler being, by nature sharing something divine." These questions obviously express religious concerns, since Socrates wonders whether he is an arrogant, violent, and defiant enemy of the gods like Typhon, on the one hand, or akin to the divine and friendly toward it, on the other. His questions also express ethical concerns, since Socrates wonders whether he is basically friendly both to others and to himself (a hundred-headed monster like Typhon is presumably not friendly even to itself). For, since human beings have competitive and destructive desires, friendliness to oneself and to other humans requires that one moderate one's desires and behavior in the light of norms that may be called ethical. And since Socrates did his very best to answer these ethical and religious questions, we can infer that ethical and religious issues were of the utmost importance to him, and that his recognition that he lacked knowledge in these important issues constituted part of his willing the downfall.

When Climacus says that "Socrates *did his very best* to gain knowledge of human nature and to know himself," he implies that Socrates wonders whether he is by nature called to be ethical and religious, and/or whether he has in fact adequately answered that call. Or we might say that he is inquiring both what the best sort of life is for human beings, and whether he is himself living the best life.

As Climacus sees it, the fact that Socrates asks these ethical and religious questions about the best life indicates that he acts, or is willing to act, on his answers. For Climacus claims that Socrates had "rare integrity" and "artistically exemplified what he understood" with "wonderful consistency" (PF, 24, 10). And if Socrates maintains a wonderful consistency and integrity between his understanding and his actions, then he must be prepared to act on any answers he might find to his ethical and religious questions. Therefore, according to Climacus, the inquiry that leads to Socrates' willing the downfall of his reason is a practical inquiry.

By presenting Socrates as asking himself the ethical and religious questions we have been examining, Climacus presents Socrates as having intimations of sin. Officially, Climacus claims that neither Socrates nor anyone else can be aware of sin without revelation (PF, 47). Despite his official position about sin and revelation, it is nevertheless clear that Climacus in fact portrays Socrates as suspecting his sinful condition. For sin in part means ethical turpitude, and Climacus presents Socrates as suspecting his ethical turpitude. *Sin* means misrelation to the divine, a proud rejection of divine norms, guidance, and assistance. And Climacus presents Socrates as suspecting that he is misrelated to the divine owing to Typhonic arrogance. Again, sin means to lack the condition for eternal happiness, and Socrates as presented by Climacus is beginning to suspect that he lacks this condition, since he is aware that despite his best efforts he still does not know either what the best life is for a being such as he is, or whether he has made any progress in living that life. The *Postscript* seems to confirm Socrates' closeness to the idea of sin when it says that Socrates "discovered within himself . . . a disposition to all evil" (CUP, 131). Similarly, *Sickness unto Death,* even as it denies that Socrates had a conception of sin, says that he had an awareness of the *difficulty* "connected with the transition from understanding to doing," which difficulty is nothing other than sin (SUD, 83). Indeed, as I have already pointed out in the previous chapter, the *Sickness* even suggests that Socrates "despair[ed] over his sin" (SUD, 116). Presumably an important aspect of despairing over one's sin is (a fairly accurate) awareness of it. Furthermore, since despair over sin is a very good definition of willing the downfall of one's understanding, by suggesting that Socrates despaired over his sin, Anti-Climacus thereby suggests that Socrates wills the downfall. Thus Kierkegaard's pseudonyms have a tendency both to deny and to imply that Socrates has an idea of sin and of his own sinfulness.

Climacus claims that Socrates constantly "presupposes that the god exists," but does not tell us why the skeptical and ignorance-practicing Socrates would comport himself so surprisingly in the governance of his ideas (PF, 44). That the rational and skeptical Socrates would constantly presuppose this without proof is a very strange thing indeed. At this point we may conjecture that Climacus wishes to suggest that Socrates constantly presupposes the god's existence because he is incipiently aware of, or suspects, his sin and his consequent need of divine aid in order to achieve his highest end. At any rate, Climacus connects Socrates' ignorance with Socrates' believing he had a "divine commission" (PF, 10). Perhaps Socrates was aware with Kierkegaard that "to need God is a human being's highest perfection." Thus Socrates' willing of the downfall of his own understanding seems to consist in his doubting his capacity to know and rightly relate to the highest good without divine assistance. Incidentally, in *For Self-Examination,* Kierkegaard puts the following words into the mouth of Socrates: "I rely on the assistance of the god" (FSE, 10), and to rely on the god requires being aware or suspecting one's own incapacity.

"Religiousness A" or the Downfall in the *Postscript*

Although the *Postscript* does not mention the downfall by name, it has the idea of it, and calls it "Religiousness A," which represents for Climacus the deepest and most perfect downfall of the understanding possible without revelation.

Religiousness A follows the ethical stage of spiritual development, in which a person *struggles* to become good and happy in the confident expectation of *victory* (CUP, 288). According to Climacus, the struggles of the striving ethicist ultimately fail and thus lead to an opportunity to become humble, and Religiousness A is a development and elaboration of humility. One aspect of the humility of Religiousness A is "guilt-consciousness" (CUP, 526, 528–529, 532–533). Another is the awareness that without God one is "capable of nothing" and a consequent effort to "rely on God" in all things (CUP, 467–478). It is crucial that both guilt-consciousness and the sense that without God one is capable of nothing grow, not out of abstract thinking, but out of ethical struggle and striving. Thus the hints about the practical character of the downfall in *Fragments* are made more explicit in the account of Religiousness A in the *Postscript.*

The humility of Religiousness A is obviously a propaedeutic to Christianity. Guilt-consciousness is a preparation for "sin-consciousness" and for requesting and receiving *forgiveness* of one's sins (CUP, 524, 538–539). Relying on God in the awareness that without God one is capable of nothing prepares a person to ask for and to receive grace in order to grow in goodness, wisdom, and happiness. In general, the humility of Religiousness A is a preparation for the deeper humility of Christianity, which requires the subordination of oneself in humble obedience to the Divine Person of God. The following quotation aptly summarizes nearly all that we have discovered about the humility of Religiousness A: "An eternal happiness is specifically rooted in the subjective individual's diminishing self-esteem acquired through the utmost exertion" (CUP, 55).

In the *Postscript,* Climacus is more explicit not only about the character of the downfall, but also about Socrates' willing it, when he claims that Socrates was an "ethicist . . . bordering on the religious," by which he means that Socrates was losing his confidence that he would succeed in his struggles to become good, wise, and happy on his own, and beginning to suspect his guilt and need for God (CUP, 503).

Virtually all of the books of Kierkegaard formulate artful variations on the idea of the downfall of the understanding. In *Fear and Trembling,* the "movement of finitude," or of *faith,* in which a person "reflects upon God" and not "upon himself," corresponds more or less with the downfall of the understanding that makes way for *humble* reliance on God (FT, 37). By the way, *Fear and Trembling* is quite clear that a crucial quality of the knight of faith is his *humility,* which is "that power whose strength is powerlessness" (FT, 34, 49, 73, 16). *The Sickness unto Death* similarly explains that "the self must be broken in order to become itself," or that "effective despair, radical despair" is the "thoroughfare to faith" and healthy selfhood (SUD, 65, 59, 67). In language closer to *Fragments,* it also says that when a "person is brought to his extremity, when, humanly speaking, there is no possibility," then "losing the understanding" means to "believe that for God everything is possible" (SUD, 38). But in order to become eligible for divine assistance there must be a strenuous *straining* of the "understanding to find help" (SUD, 39). This "losing of the understanding" is clearly a variation on the "downfall of the understanding." And the *straining* of the "understanding to find help" at a person's *extremity* is similarly a reformulation of the idea of ethical and religious striving.

The Power of Suggestion

At this point the reader might be wondering why Climacus merely suggests in *Fragments* that Socrates wills the downfall and does not forthrightly assert this, and why Climacus gives the impression that willing the downfall is a theoretical and not a practical or holistic act. In order to see why Climacus only suggests these things when he could have said them plainly and simply, we must revisit some ideas from earlier chapters.

As we have seen, Kierkegaard uses Climacus to find, or meet, philosophical readers where they are, while Climacus for his part captures the interest of philosophical readers with the figure of Socrates, the greatest and most famous philosopher. Obviously, the Socrates with whom Climacus meets such readers must appear, at least initially, to conform to their expectations. If Climacus were immediately to claim that Socrates parts company with philosophy by willing the downfall of his own understanding, Climacus would lose the respect and the attention of his targeted readership. Therefore he gives his readers what they want: a seemingly philosophical Socrates—at least at first.

Meeting philosophical readers where they are requires that Climacus give the appearance that the downfall has to do primarily with theoretical reason. For to philosophers who have studied their Kant, the idea that reason is incapable of metaphysical knowledge of the *ens realissimum* is a familiar thesis. But the idea of despairing over one's ethical and religious weakness is foreign to a philosophical way of thinking. Therefore Climacus initially suggests that the downfall is an enactment of the Kantian idea that it is necessary to deny reason in order to make room for faith, instead of an existential idea that spiritual striving leads to despair and a felt need for grace. By the way, we should bear in mind here that the idea that theoretical reason must be denied in order to make room for faith is not so much a distortion of willing the downfall of the understanding as a subordinate element within it.

Having distorted (or incompletely expressed) his message by adapting it to his readers' mentality, Climacus works to bring his readers to an awareness of his true and complete message by means of hints and suggestions. The slow work of discovering these hints and of puzzling out their significance gives readers time to adjust to Climacus's surprising message and perhaps enables them to take this message seriously, appreciate it, and honestly evaluate it. Many readers will either not notice Climacus's hints and suggestions of his hidden message or not work out their significance. But even they may be subtly affected by the subliminal suggestions of Climacus and thus become prepared to take his message seriously if they encounter it in more direct language of the *Postscript*.

In chapter 3 of *Fragments*, Climacus is supremely artful in the way that he adapts to his philosophical readers and then uses suggestion to influence them. Nearly all of chapter 3 is framed by two similar, but importantly different, analogies that compare "erotic love" to the downfall of the understanding.

According to the first analogy a "person lives undisturbed in himself, and then awakens the paradox of self-love as love for another, for one missing" (PF, 39). These words refer to the Socratic version of the downfall that Climacus has just indirectly described in the opening paragraphs of chapter 3. Let us analyze this analogy item by item.

"A person lives undisturbed in himself. . . ." To live undisturbed in oneself is to live trapped in oneself, wholly immanent in one's own egoism, and therefore not loving or knowing others as others, or for what they are, but only as things to be observed, exploited, or avoided. In other words, the extreme egoism of unadulterated self-love prevents the self-transcendence that loving and therefore knowing others requires.

". . . and then awakens the paradox of self-love as love for another. . . ." This "paradox of self-love as love for another" is *erotic love*. Erotic love constitutes a transcendence of the original boundaries of self-love. But since eros loves the other only as itself, and not as other, erotic love is only a partial transcendence of self-love. *Works of Love* explains this partial transcendence by saying that the erotic lover gets a "new . . . self" (WL, 56). This new self includes both the lover and the beloved and therefore transcends the lover's original self, but is still *preferential* and therefore selfish vis-à-vis the *neighbor* (WL, 56).

Like erotic love, the downfall of the understanding constitutes a partial self-transcendence. The partial self-transcendence of the downfall seems to be a reaching out to the divine beloved in order to subordinate oneself to it and become aware of it as much as possible as it is. Thus the downfall of the understanding constitutes a step toward the perfection of the understanding. For even to attempt to know the divine other as other constitutes an amendment and transcendence of egoistic understanding.

This reaching out to the divine other encounters an obstacle: The deity is "one missing." In ordinary cases of erotic love, the beloved is not missing. Therefore, it seems, Climacus is talking about erotic love not as it is ordinarily understood, but as understood by the poets of unhappy love, or by Socrates in the *Phaedrus,* where the divine beloved is not present in the way an earthly beloved is present, but as a distant goal. This Socratic usage of *erotic love* is appropriate, since the analogy is meant to explain the downfall of the understanding as willed by Socrates.

Thus the analogy begins with self-love, then directs our attention to something higher, namely ordinary erotic love, and then again directs us to something higher still, erotic love as described by the poets or Socrates, and finally directs us to the still-higher possibility of loving the deity as one present, even face to face. You might say that the analogy suggests a ladder of love similar to the *climacus erotis* of the *Symposium*.

The fact that the divine beloved is one missing for Socratic lovers of the divine means that they cannot fully transcend themselves by actually loving and knowing the divine beloved face to face, but they can only yearn or strive to do this and fail. Since the divine bridegroom is one missing, the Socratic downfall of the understanding cannot be consummated in the divine rites of love.

At the end of chapter 3, after a long interlude (PF, 39–47), Climacus presents a second analogy comparing erotic love to the downfall of the understanding. This second analogy intimates that Christian faith is the perfection and consummation of the Socratic downfall of the understanding. Whereas in the first analogy, the god is one missing, in the second analogy, the deity is present, at least partly, because it takes the understanding *captive*. Being taken captive by the divine is a much higher degree of subordination to the deity than merely longing for it and requires a higher degree of humility. For to long for the highest is less humiliating than obeying and serving it. Thus the second analogy describes a deepening or perfection of the downfall (from the Christian point of view) of the understanding described by the first analogy. Climacus's name for this deeper subordination of the understanding to its captor is *faith,* as he indirectly indicates when he says that the understanding is taken captive by an unnamed *passion,* and then calls this captor a "happy passion" and *faith* in the next chapter (PF, 48, 59).

The contrast between the first and second analogy suggests that Socrates can complete or consummate the downfall of the understanding that he is trying to will only in Christian faith. It suggests that Socrates is vaguely aiming at faith and is ready for an invitation to faith, even that he is longing for Christ. But since for him Christ is absent and unknown, Socrates' desire and resolve to will the downfall remain inchoate, incomplete, and yet to be fully tested. Consequently, the passion of his understanding wills the downfall, as Climacus says, "without really understanding itself" (PF, 38).

The text between the two analogies that we have been examining marks out a path from the Socratic downfall to the Christian downfall of the understanding and attempts to lead readers along this path.

The interlude between the analogies meets philosophical readers where they are by beginning with a more or less philosophical critique of arguments for the existence of God (PF, 39–44). Even supposing this perplexing critique is correct, it still does not rule out the possibility of direct or experiential knowledge of God. It may even be meant to suggest such a possibility. Climacus concludes his general refutation of proofs for the existence of God with the perplexing claim that Socrates, well aware of the inadequacy of such proofs, nonetheless "constantly presupposes that the god exists" (PF, 44).

Climacus then goes on to assert more general and more drastic limits to human understanding. But he asserts those limits in exciting language calculated to make readers desire to transcend them and suspect that they can transcend them, or at least in such a way as to induce them to relate passionately to those limits. This is to say that he plays games with limits, or limit-games, in order to awaken and direct what in the last chapter we called the climacean capacity. For instance, he claims that the "paradoxical passion of the understanding . . . correctly perceives the unknown as frontier" (PF, 44). A frontier is not an impassable barrier, but a transitional region linking the known to the unknown. Therefore, by describing the unknown as frontier Climacus suggests that it is something to be explored by bold adventurers of the spirit. Hence the "frontier is expressly the passion's torment," but "also its incentive" (PF, 44).

Climacus proceeds to discuss the "absolutely different," which he claims "the understanding cannot even think." And yet Climacus seems to think about it, and he tries to bring his readers along with him. Moreover, by claiming that the understanding "cannot absolutely transcend itself" so as to *securely grasp* the *difference* between the unknown and the known, he suggests that the understanding can partially transcend itself in order to grope toward and maybe even glimpse the "absolutely different" (PF, 45).

Climacus then surprises readers with the claim that the cause of the "absolute difference" between human beings and the transcendent unknown is not human finitude and temporality, but *sin* (PF, 47). Climacus has prepared for this surprise cunningly, and he uses it artfully.

He employed the paradoxes about transcendence to disorient his readers and work them up into a passionate desire for the transcendent, and then he springs on them the idea that sin is the cause of their confusion and ignorance about transcendence. Thus Climacus attempts to turn bored unreceptivity to a Christian cliché into a deep and concerned consciousness of sin.

Climacus explains that it is because Socrates *lacked* the "consciousness of sin" that he "became almost bewildered about himself when he came up against the different" (PF, 47). This is a problematic explanation of Socrates' confusion about himself. To be sure, if Socrates had had a clear consciousness of sin, he would not have become bewildered about his ethical and religious condition. But, if he had utterly lacked the consciousness of sin, surely he would not have been afflicted with the suspicion that he might be as monstrous as a hundred-headed hubristic enemy of the gods. Thus Climacus suggests that Socrates was partially aware of his sin.

There is yet another suggestion that Socrates suspects sin in the appendix to chapter 3: "Through the moment, the learner becomes untruth; the person who knew himself becomes confused about himself and instead of self knowledge he acquires the consciousness of sin" (PF, 51). This passage, put together with the recurrent reference to the *Phaedrus* in chapter 3 of *Fragments* of which it is an echo, clearly suggests that Socrates, with his deep confusion about himself, was at least partway to the *moment* in which one acquires the *consciousness of sin*. Thus Socrates wills the downfall of his understanding by suspecting sin. Moreover, in partly surpassing his limitations by intimating them, Socrates points to the unity of climbing and falling referred to at the beginning of this chapter: "A reed, but a thinking reed."

We have now completed our survey of the interlude between the two analogies. As I indicated previously, the purpose of the interlude is to trace out a path from theoretical inquiry to Christian faith, and in tracing out this path to invite readers to tread it. The path has several stages: Climacus meets philosophical readers where they are with a sort of philosophical critique of arguments for the existence of God; then he tries to deepen and transform this philosophical interest in arguments into a passionate intimation of transcendence; then he attempts to transform this passionate intimation of the absolutely different into effective consciousness of sin; and, finally, he suggests that the Christian downfall is both the solution to the problem of sin and the key to awareness of the elusive transcendent.

The Downfall of the Understanding Called Offense

In addition to the Socratic and Christian versions of the downfall of the understanding, there is a third version. Climacus refers to it when he claims that "in one way or another the collision" between the *understanding* and the *paradox* "must become" the understanding's *downfall,* and when he claims that the *encounter* between the *paradox* and the understanding can be *happy* or *unhappy* (PF, 37, 49). The happy encounter is the downfall called *faith,* and the unhappy encounter is the downfall called *offense* (the Socratic version is presumably neither happy nor unhappy, but aims at happiness) (PF, 59, 49). Anti-Climacus explicitly calls "being offended at" Christ a *downfall*—a downfall, however, not of the understanding, but of the whole person (PC, 77).

In the appendix to the third chapter of *Fragments,* "Offense at the Absolute Paradox (An Acoustical Illusion)," Climacus describes offense as a deeply self-deceived condition of mind and therefore as a sort of downfall of reason. He claims that the absolute paradox offends reason as an absurdity, and that reason cannot *discover* on its own that the paradox is *absurd,* but must learn this from the *testimony* or revelation of the paradox (PF, 52). But, he adds, the offended person is eager to assert that he has discovered, on his own, the absurdity of the paradox. In other words, the offended person wishes by rejecting the paradox to assert an autonomy and independence that (in the opinion of Climacus) he does not in fact possess. Ironically, here where the offended person asserts his independence most strongly, he is (according to Climacus) most passive and dependent. Thus Climacus presents offense as a delusion of rational autonomy, and therefore as a downfall of reason.

The appendix describes another way in which offense is a downfall of the understanding. Climacus explains that offense is "unhappy love" of the *paradox* (PF, 49). *The Sickness unto Death* makes a similar point when it says that offense is analogous to *envy,* defined as "secret admiration" and "unhappy self-assertion" (SUD, 86). Thus offense is a self-contradictory refusal to acknowledge that one's admiration of the paradox requires happily surrendering to it and joyfully adoring it. Similarly, by calling offense an "unhappy love" that "does not understand itself," Climacus implies that if the offended person did understand himself, he would admit his love of the paradox and submit to it. Thus Climacus thinks that offense is a self-contradictory, self-deceived condition of the understanding, and in this way a downfall of the understanding (PF, 50). Furthermore, by portraying faith in Christ as a happy love and there-fore as a consistent spiritual condition, and offense as unhappy love and therefore as an inconsistent spiritual condition, Climacus portrays faith as more rational than offense.

Since one downfall of the understanding is a happy love, and the other a proud, self-assertive, and unhappy love, we can infer that the understanding, according to Climacus, comprises two elements in ten-sion with one another: a desire for happiness and a desire for autonomy or self-sufficiency. The encounter with the paradox reveals the incompat-ibility of these two elements, and the necessity that one or the other of them must fall. Faith then is the downfall of the desire for self-assertion, while offense is the downfall of the desire for happiness.

One might suspect that no one would ever deliberately choose un-happy self-assertion over happiness. Climacus concedes that no one whose *passion* was not at its "ultimate potentiation," or peak, would do this (PF, 37). For without powerful passion, a person lacks the resolve for such a terrible deed. But, thoroughly impassioned, a person can gain extraordinary strength and courage, since the "ultimate potentiation of every passion is always to will its own downfall" (PF, 37). In *Sickness unto Death,* Anti-Climacus chillingly and I think convincingly describes a passionate, offended, and demonic consciousness which in order to rebel against God wants to be (or to remain) unhappy so as to have a grievance on which to base its rebellion (SUD, 72–74). Many atheists and political revolutionaries have admired Aeschylus's Prometheus for steadfastly defying the tyranny of Zeus under torture for 30,000 years, thus declaring their wish to be as resolute as Prometheus in their dedica-tion to autonomous independence from divinity. Milton's Satan likewise would rather "reign in hell than serve in heav'n," and for this preference was regarded by many of the Romantic poets as the true hero of *Paradise Lost*.[4] Dostoevsky's Ivan claims that if God were to offer him a *ticket* to Paradise he would *return* it in order to express his defiance of the ways of Providence.[5] Perhaps the best example of an actual, historical person who had the passion and power to return his ticket is Nietzsche, who valued nobility more than happiness (at least as ordinarily conceived) and seems to have thought that nobility does not even aim at happiness. Moving closer to home, perhaps self-examination might reveal that some of us have occasionally preferred sorrow to joy, if by being unhappy we could dramatically reveal that another person has wronged us and in this way establish our noble superiority to him. Thus the model of freedom offered by Climacus according to which freedom's fundamental choice is between unhappy self-assertion and happy self-surrender is not as implausible as it might have seemed at first sight, and it may even be profoundly perceptive of the human condition.

It might seem that the choice between offense and faith is a choice between unhappy greatness and happy, unheroic lowliness. This is not, however, how Kierkegaard and Climacus see it. For they think that it requires great heroism and humble courage, not weakness, to quest for and slay the dragon of pride that devastates the soul of a fallen human being.

The Compatibility of Climbing and Falling

A critic might object that Climacus contradicts himself by presenting Socrates both as transcending his limits and as humbly accepting them. I would reply that there need be no contradiction here as long as the limits that Socrates transcends are not the limits that he respects, or as long as he transcends the limits in one way and is bound by them in another. The Socrates of *Philosophical Fragments* does indeed surpass many of the limits declared for him by Climacus, but for all that he does not manage either to invent Christianity or to save himself by his own unaided efforts. Therefore in the end Socrates as presented in *Fragments* remains within the boundaries within which Climacus confines him.

A critic might also object that I claim both that Climacus understands that it is impossible to draw rigid limits to human knowledge and that he thinks the downfall of the understanding means accepting that the understanding has certain limits. My response is that both the claim and the arguments for the claim that it is not possible to know the absolute limits of human knowledge are mine, not Climacus's. Therefore Climacus does not contradict himself on this point.

But, the critic might continue, if the claim is yours and not Climacus's, then that claim cannot help us to understand Climacus. My response is that Climacus writes in many ways as if he would assert, or was near to asserting, the impossibility of knowing the limits of human understanding. For example, he posits limits to human understanding so as to reveal a capacity to transcend those limits, thus calling into question our capacity to set such limits. In the *Postscript*, he writes that "every human being . . . can draw the distinction . . . between what he understands and what he does not understand" (CUP, 558; cf. CA, 3). But he does not write that every human being can draw the distinction between what he could understand and what he could not understand. This difference between a modest and humble "does not understand" and a proud and presumptuous "could not understand" suggests that Climacus is aware that it is problematic if not impossible for reason definitively to determine its own limits. Similarly, Climacus asserts not that Socrates denies that he has the condition for the truth, but that Socrates admits that he does not know himself despite his best efforts. Thus Climacus does not present Socrates as a skeptic dogmatically denying his ability to know himself, but as a "simpler and gentler creature" who merely admits that he does not know himself despite the utmost exertion, and perhaps suspects that he cannot know himself (PF, 39).

Yet another indication that Climacus thinks a rational determination of the absolute limits of reason is problematic is that he does not argue for such limits in *Fragments*, and yet we might expect that he would provide arguments if he had any. Finally, even supposing Climacus thinks that becoming a Christian would mean accepting that human understanding has certain absolute limits, he also seems to think that the incipient Christian accepts or perceives this with the help of God, or on the basis of belief in revelation, and not on the basis of natural, philosophical knowledge. Furthermore, he thinks that incipient Christians become aware that they were untruth even as they cease to be untruth. Thus there are many indications that Climacus thinks that claims to philosophically establishing absolute limits to human knowledge are dubious and even hubristic.

Ultimately, to will the downfall of one's understanding is not to posit a philosophical or theoretical thesis about necessary and universal limits of human knowledge, but to make a personal decision to rely on God.

Moreover, it is to decide this, not primarily on the basis of epistemological arguments, but as a result of one's own personal failures in existential striving. In other words, willing the downfall of the understanding is the dénouement of a story in which a person strives with all their might to become good, wise, and happy on their own; fails in this endeavor; and then becomes humbly open and receptive to divine aid, which not only lifts up strivers who are cast down, but teaches them their absolute need for God.

EIGHT

The Proof of
Paradoxical Reason

If ye continue in my word, then are ye my disciples indeed;
and ye shall know the truth, and the truth shall make you free.
(John 8:31–32)

I am the way, the truth, and the life. (John 14:6)

The truth in the sense in which Christ is the truth is
not a sum of statements . . . but a life. (PC, 205)

This is eternal life, that they may know thee, the only true
God, and Jesus Christ, whom thou hast sent. (John 17:3)

That is, only then do I *know* the truth, when it becomes a *life*
in me. (PC, 206, commenting on John 17:3; emphasis added)

Kierkegaard appears to reject the requirement of reason that he critically
evaluate the beliefs grounding both his own and his rival's ways of life.
But in fact he affirms this requirement.

We have already examined some of Kierkegaard's reasons for appearing to reject rational evaluation of ways of life. He thinks that he
needs the incognito of irrationalism to help his readers become more
rational, but if he unambiguously set about critically assessing lives with
arguments *pro et contra* he would blow his cover. He also thinks that the

task of reason is not so much to think the truth as it is to live it. Of course living the truth includes thinking it, but it also embraces feeling, willing, and enacting it. Since he wishes to encourage his readers to live what they know and believe, and since he is aware that they are very prone to substitute thinking for living, he avoids writing in such a way as to promote or excuse an obsession with thinking. Obviously, guarding in this way against an obsession with thinking does not permit publishing forthright and extensive rational evaluation of ways of life.

We must suspect that the quality of critical assessment will decrease when its role in rationality is drastically demoted. If one gives the activities of proving, assessing, and arguing little time and attention, surely one will become less adept and successful at them than one would by devoting oneself to them. Thus Kierkegaard seems to have sacrificed rational evaluation on the altar of subjectivity.

Kierkegaard is willing to make this sacrifice, if necessary. But it is not clear that it is necessary. For we succeed better at some things by not devoting ourselves wholly to them, or by situating them mid-range within a hierarchy of values. For example, single-minded devotion to physical health is not always the best means to this goal. Striving for other things might yield a more robust constitution than a fanatical pursuit of muscle tone, skin care, and low cholesterol. Likewise a budding romantic relationship might get on better if one does not prematurely put too much stock into it. Again, it could be that one will be a more astute philosopher if one cultivates familiarity with other disciplines, arts, and sciences than one would be by reading, writing, and talking only straight philosophy. Finally, to quote Richard Lovelace, "I could not love thee, dear, so much, loved I not honor more." Applying all this to our current question, it is possible that we will know the truth better if we love it so much that we attempt to feel, will, act, and even be it, than we would if we loved it only enough to think about it a lot.

In this chapter, we will examine yet another reason that Kierkegaard appears to flout the rational duty of critical assessment: namely, the unusual character of his conception and practice of proof. When the truth is a sum of statements, one proves it primarily by arguing for it; but when the truth is a life, one proves it primarily by living it. Given that the goal of objectivity is theoretical contemplation of ideas, while that of subjectivity is holistically living them, we should not be surprised that objectivity and subjectivity differ considerably in their manner of evaluating ideas.

My examination of Kierkegaard's subjective mode of evaluation will consist in arguing for and against it, publicly. And this is to say that I am going to assess subjectivity objectively. "But," someone should protest, "doesn't such a manner of proceeding distort subjectivity, and even betray it?" The event will decide. I for my part think that reason is one, and, this being so, that it is possible to see from within objectivity itself many of its weaknesses and many of the strengths of subjectivity.

Objective Evaluation

To understand thoroughly the subjective mode of evaluation and why Kierkegaard affirms it, we must understand the objective mode of evaluation and why he rejects it.

The goal of what I am calling the objective mode of evaluation is to know the world as it is in itself, or as it is for all people, or would be for all people who think correctly. Thus we might say that its *goal* is universal truth. Knowing the truth as it is *requires* that one transcend one's peculiarity and particularity, or, perhaps, that one adopt a third-person point of view on the world. Objective thinkers attempt to reach this goal and to fulfill this requirement by means of public, logical argumentation. For logic is rooted in the nature of things, or at least in human nature, and not in personal whims and caprices, and when a proposition is logically deduced in public from the common fund of premises, it seems well on the way to being established as the same for all people.

Kierkegaard agrees almost wholly both with objectivity's goal of universal truth and with its requirement of self-transcendence. But he agrees only in part with objectivity's way of pursuing its goal and meeting its requirement. It is because he agrees so much with objectivity, has so much in common with it, that it is correct to say that both objectivity and Kierkegaard's subjectivity are forms of rationality. This agreement also has the consequence that when Kierkegaard disagrees with objectivity and criticizes it, he does so largely from the inside, that is, on the basis of premises and modes of argument that he (and his subjectivity) share with objectivity. Thus the opposition between subjectivity and objectivity is more like a lovers' quarrel than a xenophobic war.

Though Kierkegaard believes in the validity of logic, and is confident that much can be accomplished by means of it, he also thinks that it is critically important that there has never been, nor can there ever be, a public demonstration of the answers to certain crucial questions: Is there a personal God who created and maintains the world? Does a human being have an immortal soul? Is there a best life for human beings, and if so, what is it? Do we have any absolute duties, and if so, what are they? By the way, Kierkegaard sometimes argues for these limits of logic. But since few people disagree about these limits, and since it seems to me that Kierkegaard's arguments for them are less clear and no more insightful than those of other philosophers, I will press on to what I perceive to be the strong points of his critique of objective evaluation.

Although most people agree that there are no public demonstrations of God, immortality, and ethical freedom, few people agree on what is to be done about this deficit in the fund of public truths. Faced with the nonexistence of these demonstrations, objective thinkers often resort to *probability*, with such thoughts as the following: "Even if we cannot demonstrate the truth or falsity of Christianity, at least we can show or know that Christianity is probably true, or likely false, as the case may be."

Kierkegaard thinks that probabilistic thinking about Christianity is deeply mistaken (PF, 52, 94–95). It is reasonable to assign probability to a specific event when we know many things about the generic character of that event and its parameters. For example, it is reasonable to assign probability to rolls of dice because we know many things about dice in general: about the flat surfaces on which they are typically rolled, about how other dice have behaved in the past when rolled on such surfaces, and about the laws of motion that govern the interaction of rolled dice and planes. In short, it is reasonable to assign probability to an event only if we know certain things about it and the field of reality to which it belongs.

The problem with trying to assign probability to the existence of God, immortality, or freedom is that we do not have the requisite field knowledge. We do not have experience of many worlds in which there are freedom, an afterlife, or a god and of many worlds in which none or only some of these things exist. Lacking this experience, we also lack the generic knowledge of gods, afterlives, freedom, and worlds that we would need in order to devise a probabilistic calculus for them.

Someone might object that though we do not have generic knowl-edge of gods, we do have it of people, and Christianity describes God as a person. Furthermore, just as the Christian God is supposed to cre-ate and providentially sustain the world, so human beings make and maintain artifacts. Therefore we do have a kind of generic knowledge of creative and providential persons that we might use for determining the probability of the existence of the Christian God and therefore of an afterlife and freedom too. Depending on whether the world is sufficiently or rightly similar to a human artifact, we may conclude that it is likely that the world is divinely created and sustained, or that it is not.

But, I reply, what are the right degree and the right kind of similarity, and how are these things to be determined? The kind of thinking that compares human and divine art is analogy, and it is not clear what the rules for using analogy in a probabilistic calculus should be. When we try to determine the probability of a given roll of dice, we compare the dice in question to other rolled dice that are very similar to them, or that belong to the same species. And comparing two members of one species is not analogy, or else is the very strongest sort of analogy. But compar-ing human beings to God is not comparing entities that belong to the same species, and even though Christianity teaches that human beings are created in the image of God, it also teaches that there is an infinite dissimilarity between human and divine things, so that analogy between human beings and God is weak, or at least tricky, and therefore a dubious basis for probabilistic thinking. Therefore it is at least highly doubtful that there can be a science of probability for assessing the odds that the world is created by a God who gives duties, freedom, and immortality to human beings. Thus the objective attempt to assign probability to God, duty, immortality, and freedom is a doubtful project.

Not everyone who resorts to probability admits it. For example, someone might say the following: "For me it's not a question of prob-ability. When the evidence for something is strong, I believe it, and when it's not, I don't. I don't believe the Christian claims about Christ because the evidence for them is weak, and against them, strong. It's as simple as that." But are things really so simple? What counts as strong evidence? If strong evidence is not the same as a demonstration, then how is it differ-ent from *an indication of probability*? There are signs that Christianity is false and signs that it is true. But how does one read the signs and come to a judgment about their significance without implicitly thinking to oneself: "On the whole, it seems to me more likely that Christ was (or was not) who he said he was"? I am not asserting that it is impossible to avoid probabilistic thinking when one reads the signs about Christ. Instead I am suggesting that most people do not, and challenging readers who think they do to explain how.

The principal reason that there are no public demonstrations for or against God, freedom, or immortality is that the common fund of premises is too scanty. In other words, people do not universally, or even mostly, agree to a set of premises on which a demonstration for or against the existence of these three things could be founded.

Thus arises the question how diversity in premises or principles affects the quest to know the answers to the most important ethical and religious questions. Does this diversity entail that knowledge or even rationally justified belief in these concerns is impossible? And if so, what follows from this? Or is there some way through or around the difficulty posed by diversity in ethical and religious principles?

Objective philosophers approach the problem of principles in many ways. Some of them attempt to disprove the apparent diversity of principles by using logical analysis to search for a consistent set of assumptions that underlie all human thinking in all times and places. Others attempt to devise rules for determining what should and should not count as a rationally justified principle. Still others attempt to discover, and perhaps develop, a faculty for knowing principles. For example, Descartes thinks that he has found such a faculty in the human capacity for clear and distinct conception. Having found this capacity, he then exercises or develops it and trains himself in the use of it. Similarly, Husserl searches for and thinks that he has found a faculty for principles in a mode of thinking that *brackets* the question whether the objects of consciousness exist independently of consciousness. And, like Descartes before him, he exercises this capacity and trains himself in the use of it.

However much objective philosophers may differ in their manner of approaching the problem of principles, they are all similar in that they do not approach it as whole persons. More fully, they do not seek knowledge or optimal awareness of principles by cultivating moral virtues that embrace feeling, willing, and acting—for if they did this, they would be subjective, not objective. Kierkegaard thinks that this partiality for mere thinking is the fatal flaw in the objective mode of evaluation. We shall see why he thinks this as we go on to examine how his subjective mode of evaluation handles the problem of principles.

The Subjective Mode of Evaluation

The subjective mode of evaluation is similar to the objective mode in that it seeks universal truths that transcend the peculiarities of individuals. But it is dissimilar in how it goes about seeking this goal. Whereas objective evaluation is third-person, subjective evaluation is first-person—in the sense that it stresses the rational necessity for every person to judge for himself or herself and draws and enacts the consequences of this necessity. Whereas objective evaluation seeks knowledge only or mainly with the intellect, subjective evaluation seeks it with the whole human self—thus subjectivity is both first-person and whole-person. And, finally, whereas objective evaluation does not focus on principles, but on what can be deduced from them, subjective evaluation regards the knowledge of principles (or justified belief in them), and not what can be inferred from them, as the most important knowledge.

Let us begin our assessment of subjective evaluation—both as I just described it and as Kierkegaard actually practices it—by considering some objections to it.

We human beings are liable to all sorts of error. We overlook inconsistencies and obscurities in our ideas. We fail to raise obvious objections to our beliefs and neglect to consider reasonable alternatives to them. We do not follow our thoughts through to their logical conclusions. And we mistake our individual idiosyncrasies for universal necessities. Besides the errors to which universal human nature is prone, individuals also have their peculiar weaknesses—weaknesses which, moreover, tend to be magnified by solitude and mitigated or corrected by dialogue with others. Given our general and particular limitations, and the tendency of solitary inquiry to exacerbate individual fantasy, it seems rational for us to pursue truth in cooperation with others, in the hope that each may correct for the others' defects and limitations. But subjective evaluation does not sufficiently respect this need for collaboration. As a first-person, solitary, and self-reliant pursuit of truth, it is highly prone to errors that could be avoided by more collaborative methods. And since the subjective mode of evaluation does not avail itself of rational procedures of correction, it is not rational.

Even if subjective evaluation itself could in theory stand up to and refute the preceding objection, Kierkegaard's own practice of subjective evaluation is extreme. For he rarely argues for his ideas, seldom solicits objections, and replies to objections far less than a rational inquirer should.

Though holism in a vague and general sort of way is a fine idea, careful thinking about it reveals various problems. What does it mean to seek truth as a whole person? Are all parts of the person helpful in the pursuit of knowledge? Or is not a human being an animal with specialized organs, some of which are apt for truth-seeking, others not? Take feelings—are they good inquirers? Hunches based on feeling are notoriously unreliable, and no sane and self-respecting philosopher puts much stock in them. Therefore, using the whole person in the pursuit of truth is not a good idea after all.

If everyone practiced subjective evaluation, the problem of diversity would be intensely exacerbated: diversity would abound, and every single individual would go his merry way, thinking that he was right, others wrong, and never openly engage in the rational dialogue in which his errors might be exposed and corrected. Another way of putting this objection is that if the most important source of crucial ethical and religious truths is something like intuition, then we will be left with no way of assessing competing intuitions, so that diversity will not only triumph, but tyrannize. Moreover, replacing argument with intuition is giving authority to vagueness, irresponsibility, and idiosyncrasy.

These objections to subjective evaluation are serious and weighty. My responses to them begin here, but will not be complete until the end of the chapter.

Let us begin with the objection that reason demands of Kierkegaard that he do more in the way of publicly arguing both for his own claims and against the claims of his opponents. I suspect that this objection is correct, but I am not sure. Let us be clear before going further that Kierkegaard does in fact publicly present some arguments *pro et contra* in his writings, but not as many as other philosophers do, and he argues more against others' ideas than he does for his own. It is possible that Kierkegaard arrives at many of his ideas by means of arguments with himself that he does not share with others. We should not be quick to assume that a genius, armed with a keen intellect and a library full of great books, cannot reason on his own very carefully to sound conclusions, even though it is certainly true that solitary reasoning has certain dangers that public argumentation does not.

Even granting that Kierkegaard himself errs by making too little use of public argumentation, it does not follow that subjective evaluation essentially involves this error. Perhaps another subjective thinker might do better than Kierkegaard does and use public argumentation in just the way it ought to be used. Kierkegaard is merely an example of subjective evaluation, not its Platonic idea. Kierkegaard might have been on to something, but not spot on it.

It is almost certainly true that, ideally speaking, Kierkegaard argues too little both for his own beliefs and against the beliefs of his rivals, at least in public. But the ideal is not always possible, and doggedly pursuing the ideal sometimes achieves less than compromise. In other words, it may be that some compromise in inquiry is humanly necessary, so that the question is not *whether* to compromise, but *what* to compromise and *how*. In the case in question, it may be that, once one begins to argue publicly, the temptation to share responsibility for one's beliefs with others necessarily becomes overwhelming, so that the public arguer inevitably ceases to judge for himself; or it may be that for this or that person, the temptation will be irresistible. If so, and if judging for oneself is more important in the search for truth than the benefits of public argumentation, then the most rational mode of evaluation possible (for all or some people) must forego or limit public argumentation for the sake of preserving autopsy. In other words, it may be more rational in the search for truth to compromise public argumentation than to compromise *sapere aude*.

Kierkegaard is clearly right that people tend to use public argumentation as a way of trying to diminish or abolish their responsibility for their own beliefs by sharing it with others. He is also correct that every person must judge for himself or herself. Even when someone tries to trust another person's judgment more than, or instead of, his own, he must trust himself to judge the reliability of the other person, and trust the other person on the authority of his own judgment. Thus one believes all that one believes primarily on one's own authority, even if one decides to credit another's opinion rather than one's own on some point or other. And since this is so, many cases of trusting others will turn out to be irrational attempts to avoid the necessity to judge for oneself. And since one can use public argumentation as a way of denying the necessity of personal responsibility, sometimes at least it will be rational to avoid public argumentation. Therefore, even if Kierkegaard is wrong in the particular way that he avoids public debate, he is right in a general sort of way about the need to be wary of it.

Later in this chapter I shall argue that the desire to avoid sharing responsibility is intense, hard to eradicate (or moderate) because of the force and ubiquity of its causes, and that this desire has great power to pervert public argumentation. Assuming that all this is correct, it does not seem clear to me how to determine the right balance between arguing publicly and preserving independence of judgment. I therefore must leave it to you to judge for yourself how strong you are, or can make yourself, to resist the temptation to share responsibility for your beliefs ith others in an irrational manner when you engage in public argumentation, and what role you should assign to public debate in your own search for truth.

The most basic reason that Kierkegaard argues relatively little for his beliefs is that he thinks that many of them are to be known, to the extent that they can be known, directly, or experientially, and not on the basis of logic working from a common fund of premises. If Kierkegaard is correct about this, then it would be irrational for him to argue for ideas whose nature demands that they be known or justified by means other than logic. By the way, given that Kierkegaard thinks that many of his key convictions are to be known noninferentially, it begins to make sense that he argues more against what he takes to be error than he argues for what he believes to be true. For it could be the case that many errors are logically refutable even when the corresponding truths are not logically demonstrable, so that the function of logic in ethics and religion might be more to clear the way to truth by refuting error than directly to reveal the truth.

In order that we may begin to see how Kierkegaard might respond to the charge that subjective evaluation exacerbates the problem of diversity, let us consider this revealing passage.

What, specifically is the ethical?—Well, if I put the question in this manner, I am asking unethically about the ethical, I am putting the question just as the whole confusion of the modern age does, and then I cannot put a stop to it. The ethical presupposes that every person knows what the ethical is, and why? Because the ethical demands that every man shall realize it at every moment, but then he surely has to know it. The ethical does not begin with ignorance which is to be changed to knowledge but begins with a knowledge and demands a realization. Here it is a matter of being unconditionally consistent. The slightest uncertainty in attitude— and then the modern confusion has gotten hold of us. If someone were to say: I must first know what the ethical is—how plausible—especially since from childhood we are all accustomed to being arguers. But the ethical answers altogether consistently: Scoundrel, you want to make excuses and look for excuses. If someone were to say: There are quite different concepts of the ethical in different countries and in different ages. How is this doubt halted? It can result in scholarly folios and still not stop, but the ethical seizes the doubter with ethical consistency and says, what concern is it of yours? You shall do the ethical at every moment, and you are ethically responsible for every moment you waste. (JP, 1:649, 10)

This *Journal* entry shows that Kierkegaard thinks that awareness of ethical truths is not the result of argument, that he is aware of the fact that people believe there is a problematic diversity in ethical convictions, and that he thinks this diversity is either not real or not a problem calling for a lengthy, argumentative, philosophical solution. His own solution is quite surprising. He says that he thinks everyone already knows the ethical. By this he does not mean, as various passages in his writing about the difficulty of developing the conscience indicate (JP, 1:684), that everyone is fully and transparently aware of all ethical truths. Instead he means that everyone knows enough of the ethical to act on what they know, and that the way for them to know more is for them to act on what they already know. Kierkegaard's theory of the stages of ethical and religious existence is precisely an attempt to suggest how all genuine ethical and religious striving converges on one truth. Moreover, if Kierkegaard is right that there is a personal God who honors and assists people who make an honest effort to hear and obey their conscience, then of course he is also correct that all genuine ethical and religious striving converges on universal truth. And even if there is no God, but there is universal human nature, it could still be the case that the best way to learn to live in accordance with human nature would have to include serious existential effort to live in accordance with conscience.

At this point, we might also note that if subjective evaluation meant whimsical, arbitrary, or relativistic individualism, it would certainly produce a very problematic diversity. But being a single individual who judges for oneself is not the same as being a relativistic individualist, as we shall see.

The Connection between Character and Cognition

In this section I will argue that there is a deep connection between character and cognition, that striving to develop the right kind of ethical character is the best way to prepare oneself to evaluate ethical and religious ideas, and that since subjectivity strives to develop such character, while objectivity does not, subjectivity has a decisive advantage over objectivity in the evaluation of ways of life.

Before going into the details of the argument for the claim that development of ethical character is crucial for the rational project of evaluation, let us look at this argument written in broad strokes. Its first premise is that desires, fears, emotions, actions, and habits have an influence on what and how a person thinks, or on what a person can see, understand, know, or become aware of. In other words, some desires, habits, emotions, and actions are conducive to truth, and some are inimical to it. A good indication, familiar to many of us, that this is true is provided by the Platonic dialogue called the *Meno*. For in the *Meno* it is arguable and maybe even obvious that the character after whom the dialogue is named fails to learn as much as he could by talking to Socrates, not because he is especially stupid or dull-witted, but because he is lazy, self-indulgent, vain, unwilling to take responsibility for himself; because he refuses to blame himself for his own errors; because he is too proud to admit his ignorance; and because he is consequently unable to make the new beginning required of philosophy in which one attempts to think for and from oneself. In short, the *Meno* is a dramatic illustration that weak and base character undermines the philosophical endeavor. The second premise of the argument is that it is possible to alter, at least partly, one's desires, fears, emotions, actions, and habits through practical discipline and exercises. In other words, we can to some degree alter our character by intelligently making changes in the way that we act. One important conclusion to be drawn from these premises is that it is possible to improve one's understanding (philosophical or otherwise) by a practical discipline that includes exercises. A further possible conclusion is that the more one's practical discipline embraces one's life as a whole, the more that discipline will improve one's (philosophical) understanding. And finally, since subjectivity is a practical discipline that embraces one's whole life, whereas objectivity is abstract, absentminded, and theoretical, subjectivity is a better way to seek (philosophical) knowledge of crucial human truths than objectivity is.

It is obvious that people often fail to see something just because they are afraid to see it, or because it would be too upsetting or too disturbing to acknowledge it. In other words, people often believe comforting illusions through cowardice, or because they lack the courage to face a harsh or frightening truth. Freud was so impressed by this human tendency to deny obvious but threatening truths that he coined a technical term for it: resistance. Ivan in the *Brothers Karamazov* provides a good example of resistance when he stupidly and stubbornly refuses to admit that he provoked Smerdyakov, his half-brother, to murder their father. Kierkegaard for his part thinks that the deep thinker must be a spiritual *knight* with the strength and *courage* to think *terrible* thoughts that others cannot endure to think.

Once philosophers become aware of the need for courage and nobility, their next step is to strive to develop these virtues in their lives or practices. One's inborn nature and one's upbringing have a lot to do with whether one is high-minded and brave. It is also probably true that courage in practical life, for instance derring-do in a dark alley or in war, is importantly different from philosophical courage. Nonetheless, one can cultivate a kind of courage in practical life that is useful in philosophical inquiry. For example, we can make it a habit as we go about our daily activities to ask ourselves whether we failed to do something that we had planned to do, or would like to have done, or ought to have done, because we suspected that doing it would reveal something about us that we were afraid to discover or acknowledge. Sometimes we might go further than merely asking ourselves these questions and proceed to perform a fearful action that we would usually avoid so as to get the better of our fear. To give a more specific example, someone might refrain from asking his wife important questions about their marriage because he is afraid to hear and face her answers. Similarly one might remain silent in a philosophical conversation because one is afraid that by speaking one will be revealed as ignorant, stupid, or foolish, thus forfeiting the opportunity to learn, perhaps at the expense of being a little embarrassed. Therefore, by facing threatening truths in seemingly nonphilosophical activities such as talking to one's wife about one's marriage one can cultivate a courage that will be useful in more obviously philosophical activities.

Just as cowardice in life can lead to cowardice in philosophy, so it is with dishonesty. It is hard to believe that a person who often lies to himself about his own actions and qualities, about the actions and qualities of other people, and about his social and personal relations to other people will be honest when he tries to answer the most important philosophical questions. Since he has developed the habit of lying to himself and thus disrespecting the truth in his practical life, his mendaciousness is likely to carry over to his philosophizing. In other words, the person who cannot acknowledge the truth in personal relations is not the sort of person who can acknowledge it in questions of the greatest importance about human life. Moreover, understanding the deepest human things requires not just acknowledging the truth, but loving it, craving it, needing it deeply, and energetically seeking it. And someone who hates and avoids the truth in practical life can hardly love and seek it in philosophy. To take these thoughts just one step further, we have to suspect that the person who habitually lies to himself about his life will use his philosophy to excuse, defend, justify, or conceal these lies. For he has lies to defend, and philosophy provides him with weapons for defending them.

Owing to the connection between honesty in practical affairs and truthfulness in philosophy, philosophers would be well advised to strive to be honest with themselves in the whole of their lives and not just when they are reading, writing, or talking about philosophy. What is more, it seems that philosophers must not only endeavor to be truthful as they go along in life, but also set aside designated times for self-examination. During such times, their task is to look suspiciously into their behavior and their spontaneous ideas about their behavior in order to see whether they are deceiving themselves about what they have done or why they have done it. And if they discover self-deception, they must go further and seek the causes and the means of this self-deception, and then use what they learn from this investigation to look for other self-deceptions, both in their spontaneous impressions about their lives and in their philosophical thinking. Thus it behooves philosophers to make it an exercise, a practice, or a discipline to examine themselves regularly. Kierkegaard recommends serious and frequent self-examination, gives detailed advice on how to go about it, explains or hints at how self-deception works, and forcefully emphasizes the need to cultivate honesty with oneself and before God.

Self-deception does not have its source just in thinking. We deceive ourselves not only because we think badly, but also because we act badly. More accurately, we tend to deceive ourselves about things that we have done or would like to do and of which we do not approve, or of which we are ashamed (or would be ashamed), or that do not match the picture that we paint of and for ourselves. In other words, whenever we have done or want to do something shameful, we are strongly tempted to rationalize, ignore, or distort it. What is more, if we make a habit of doing things of which we are ashamed, it becomes much more tempting and much easier to deceive ourselves about these things. Or should I say that it gets easier to do shameful things the more one does them precisely because one deceives oneself about them?

Owing to the fact that human beings tend to deceive themselves about actions of which they are ashamed, seekers of truth should seriously consider making it a practice not to act in ways so shameful to them that they are strongly tempted to deceive themselves. In other words, philosophers should consider adopting a discipline or rule of behavior that develops in them an integrity of character that supports the search for philosophical knowledge. Kierkegaard has colorful names for such integrity, namely, our old friends, *subjective truth* and *subjectivity.*

The philosophical search for knowledge absolutely requires that one think, see, and judge for oneself. In other words, you cannot be a serious truth-seeker if you are too easily persuaded by intellectual authorities, or if you are overly dependent on or influenced by the opinions of others. As Kierkegaard puts it, "only when I discover" the *truth* about myself "is it discovered" for me (PF, 14). And yet it is very human to be deeply influenced by the opinions of others. There are many forces at work that make human beings treat their fellows as authorities. The most basic of these is our nature, or second nature, as social beings. The process by which children are socialized involves getting them to accept many ideas and behaviors on the authority of adults. Thus almost all of us begin life by being taught not to think for ourselves and therefore by developing a habit of unthinking trust. Furthermore, as social beings we need friendship, companionship, and community. The need to be liked, loved, accepted, approved of, respected, recognized, or to belong strongly encourages us to adopt the opinions of others. For adapting oneself to the opinions and behaviors of other people or of a community is a very effective way of being accepted by them. Conversely, rejecting or disagreeing with the opinions of others is usually a very effective way of being rejected by them. Moreover, there are many people—e.g., politicians, advertisers, and propagandists—who make it their business to become authorities that we irrationally accept. Thus the human need or desire for society constitutes a strong inducement to treat others as authorities. And this is to say that the social character of human beings is at least partly at odds with philosophy or truth-seeking, which requires that one question or challenge custom, fashion, prejudice, tradition, and other authorities.

The social instinct takes many forms that are inimical to truth-seeking. For example, human beings often desire to have power and influence over others or more power and influence than others. One means of such power is persuasion. And to persuade others often requires that one flatter them, that is, that one lie to them, thereby compromising one's own beliefs. Thus the desire for power turns us into rhetoricians. As rhetoricians, we are constantly trying to discern, not what is true, but what will be believed, accepted, or embraced by others. Thus rhetoricians develop the habit of disrespecting truth so as to succeed in achieving power and influence through persuasion. And since the desire for power and influence is a common and strong human desire, human nature itself tempts not just a few specialized rhetoricians to compromise the truth, but virtually everyone. Nonetheless, some people are more exposed to the rhetorical temptation, like politicians, teachers, and philosophers. Kierkegaard is especially wary of the need to chasten the desire to acquire power through persuasion.

Another crystallization that the social impulse can take, especially among philosophers, is a desire to win arguments so intense that it can trump the desire to discover and accept the truth. I assume that anyone who has taken part in the philosophical search for knowledge in cooperation with others is well aware of how the desire to win an argument can make *other people* stubbornly resistant to an obvious or well-proven truth.

Yet another permutation of the social instinct is the human tendency to take offense, or to be insulted, or to be spiteful or resentful. Although the offended person may not attempt to win the approval of others through his opinions and actions, he nonetheless defines himself and his opinions in relation to the person who has injured him. The offended person wants revenge, or public vindication, or to expose the guilt of others, and adapts himself, his actions, and even his opinions to the goals of getting revenge or vindication for himself and condemnation of others.

Resentment can affect not only our social relations with others, but also our philosophical endeavors. Nietzsche suggests that Epicurus's whole philosophy, which he wrote out in some three hundred books, was almost nothing but a refined and sophisticated expression of "rage and ambition against Plato."[1] Philosophical resentment works something like this. A philosopher feels so injured by the excellence of another thinker, or by his own lack of fame, that he develops a pathological need to get revenge, at any cost, therefore even at the expense of truth. Out of this desire for revenge, against Plato, or against the world as a whole, might grow an idea, or even a whole philosophy, whose purpose is to offend the offender, or to put the offender in as bad a light as possible, even at the cost of lying. Kierkegaard claims that Christianity is rejected—when it, and not some facsimile of it, is rejected—because of *offense* at God and the Gospel.

In order to achieve independence of philosophical judgment, it is arguable that one must also achieve independence of character. The person who lives only or mainly in the eyes of others cannot suddenly begin to see through his own eyes when he sets out to philosophize. The person who defines the rule of his behavior according to the dictates of public opinion cannot miraculously dissolve his habits of dependence when he begins to think philosophically, but will think within the fetters of that dependence. The person who is offended at the world because of the way that his parents, friends, wife, co-workers, colleagues, or God treated him will distort the world and his life in it when he tries to understand these things through philosophical reflection. The person who makes it a practice of slavishly adapting himself to others in his life will only rationalize and theorize that slavish practice when he tries reflectively to grasp his life with others. The person whose chief goal in life is to persuade others by compromising the truth ends up at least half-believing his own lies. The person who is too lazy and cowardly to live by his own judgment and at his own discretion will hardly find the strength and courage to judge for himself when he tries to climb up out of life to get a large view on it. And so on. Therefore, seeing for oneself requires acting for oneself, as Kierkegaard would say, by one's own self-activity, at one's own risk, and on one's own responsibility. In short, autopsy requires autopraxy.

Given philosophy's need for independence of judgment, the person who aims at philosophical wisdom would be well advised to adopt a way of life that cultivates magnanimity, self-reliance, or noble aloofness of character. As Nietzsche put it, the genuine philosopher cannot encumber himself with a wife.[2] Or as the Buddha put it, the life of a householder is cramped and *dusty*, but the life of the person who has "gone forth" from "home-life" is "wide-open and free" (e.g., "To Sangarava," MLD, 821). Or as Kierkegaard puts it, spiritual truth requires the rigorous discipline of solitude. By the way, I am not saying here that marriage and friendship are utterly incompatible with independence of judgment, only that they threaten to become so.

So far we have examined only the positive side of independence of character. It also has a negative side. The person who has, or who strives to achieve, independence of character and of mind might end up making the opposite error of being too partial to his own ideas. He might think something is true just because he said it and not the crowd, or just because he wrote it and not a hack, or just because he thought of it and not some rival. Just as you can irrationally suppose that something is true because others think it, so you can irrationally suppose that something is true because *you* think it. I can be too partial to my own opinions in almost the same way that I can be too dependent on the authority of others. All people, not just those who cultivate independence, are tempted to be irrationally partial to their own ideas. But the independent ones are especially vulnerable to this temptation. Thus arises the paradoxical task of being self-reliant but not self-preferential.

In Plato's *Laws*, the Athenian Stranger argues that every human being is naturally inclined to "excessive friendship for oneself," that we all tend to excuse this extravagant self-love, and that this irrational partiality or preference for oneself is the source of everyone's supposing that his "lack of learning is wisdom." As a result, the Athenian Stranger continues, "we think we know everything when in fact we know, so to speak, nothing."[3] This is to say that Socratic ignorance requires overcoming one's excessive love for oneself or that one surmount one's irrational partiality for one's own ideas.

Thus the philosophical search for truth requires resisting excessive self-love or striving to transcend the natural but irrational preference for oneself. In other words, the philosopher must try to get his or her ego out of the way so that the things can show themselves from their own side. The philosopher must stop thinking that something is true because he or she thinks it, said it, or wrote it, and seek a truth that shows itself when one ceases to be attached to one's own thinking as one's own thinking.

The Athenian Stranger argues that this irrational love for and partiality toward oneself is the cause not just of ignorant people presuming that they are knowledgeable, but of all sorts of wrongdoings.[4] Certainly it is true that we act, at least often, out of a partiality for ourselves which would be hard to justify on rational grounds, and which we excuse in ourselves but which we would blame in others. But, if the same unreasonable egoism influences both our thinking and our acting, and if we desire to overcome this self-flattering blindness in our philosophical vision, then it makes sense that we might make it a practice to resist it in our actions so that we might transcend it in our thinking and philosophizing. In other words, it would be naïve to think that one can be indulgently partial to oneself in all the activities of one's personal and practical life but heroically impartial with respect to oneself in one's philosophical investigations. Therefore, if we are going to transcend extravagant self-love in our philosophy, then we must make an effort to overcome it in our actions. Or, more modestly, it is plausible that an effort to treat oneself impartially in one's personal relations with other people might support the effort to become an impartial witness to the truth in one's philosophy or thinking.

By the way, even if some sort of selfishness is the rational attitude toward life, it will still be true that philosophical knowledge requires transcending irrational versions of preference and partiality for oneself. In other words, even if the rational way to live is always to be sure to look out for number one, still it would be necessary not to think that something is true just because it seems true to the center of the universe upon shallow and hasty reflection.

It is obvious that Kierkegaard's noble and solitary truth-seekers are seriously at risk of becoming proud in a way that is inimical to truth. But, I take it as equally obvious that these truth-seekers are aware of this difficulty, stressing as they do the need for humility, and being, as they are, careful interpreters of the religion of humility—Christianity. Nor are they merely aware of the danger, but they work against it with all their might by striving for humility.

Having clarified the importance of practical exercise or discipline for philosophical inquiry, I will go one step further and argue that a person's whole life forms the basis of his or her (philosophical) quest for wisdom. Not only Kierkegaard, but the Buddha, Plato, and Nietzsche think that it is not enough for the philosopher to adopt a few practices or to do a few exercises in support of his or her philosophizing. Rather they think that it is necessary for philosophers or seekers of truth to make their whole lives a discipline or training for philosophy (or truth-seeking). Or more modestly, they think that the best support of philosophical thinking is a philosophical life. Whether or not they are right seems to me to be a question to be decided by the trial of one's own experience. But for now I will tentatively offer an argument for the necessity of a total program or of a comprehensively philosophical way of life. The argument is drawn mostly from Plato's *Republic*.

According to the *Republic*, there are three basic kinds of human desire: desires for truth; desires for victory and honor; and desires for physical pleasures like those of food, drink, comfort, and sexual intercourse. These desires often conflict with one another, with the result that most of us are pulled by our desires in many directions at once and thus weakened and confused. More relevantly, desires for honor and desires for physical pleasures draw psychic energy away from the desire for truth and consequently thwart, interfere with, or otherwise undermine the pursuit of truth. Therefore it is prudent for philosophers to make an effort to strengthen the desire for truth and establish it securely on the throne of their souls. In some cases this will mean trying to eradicate unnecessary desires that conflict with the desire for truth: for example, a desire for gambling, or for political power, or for the spectacles of sport, or for the entertainments of television and the internet. In other cases it will mean moderating necessary desires. For example, philosophers will attempt to have simple and modest desires for food, so that they are not enslaved by the laborious burden of satisfying the demanding and fastidious palate of a gourmand. And in still other cases it will mean subordinating, harmonizing, or adjusting various desires to the desire for truth. For example, instead of attempting simply to eradicate the desire for honor, one might instead make it a point of honor never to lie to oneself, or not to tell some sorts of lies to other people.

In the words of the *Republic,* the pursuit of the truth requires a *conversion,* a "turning around" of the "whole soul," so that the "eye of the soul" is pointed in the direction where truth is to be discerned.[5] This effort to turn the soul around largely means directing the passions, motive powers, and habits of the soul toward the goal and activity of seeking and living the truth. Alternatively, we might say that in order to transcend oneself in philosophical knowledge one must master oneself in practical discipline. For in order to go beyond oneself one must have an integral and definite self to transcend. And since Kierkegaard's subjectivity is precisely a striving to turn the whole soul toward truth, it seems to be deeply in accord with Plato's regimen for the philosophical search for truth and, as I have argued, deeply in accord with human nature. Kierkegaard does not think of himself as a philosopher, but, even so, the present argument suggests that all truth-seeking about the deepest human concerns, including philosophical versions of this search, requires subjectivity in order to achieve its own ends.

Someone might object that since we know that some great philosophers had bad characters but good ideas, the connection between cognition and character cannot be especially strong. Even if it is true that great philosophers had bad character but true ideas—and I do not know that it is true, or how true it is—it does not follow that they would not have been still-greater philosophers if they had had better character. Presumably there is something irrepressible about genius. Genius will do something amazing and worth studying, even when it is misguided or perverted. If it is possible for anyone to transcend himself or herself in knowledge, exceptional philosophers might also occasionally transcend their cor-

202 · THE PARADOXICAL RATIONALITY OF SØREN KIERKEGAARD

rupt character. Moreover, the influence of character on cognition is not equally strong in all fields of inquiry. For example, corrupt character perverts cognition of human nature and of the best life for human beings far more than it perverts cognition of scientific, mathematical, and linguistic truths. Someone might also object that my claims about cognition and character are a sort of generalization of the ad hominem fallacy. In reply, I say that this fallacy attempts to infer the falsity of an idea on the basis of the character of the person who propounds it, but cultivating one's own character so as to be a better judge of truth does not require this inference about other people.

A Way of Knowing Principles

I have argued that subjectivity develops moral virtues that support knowledge of human nature, its place in the world, and the best life for human beings. Now I will argue that subjectivity develops and trains faculties of noninferential knowledge, and that, properly developed and used, these faculties are means of rational evaluation of ways of life.

Much of subjectivity's development and training of the capacity for principial knowledge takes place in the activity of self-examination, one of whose organs is conscience. Kierkegaard writes that "there is no accomplishment . . . which requires such extensive and rigorous schooling as is required before one can genuinely be said to have a conscience" (JP, 1:684). Subjective self-examiners attend to their conscience when they ask themselves such questions as the following and seriously attempt to answer them: Do my actions measure up to my ideals and to my conception of my duties? Have I failed to fulfill any of my duties, and, if yes, why did I fail to fulfill it? What do I regret, or what do I feel guilty about, and according to what standard? In my thinking do I habitually dilute or scale down the ideals of my conscience, and if so, what do those ideals look like undiluted? What ought I to do now, or what should I be preparing to do? By asking themselves these questions, subjective strivers attempt to discover what they honestly think about ethics and religion and about their own personal relation to ethics and religion. And by asking such questions and conscientiously attempting to answer them regularly and as a discipline, they hone and strengthen their conscience as a capacity for insightful honesty about ethical and religious principles.

Subjective strivers also consult their moods and emotions by asking questions such as these: How do I feel about various ideas and actions? Why do I feel as I do? What do my feelings reveal about my thoughts and convictions? Do my feelings agree with my thoughts, and if they do not agree, do they reveal an insincerity, ambivalence, or difficulty in my thinking? Among the most revealing moods or emotions, according to Kierkegaard, are guilt, sorrow, boredom, anxiety, and despair, about the last two of which he wrote whole books.[6] Kierkegaard also recommends that one attempt to bring one's emotions into line with what one takes to be one's deepest convictions, so as to manifest the affective dimension and consequences of those convictions and thereby test them.

Consulting their emotions helps subjective strivers to detect self-deception. For, as Freud showed very well, self-deception tends to leave traces in our emotions, which can be followed to their source. When we feel anxious, angry, or sorrowful without knowing why, this may be because we are somehow hiding from ourselves the source of our disease, or unease. Therefore, by pursuing such feelings to their source, we can often learn what we have been hiding from ourselves, how we have been doing it, and why.

According to Kierkegaard, no matter how well we think, we cannot learn what we really think merely by thinking; we must also act. This is to say that the subtlest and most reliable strategy of self-examination is (or includes) ethical and religious striving, or subjectivity. Subjectivity tests ethical and religious ideals by living them. Since these ideals are not ideas to be contemplated, but principles to live by, the best way to evaluate them is actually to live by them. By living an ideal, one puts oneself in a position to learn things about it and oneself that an abstract consideration of these things would not reveal with equal clarity and authority: Is this ideal in fact the sort of thing for which I can passionately live and courageously die? Does it give lasting and deeply felt meaning to my life? Does it really have the power in practice to unify and consolidate my soul, so that I could (strive to) will it absolutely, without compromise, and without reservation for my whole life?

To achieve its goal, self-examination must detect and defeat self-deception. And to do this it must study the causes, effects, mechanisms, signs, and symptoms of self-deception, as well as the kinds of things that it typically seeks to conceal, and then apply this knowledge in further

204 · THE PARADOXICAL RATIONALITY OF SØREN KIERKEGAARD

self-examination. In other words, a self-examiner might find that he has deceived himself about some things, ask himself why and how he was deceiving himself, and what were the signs of his self-deception. Then he will use all this knowledge of the why, the how, and the signs of some instances of self-deception to discover further instances of it. The science of self-deception is a crucial part of subjectivity as understood by Kierkegaard.

Most of the knowledge of principles sought by subjective thinkers is self-knowledge. Kierkegaard thinks that all important knowledge is, or is closely connected to, self-knowledge (SUD, 31). The subjective thinker strives to know, more than anything else, what she really thinks, what are the ultimate motives of her actions, and what she really feels and why. Consider the following passage:

> there never [has] been an atheist, even though there certainly have been many who have been unwilling to let what they knew (that the God exists) get control of their minds. . . . With respect to the existence of God, immortality, etc., in short, with respect to all the problems of im-manence, recollection applies; it exists altogether in every man, only he does not know it, but it again follows that the conception may be very inadequate. (JP, 3:3606)

Therefore it is "infinitely ridiculous" to try to prove these things. Thus Kierkegaard thinks that knowledge of God and other important things is or comes from self-knowledge, and that this self-knowledge is natural, so that if it is absent this is because of self-deception. Therefore making it present is typically a process of undeception carried on in relation to God, so that "the true autodidact is precisely in the same degree a theodidact" (CA, 162). In other words, "to come into relation to God is a voyage of discovery" that is also an "inland journey" into oneself partly for the sake of self-knowledge (JP, 2:1451).

A critic might object at this point that even if the subjective thinker is ever so correct about what he really thinks, he might be ever so wrong about the truth. In reply I would say that the same sort of objection can be made to any method of knowing reality: Even if you have followed your method of truth-seeking impeccably, you might still be wrong about the truth. For even if you think you have followed your method correctly, you may not have. And even if you think that your method, correctly fol-lowed, guarantees truth, you might be wrong about this. Furthermore, attempting to discover what one really thinks does not entail insulating and isolating the self. Subjective truth-seekers who strive to know what they really think also strive to encounter reality by examining it, reading what others have written about it, and so on. In other words, they seek self-knowledge not just by examining themselves, but by studying other things. They also test the fruits of their self-examination dialectically, to see whether their ideas about themselves are consistent with one another, and whether they still believe them after they have seen their inter-relations and implications. Thus logic ends up playing an important role in subjective striving for self-knowledge. Finally, if the Platonic dialogues are even close to realistic in their portrayal of life, most human beings do not know or strive to know what they really think, so that striving for self-knowledge should give subjective seekers of truth an immense advantage over objective seekers of truth who do not seriously attempt this.

By the way, Socrates' description and practice of his "second sailing" comes pretty close to Kierkegaard's making it a priority in ethical and religious inquiry to discover what he really thinks, and so do the cogito of Descartes, the *epoche* of Husserl, and the *internalism* of some analytic epistemologists.[7] To sum up, the search for self-knowledge for Kierkegaard is not the whole of ethical and religious inquiry, but the key to it, its organizing principle, an added dimension to merely objective inquiry.

A critic might also object that striving to know what one really thinks seems like a way of knowing oneself merely as an individual. How then can Kierkegaard discover universal truths about human nature merely or mainly by studying himself? How can it be that "the issue pertains to me alone, partly because, properly presented, it will belong to everyone in the same way" (CUP, 17)?

As I indicated, Kierkegaard's method of honesty is not utterly isolationist. He minutely observes other people, carefully ponders about them, and reads their books in order to try to know them, himself, and human nature.

A crucial tool for Kierkegaard's study of other people (or of possibilities that one is not currently actualizing) is *imagination,* which he calls the "capacity *instar omnium* [for all capacities]. When all is said and done, whatever of feeling, knowing, and willing a person has depends upon what imagination he has, upon how that person reflects himself— that is, upon imagination" (SUD, 31).

Kierkegaard and Climacus do not regard imagination primarily as a creative faculty, but as a faculty of awareness or perception. The chief function of the imagination is to *perceive* an "image of perfection," or of an *ideal*, which can be "handed down by history" or "formed by the imagination itself" (PC, 186). More specifically, it is through imagination that one becomes "aware of" one's "self and of God"—the self that one might become, and of God through whom and *before* whom one becomes one's self in *imitation* of the ideal (SUD, 41).

According to Climacus, it is "poetic imagination" that enables one "to become contemporary with the event that occurred 1,812 years ago," namely the incarnation and crucifixion of God in Christ (CUP, 65). Anti-Climacus, who ascribes this same power to imagination, writes that to become "contemporary with Christ" is to "see you [i.e., Christ] in your true form and in the surroundings of actuality as you walked here on earth . . . *see you as you are*" (PC, 64, 9; emphasis added). Silentio also indicates that he uses poetry or imagination to help his readers become contemporary with Abraham and his heroic acts of faith (FT, 9, 30, 39, 63, 66). Thus Kierkegaard claims that imagination can enable one to transcend one's time, place, and the assumptions and habits of thought that belong to one's situation in order to see Christ, Abraham, or any other model of perfection more accurately, or even as it is.

In order to see the ideal as it is one must transcend oneself and one's temperament, prejudices, and other individual limitations. One way of doing this is to see things as other people—actual or possible—see them. This does not mean seeing things as you yourself would see them in the situation of the other, though even this can be helpful, but seeing as the other sees, seeing, as Buber puts it, "from the other side."[8] This ability to see as others see is crucial for evaluating ideals, since otherwise one will fail to appreciate some ideals owing to one's habits and other accidental limitations. Without this self-transcending act of imagination, even putting an idea into practice is not an adequate way of testing and evaluating it, since actively to test an idea but in the wrong spirit or in the wrong frame of mind or without an affective appreciation of it can hardly count as a fair and adequate trial.

Kierkegaard implicitly claims in many ways to be able to see as another person sees. When he writes pseudonymously he does not merely attribute ideas to a fictitious character, but he aims to inhabit that persona and speak from within it. One of his pseudonymous authors, Vigilius Haufniensis, explicitly describes the process of *inclining* or *bending* toward another person in order to see as he sees (CA, 54–55). In *Practice and Christianity*, Anti-Climacus adopts the point of view of no fewer than ten different fictional people who lived at the time of Christ in order to assist his readers to transcend themselves and see as others see (PC, 42–52). There are also many other exercises of imagination in this work and in other books of Kierkegaard that seemingly have the purpose of aiding self-transcendence through practice in imagination. For example, Anti-Climacus frequently bids his readers to imagine themselves doing or saying something in a certain situation and to imagine what another person might say, feel, or think in response. He even asks his readers to imagine themselves helping another person to imagine something and so on.

The imaginative power of seeing as others see, if it is real, learnable, and trainable, will obviously be of great assistance in solving or ameliorating the problem of diversity in principles. For just as the best kind of logical evaluation of another person's ideas is immanent in that it proceeds from the assumptions of the other person, so the best kind of nonlogical evaluation of another person's principle is immanent in that it sees the principle as the other sees it. And by seeing as the other sees, one does not just test the other as other, but tests the other as a possibility for oneself. Thus imagination is *reflection*, or the "rendition of the self as the self's possibility" (SUD, 31).

Some readers will doubt that there really is an imaginative capacity to see things from the other side. But it is crucial not to judge this matter by one's own accidental limitations without having made an effort to train one's imagination. It seems to me incontestable that some people are capable of a fairly thorough imaginative identification with other people, and that almost all people are capable of some degree of self-transcendence through imagination. Furthermore, as Vigilius indicates, it is possible to test one's sense of the other by presenting him back to himself and seeing whether he accepts the representation, or by observing what effect the representation has (CA, 55–56).

This is not to say that Kierkegaard thinks that imagination can perfectly substitute for the trial of actual experience. Far from it. He is well aware of, and cautions against, the "foreshortened depiction" of the imagination that can make difficult tasks seem *easier* than they actually are (PC, 187). Nevertheless, it may be wise or rational in some cases to do a preliminary test with the imagination before embarking on a perilous venture.

Kierkegaard's claim that he can find and meet readers where they are implicitly involves the claim that he can see things as his readers do. Presumably Kierkegaard's success (or lack thereof) in stealing into his reader's thoughts and surprising them with his presence, or in giving them a sense that he is familiar with their mental landscape, or even that he somehow knows how to address them where they are, serves as important evidence of the human (in)capacity for seeing as another sees. C. S. Lewis, a man of great imagination, but perhaps more sober and less inclined to exaggeration than Kierkegaard, seems to agree with Kierkegaard about the power of imagination when he writes that

> in reading great literature I become a thousand men and yet remain myself. Like the night sky in the Greek poem, I see with a myriad eyes, but it is still I who see. Here, as in worship, in love, in moral action, and in knowing, I transcend myself, and I am never more myself than when I do.[9]

Thus Lewis thinks that he can meet authors whom he reads where they are. And if he is right about this, Kierkegaard may also be right about the converse claim to meet his readers where they are.

To sum up, Kierkegaard and Climacus claim that strivers who develop the virtues of subjectivity and who train their faculties for ethical and religious principles become aware (by means other than logical inference) of ethical and religious truths. In the remaining part of this chapter we will examine, and to some extent assess, this subjective awareness of principles. If we do not ourselves have this subjective awareness, we should consider the possibility that it may be presumptuous of us to dismiss it as a mere fantasy.

Someone might object that even if subjective evaluation is justifiable or reliable in some ways, it is a misuse of language to call *knowing principles noninferentially,* or *attempting to know them thus, rational evaluation.* For, the objection continues, rational evaluation of an idea consists in considering arguments for and against that idea. In reply I say that it seems to me that rational evaluation means trying to figure out the best way to test something and then using that test. Sometimes the best test will be considering arguments. But sometimes the best test will be something noninferential, like experience, as it is, for example, when the question is whether or not I like the taste of pomegranate. Since deduction requires premises, rational evaluation, if it is to amount to much, must either show that arguing in a circle can be a method of proof, or else find a way to know or justify premises noninferentially. Moreover, even though deductive logic cannot produce its own premises, it can play a crucial role in discovering the connection between character and cognition of principles, and it can help to devise a way of building the right sort of character for knowledge of, or the best awareness of, principles. And since it is arguable that rational evaluation requires knowledge of principles, and since reason can help to devise a method for knowing principles, it is arguable that *knowing principles noninferentially,* or *attempting to know them thus,* is in fact a part of rational evaluation.

The Venture

Climacus writes that when Christianity addresses a person it *presupposes* an "infinite interest" in eternal *happiness* (CUP, 16). This is to say that in order to consider becoming Christians people must desire happiness so deeply—that is, *infinitely*—that they are willing to seek for it with their whole beings in their whole lives, sacrificing lesser goods for it when necessary. As Richard Hooker puts it, "somewhat it seeketh, and what that is directly it knoweth not, yet very intentive desire thereof doth so incite it, that all other known delights and pleasures are laid aside; they give place to the search of this but only suspected desire."[10]

There are many great thinkers and famous schools of thought that look upon the desire and hope for eternal happiness suspiciously and explain it unflatteringly. They claim that the idea of eternal happiness takes firmest root in people who are too weak to deal with the dangers of the world and the demands of civilization, or in people who are pathetic losers in life, whether it be in the physical, psychological, intellectual, political, or economic arena. These weaklings, so suspicion suggests, use the idea of eternal happiness as a consolation and compensation for their sufferings; reality is just too hard for them, and so they escape into religious fantasy.

Perhaps the masters of suspicion are completely correct about the origin and nature of religions like Christianity that promise an eternal happiness for their practitioners. In any case, they are almost certainly right about many of the practitioners of these religions or about many of them much of the time. But it is not clear that they are correct about all of them.

Let us consider what qualities Kierkegaard thinks it takes to have a genuinely infinite interest in eternal happiness to see whether suspicion can plausibly explain away such interest as a delusion. Kierkegaard thinks that infinite interest in eternal happiness requires honesty, a practice of truthfulness in thinking about oneself—about what one thinks, what one does, and what one hopes. It requires courage both to admit that one desires a sublime something that it will be dangerous to pursue and to pursue it and to suffer and make sacrifices for it. It demands a knightly nobility that despises compromise, low pleasures, and base purposes. And it requires a humility that risks being duped, or made a fool of, if that sublime something turns out to be merely a will-o'-the-wisp. Although suspicions about the desire and hope for eternal happiness make great sense in the case of people who are lazy, ignoble, and habitually lie to themselves about many things, they make much less sense in the case of people who are so honest that they daily examine their sins and so strong and courageous that they willingly suffer immensely and sacrifice everything for truth, goodness, and happiness. To explain away the infinite interest in eternal happiness of such virtuous people, the masters of suspicion need a better explanation than they have provided heretofore. But to want to explain away such people—if they exist—seems quite suspicious, and to judge what such heroes should think about experiences that they have had, but the explainer has not, is quite presumptuous. To put the point concisely, suspicious, third-person evaluation of virtuous first-person evaluation is a dubious and questionable activity.

Someone might object that it would be hard to give a plausible, reductively suspicious explanation of the desire for eternal happiness in highly virtuous people, but add that it is not so clear that there are highly virtuous people who desire eternal happiness and venture everything for it. In reply I would say that it seems pretty clear that there have been many such people. But, in any case, the crucial question here is not whether such people exist, but whether you and I have or conceal within us a capacity for such an infinite interest. For the question of eternal happiness is a subjective question for the single individual, not an objective question to be debated in a scholarly fashion.

Thus suspicion can be used against both those who desire, hope, and strive for eternal happiness and those who stick their fingers in other people's pies in the sky. Kierkegaard's writings provide the basis for an extensive analysis of the choice not to strive for eternal happiness. Given the preceding, we might expect this analysis to suggest that nonstrivers are dishonest with themselves, weak, cowardly, ignoble, lazy, and so on, on the one hand, or else proud, defiant, and demonic, on the other.

Readers may have noticed the similarity between "Pascal's wager" and Kierkegaard's *venture* for eternal happiness. There is indeed a likeness, but with at least one important difference. Pascal presents his wager almost as a cold calculation, as a mathematical cost-benefit analysis, but Kierkegaard presents his venture as a passionate endeavor and labors to awaken in his readers the passionate awareness of eternal happiness that makes venturing a "live option." Another possible, important difference is that it may be more clear in the case of the venture than it is in the case of the wager that the goal is not just bliss, but goodness.

Subjectivity and Christianity: A "Perfect Fit"

As strivers progress, they become aware, according to Climacus, that *subjectivity* and *Christianity* are a "perfect fit."

> If, however, subjectivity is truth and subjectivity is the existing subjectivity, then, if I may put it this way, Christianity is a perfect fit. Subjectivity culminates in passion, Christianity in paradox; paradox and passion fit each other perfectly, and paradox perfectly fits a person situated in the extremity of existence. Indeed, in the whole wide world there are not to be found two lovers who fit each other as do paradox and passion. (CUP, 230)

By saying that subjectivity, which is holistic rationality, and Christianity are a perfect fit, Climacus implies that Christianity and rationality are a perfect fit, that Christianity is the perfection of reason, and that the rationality of Christianity can be discovered by subjective striving.

Let us explore this perfect fit further. Subjectivity is passionate awareness of the paradox that a human being is (or is called to be) a synthesis of the finite and the infinite, the temporal and the eternal, and the particular and the universal, and a striving to make this synthesis as actual as possible in one's own person. Christianity reveals Jesus Christ the God-man as the "absolute paradox," or as the perfection of the human synthesis. And Christ shows human beings how this perfect synthesis behaves and comports itself in the world and bids them to imitate his example. When Climacus says that Christianity and subjectivity are a perfect fit, presumably an important part of what he means is that subjective strivers can discover in Christ the perfection of their efforts at paradoxical synthesis, marvel at this perfection, and hope to participate in it by imitating it, worshiping it, and gratefully receiving its assistance. More specifically, Christ shows strivers how to be exalted by being lowly, how the downfall of a person is the condition of his or her resurrection, and how love of God and neighbor is the redemption of that true love of self which launches the venture of subjectivity. And Christ offers grace for those who will humbly imitate his example.

How are we to evaluate this perfect fit argument? According to Climacus, it is neither by objective scholarship nor by philosophical inquiry, but by subjective striving for eternal happiness, which prepares a person to become aware of the perfect fit and to rightly appreciate it. For only those who personally make the venture can adequately evaluate its results. One must experience paradox for oneself, from the inside, in order to be an adequate judge of it.

God as the Postulate of Paradoxical Reason

Climacus and Kierkegaard agree that perhaps the most important thing that happens to subjective strivers is that they fail to achieve their goals. This failure is crucial for becoming aware of God and for discovering the essential fit of subjectivity and Christianity.

> In this way God is indeed a postulate, but not in the loose sense in which it is ordinarily taken. Instead, it becomes clear that this is the only way an existing person enters into a relationship with God: when the dialectical contradiction brings a person to despair and assists him in grasping God with "the category of despair" (faith), so that the postulate, far from being the arbitrary, is in fact necessary defense [Nødværge], self-defense; in this way God is not a postulate, but the existing person's postulating is—a necessity [Nødvendighed]. (CUP, 200)

This passage claims that subjective strivers eventually despair of accomplishing their ends on their own and then *postulate* God as a helper of their striving. This despair is the same as or very like what we previously knew as willing the downfall of the understanding.

The idea of God as a practical postulate may remind readers of a sort of argument for the existence of God in the writings of Kant. Moreover, *necessity* and *postulate* are terms from the lexicon of logic. Therefore, by speaking of God as a necessary postulate, Climacus implies that the subjective striver's belief in God is the result of a logical operation. Conversely, by speaking of the God-postulate as a self-defense, Climacus suggests that subjective strivers' belief in God is the result of mere psychological need. There could hardly be two more opposite suggestions, and both suggestions are seriously misleading.

Any attempt to turn subjectivity's needy postulating of God into a cogent, objective argument is going to be vulnerable to powerful objections. If it is true that all who strive as hard as they can to become good and joyful fall flat in their endeavor, perhaps this universal failure should be taken as a reductio ad absurdum of the idea that people should strive to become completely happy and ethically perfect. Or maybe some people can achieve happiness and ethical perfection, but not all, and the best sign of this natural inequality is that some people have a pathological need to postulate God. Or maybe joy and goodness are possible, for some or all people, but Kierkegaard has proposed the wrong method for achieving these lofty goals. Maybe trying really hard is not the best means to these goals, so that the need to postulate God grows, not out of the weakness of human nature as such, but out of the inadequacy of Kierkegaard's method.

Fortunately for Kierkegaard, he does not in fact propose postulating God as the result of an objective argument. In *For Self-Examination* and *Judge for Yourself!* Kierkegaard describes a Christian version of postulating God on the basis, not of argument, but of experiential awareness.[11]

A good way for us to begin understanding the Christian postulating of God is to consider what Kierkegaard writes about *doubt*. He writes that people try to "become self-important by doubting" Christian things such as the *Atonement* and the *Ascension*. He adds that "there is . . . no basis for" doubting these things, "since all such doubt is actually a self-indictment" (FSE, 69). Obviously, if there is no basis for such doubt, then there is no rational basis for it. But how could this be true?

Kierkegaard explains how to overcome doubt when he writes that "without introducing imitation, it is impossible to gain mastery over doubts," and when he claims that "those whose lives are marked by imitation have not doubted the Ascension" (FSE, 68, 190). Putting these passages together with Kierkegaard's claim that there is no basis for rational doubt of Christian things, we arrive at the suggestion that no one has the right to doubt Christian doctrine except people who have put themselves in a position to discover the truth of Christianity, namely, imitators of Christ, and that these imitators do not doubt but somehow come to know Christ.

Not only does Kierkegaard present doubting Christianity as irrational, he also implies that faith is a kind of understanding. He writes that the tension and stress arising from the attempt to imitate Christ will "have the effect that *you understand* that you cannot endure it without having recourse to *me*" (i.e., God) (FSE, 190; emphasis added). One surprising implication of this passage is that by striving to imitate Christ, people come to *understand* their absolute need for God. More exactly, they come to understand not that they need a god, and may therefore postulate one, but that they need the actual God, who speaks to them *person to person*. This is to say that failure in imitating Christ leads to a personal experiential awareness of God. Incidentally, another astonishing thing about this passage is that Kierkegaard goes so far in it as to speak *for God* in the first person, thus indicating his extremely high confidence that he knows what he is talking about.

After emphasizing the extreme importance of imitation for overcoming doubt, Kierkegaard surprisingly claims that there is a way to abolish doubt that does not require imitation:

> And not even that much [i.e., imitation] is required to stop doubt; if you indeed humble yourself before God because your life is not marked as the life of an imitator in the stricter sense, if you humble yourself under that, then you do not presume to doubt. How could it ever occur to you to report with a doubt when the answer inevitably would be: First of all go out and become an imitator of Christ in the stricter sense—only someone like that has the right to speak up—and none of these has doubted. (FSE, 70)

This passage indicates that humility is the key to overcoming doubt. This being so, we may infer that even for imitators humility is the key to their experience of God, that they see God partly owing to the self-transcendence that humility makes possible, and that they gain their humility by the bitter method of trying to imitate Christ and failing.

We might suppose that humility is the key to overcoming doubt because a meek and beaten-down milksop does not have the audacity to doubt. But imitators are great heroes and adventurers of the spirit who make Herculean efforts to achieve their goals and, like Hercules, descend into a hell of suffering as a result of their striving. Therefore we might suspect that honestly admitting one's utter weakness before God takes the greatest human strength or that only heroes of the spirit have the audacity to believe. Therefore, Kierkegaard would presumably say that humility is the condition for becoming aware of what pride cannot tolerate and therefore willfully ignores: namely, a supreme being to whom humans ought utterly to subordinate themselves.

In *Christian Discourses,* Kierkegaard offers another description (or version) of the subjective method of overcoming doubt. There he claims that it is an *irrationality* to want to deal with doubt about Christianity by *demonstrating* its truth philosophically, and that "the best means against all doubt about the truth of this doctrine" of Christianity is *self-concern* and "fear and trembling with regard to whether one is oneself a believer" (CD, 189–190). This *self-concern* consists largely in listening to and heeding a "preacher of repentance"—which elsewhere he calls *conscience*—that *dwells* "deep within every person's heart" (CD, 192). "The preacher of repentance in his inner being can help" a person "to become aware" of Christian truth, or to achieve "certitude of the spirit" (CD, 194). For example, it says to a person that "all things" "serve you for good" "when you love God" (CD, 188, 197). Thus Kierkegaard thinks that the rational way of coming to awareness of the truth of Christianity is through *conscience,* which he regards as a rational faculty (see chapter 1). Moreover, he thinks that this rational awareness of Christian truth occurs in and through self-examination or through examination of conscience.

Christians are not the only people who by striving reach the point of extreme frustration, or despair, and then receive miraculous or mysterious help (as if) from the outside. Pure Land Buddhism calls this mysterious assistance "other power," in contrast to *self-power.* In some forms of Zen Buddhism the practitioners exhaust their rational minds in an extreme effort to solve *koans,* which are certain aptly designed puzzles with no rational solution. And, having exhausted their rational minds and as it were emptied them, they find the solution coming to them of itself, as if from the outside.

I mention Buddhism in particular because most forms of it deny that there is a personal deity. With this fact in mind, a critic might suspect that Christians do not actually encounter an independently existing personal deity when they are helped out of their despair, but they merely interpret the assistance that they receive personally and theistically. Perhaps Christians impose a personalist and theistic interpretation on an impersonal or nondivine reality that they confusedly experience. Or perhaps the assistance that they receive comes from themselves, from something hidden deep in human nature. In short, perhaps they do in fact experience help, but merely imagine a (divine) helper. Christians might reply that Buddhists have a prejudice *for* emptiness and *against* God and other persons, and therefore misinterpret an essentially personal reality impersonally.

How are we to decide which party, if either, is correct? It might seem that it is more plausible that the Buddhists are right; for, if the Christians were correct, surely God would inform the Buddhists that He was in fact a person when He took the trouble to help them. But, Christians might reply, perhaps God does whisper this to Buddhists, and they do not listen—perhaps because they are unwilling to hear the disconcerting message about sin. Or maybe some of them do listen, since some Buddhists seem to believe in a sort of personal deity. Kierkegaard himself might point out that the Christian God is professedly a compromiser, and that God might condescend to appear to Buddhists in conformity with their beliefs and prejudices in order to make a beginning with them that he will finish on his own schedule. Perhaps this explanation will seem improbable to us. But, as we have seen, Kierkegaard powerfully criticizes probabilistic thinking, especially when it tries to say what a transcendent God would do or not do.

Kierkegaard would almost certainly insist at this point in the argument that it is not for nonstrivers to decide between the Christian and Buddhist interpretations of the assistance that strivers receive in extremis, but for strivers themselves, who have experienced this mysterious aid firsthand. One can very well strive to become good, wise, or happy for a long time and with all one's might before one has to make a final decision about who or what helps strivers in extreme need. Indeed it seems to be the height of irrationality to make this decision without striving, or to use the disagreement of Buddhists and Christians—who after all agree on many things and together disagree with many nonreligious ideas—as an excuse not to strive at all, especially if striving is necessary for awareness of ultimate things.

Does Kierkegaard Conscript "That Simple Wise Man of Old"?

Kierkegaard treats or uses Socrates as an ally: He presents Socrates as an image of subjectivity, and he even goes so far as to claim that Socrates has become a Christian. But, though Kierkegaard argues extensively for his interpretation of revealed Christianity, he argues very little for his interpretation of Socrates as a subjective individual on a quest for Christian faith. Therefore we have to wonder whether Kierkegaard—who often complained about the Hegelian co-option of Christianity—has illicitly conscripted or co-opted an essentially un-Christian, or even nonsubjective, Socrates. What amazing hypocrisy it would be if Kierkegaard has done the very thing to Socrates, a thinker many of his opponents respect deeply, that he thinks they themselves have done to Christianity.

I will not attempt to defend Kierkegaard at any length against this charge of unlawfully conscripting Socrates. Socrates is the most elusive, co-opted, and impersonated of Western sages, and Plato is perhaps the most inscrutably indirect Western writer. Therefore even a whole book could not pronounce confidently on the status of Kierkegaard's use of Socrates. Instead I will merely point to a few signs that Kierkegaard's use of Socrates is not ludicrous, but within the bounds of responsible interpretations of the greatest hero of Greek philosophy.

Let us consider what might seem one of the more dubious suggestions that Kierkegaard makes about Socrates: namely, that he *willed* the *downfall* of his own *understanding* (PF, 36–47). As we have seen, Kierkegaard argues to some degree for this claim by pointing out that in the *Phaedrus* Socrates says that he devotes himself to searching for self-knowledge but cannot as yet decide between two utterly opposite self-interpretations: namely, that he is simple, gentle, and akin to the gods, and that he is as complex, as puffed up with pride, and as defiant of the gods as the hundred-headed Typhon, whose name literally means *puffed up*. If Socrates is serious in these doubts that he expresses about himself, it seems likely that he is at least pretty close to willing a downfall of his understanding. If he deigned to, Kierkegaard might also remind us that Socrates "thoroughly blames" himself that he does not know "what virtue is,"[12] claims that one must *blame* oneself and not reason for one's failure to learn anything solid from philosophical inquiry,[13] speaks of the crucial importance of being *shamed* for one's pride and presumption,[14] says any number of things about his ignorance and the importance of becoming aware of one's ignorance, says that the great enemy of truth and just action is a self-complacent, self-justifying egoism—or being "one's own friend," and thinking that "it is right and proper to be so"[15]; and provides a model of repentance in his Palinode or his speech of retraction in the *Phaedrus*.[16] Thus there are many passages in Plato's dialogues in which Socrates professes ignorance, self-blame, suspicions of his own monstrosity, and repentance, and in which he warns against a self-justifying egoism that undermines truth and justice. Together these passages seem to constitute a solid basis for a responsible interpretation of Socrates as a thinker who willed the downfall of his own understanding because he suspected something very like sin.

In summary, willing the downfall of one's understanding, as presented by Kierkegaard, means striving to know and to conform to ethico-religious truth, feeling profoundly guilty for failing to achieve these goals, and then denying or seriously doubting that one has the capacity for achieving these goals. Socrates, as presented by Plato, strives to know ethico-religious truth, thoroughly blames himself for his failure to achieve these goals, and hints that he suspects that he cannot achieve them. Thus Plato presents Socrates as doing something very like willing the downfall of his own understanding.

For Kierkegaard the most important thing about Socrates is that he is a hero and exemplar of subjectivity, and for this characterization of Socrates, Kierkegaard could assemble a great deal of evidence. To pick just one striking example, when Crito asks the about-to-be-put-to-death Socrates whether he has any "last instructions" for his friends, Socrates replies:

"Just what I'm always telling you, Crito, nothing very novel: By caring for yourselves. . . . But if you're careless of yourselves and aren't willing to live, as it were, in the footsteps of the things said now and in the time before, no matter how many agreements you may make at present, and how emphatically, you won't be doing much."[17]

Thus the last instructions of "that simple wise man of old" constitute an eloquent exhortation to subjectivity. Almost the whole of Kierkegaard's authorship is a postscript to or a repetition of this Socratic entreaty.

The principal purpose of Kierkegaard's paradoxical manner of writing is to invite his readers to subjectivity, by making them aware of both of the paradoxical constitution of human nature, with its divine gifts and its Herculean tasks, and of the Absolute Paradox of the Incarnation as a prototype to be actively imitated. When striving, single individuals imitate this divine model—perhaps by first imitating Socrates, its Greek prophet—they grow in understanding, or in awareness, or in knowledge, of themselves in particular, of human nature in general, and of the author of all things. "For only then do we know the truth, when it becomes a life in us" (adapted from PC, 206, which comments on John 17:3). Thus Kierkegaard prioritizes paradoxical and holistic reason over merely theoretical reason, not only because he deems that ethical duty demands this of him, but also because he judges it to be the most effective means to the most adequate cognition of the highest things. Thus the proof of paradoxical reason is living paradoxically. Or, as St. Paul puts it: "Now faith is the substance of things hoped for, the evidence of things not seen. . . . Through faith we understand that the worlds were framed by the word of God."[18]

NOTES

1. A Pretense of Irrationalism

1. Several scholars argue that Kierkegaard does not reject reason.
Merold Westphal is one of the first interpreters to present persuasive arguments that Kierkegaard is not an irrationalist. See his *Kierkegaard's Critique of Reason and Society,* and *Becoming a Self: A Reading of Kierkegaard's Concluding Unscientific Postscript,* esp. 124–125, 181–183.

C. Stephen Evans takes on the most serious arguments that Kierkegaard is an irrationalist, and I think, compellingly refutes them. He also argues cogently that Kierkegaard assigns reason a positive role in the search for truth, and gives an account of Kierkegaard's conception and use of reason. In *Passionate Reason: Making Sense of Kierkegaard's "Philosophical Fragments,"* he claims that "our subjectivity . . . may be or become a medium that . . . opens us up to an encounter with truth" (3); that Kierkegaard "thinks that a reason that *recognizes* its passional character is a friend to humans struggling to find their place" (x); and that "Climacus in his own way . . . suggest[s] that a faith rooted in a revelation that reason cannot fully understand may indeed be rational" (95). See also his claims in *Kierkegaard, on Faith and the Self* that Kierkegaard thinks that "faith has [perhaps] ebbed" "because [people] have become impoverished in their grasp of . . . human life"; and that Kierkegaard thinks that faith "stems from a courageous attempt to face the truth about who we are and who we should be" (5, 7; cf. 329–330).

Evans has probably argued more extensively for the rationality of Kierkegaard, and explained more thoroughly the character of that rationality, than any other interpreter of Kierkegaard. Besides *Passionate Reason* and *Kierkegaard, on Faith and the Self,* his books *Kierkegaard's "Fragments" and "Postscript": The Religious Philosophy of Johannes Climacus* and *Faith above Reason: A Kierkegaardian Account* are crucial sources for understanding Kierkegaard's conception and use of reason.

Robert C. Roberts, in "The Grammar of Sin and the Conceptual Unity of *The Sickness Unto Death,*" argues that "being a Christian is a fulfillment of religiousness A" (136). And since Religiousness A is independent of revelation, Roberts is in effect saying that Kierkegaard sees natural humanity, including natural rationality, as fulfilled in Christianity. In "The Socratic Knowledge of God," Roberts also sets out to "explore and defend Kierkegaard's conception of the natural knowledge of God" (134). Roberts is especially helpful on the role of the emotions in Kierkegaard-ian rationality—see "Existence, Emotion, and Virtue: Classical Themes in Kierke-gaard" and "Dialectical Emotions and the Virtue of Faith."

Jack Mulder Jr., in *Kierkegaard and the Catholic Tradition: Conflict and Dia-logue*, has also argued convincingly that Kierkegaard's understanding of the hu-man being is a "hybrid of the Lutheran and Catholic anthropologies" (179). An im-portant aspect of this hybrid is a combination of Lutheran suspicion of reason and Socratic respect for the same.

2. In *Kierkegaard's Critique of Reason and Society*, Merold Westphal argues very persuasively that a large part of the cause that Kierkegaard appears to reject reason is that he makes it his business to critique something that "masquerades" as reason, namely, a "historically specific form of human deviousness," or "the fun-damental assumptions of the established order," or "ideology" (21, 89). This line of argument provides very good evidence that Kierkegaard does not reject reason as such, but only (what he regards as) perverse forms of rationality.

C. Stephen Evans, in *Faith above Reason: A Kierkegaardian Account*, similarly distinguishes two aspects of the concept of reason: "The concept is partly norma-tive; it connotes those patterns of thinking that ought to be emulated because they are most likely to lead to truth. A purely normative concept is, however, abstract and empty. In reality every human society holds up particular concrete patterns and modes of thinking as constitutive of reason because they are thought to realize these normative ideals" (93). Evans argues that when Kierkegaard critiques reason, or claims that faith is "against reason," he typically has in mind, not reason as such, but "particular concrete patterns and modes of thinking" of a particular "human society" that form "a barrier to achieving the goals of reason in an ideal normative sense" (93–94). Therefore, in short, Evans thinks that much or most of Kierkegaard's opposition to reason is directed at (what Kierkegaard regards as) a particular, per-verted version of reason.

3. Some scholars have come close to claiming that Kierkegaard pretends to be irrational in order to communicate rationality. In *Passionate Reason: Making Sense of Kierkegaard's "Philosophical Fragments,"* Stephen Evans writes the following:

> It is true that offended people have often tried to appropriate the term "reason" . . . and thus to claim, not just that they find Christianity absurd, but that "reason" does so. Climacus thinks that the best thing to do in this case is to make a present of the term "reason" to the opponent, and insist that Christianity is not "reasonable" and should not be made so. Given the variety of senses of "reason" and thus the variety of ways something can be said to be unreasonable, I do not think that Christians can afford to be so polite as to allow the offended person to appropriate the term. Certainly, from Climacus' own point of view, it is not the case that the offended person is reasoning in an essentially objective, neutral manner, while the person of faith is biased and sub-jective, since offense is just as much a passion as faith. Both offense and faith represent forms of passionate thinking, and it is unclear why the unbeliever's form of thinking deserves the honorific title of "reason," however much the unbeliever would like to ap-propriate the term. (91)

Thus Evans thinks that Kierkegaard concedes rationality to his opponents and accepts their assessment of Christianity (and of him) as irrational. Evans obviously does not approve of these concessions, and he does not attempt in print to explore how it might be reasonable or strategically prudent for Kierkegaard to make these concessions.

In *Kierkegaard's Critique of Reason and Society,* Merold Westphal expresses more sympathy than Evans does for the Kierkegaardian concession: "If the Reason to which we appeal in our social and political thought is the authoritative voice of an established order that has made it difficult for Christianity to hear the requirements of discipleship clearly, Kierkegaard will call for a dose of the absurd and the irrational in our social ethics. He will surely be misunderstood in doing so—by those who find it more convenient not to get his point" (27). Westphal does not go on to explain why this concession might be a good idea or effective. Moreover, he implies that the concession is not helpful to people who are inclined to regard ethics and faith as irrational; whereas in fact the books in which Kierkegaard concedes rationality to his opponents are written precisely to be helpful to readers Kierkegaard does not deem to be receptive to his message. Therefore, we should expect his concessions to be merely provisional and suspect that he intends them to be overturned.

In *Love's Grateful Striving,* in a context in which she is addressing many misunderstandings of Kierkegaard's *Works of Love,* M. Jamie Ferreira claims that "we need to try to see . . . why [Kierkegaard] is so willing to take the risk of being misunderstood" (9). It is surprising that scholars of Kierkegaard seldom ask similar questions about other books and other aspects of his thought, especially his thought about reason and its role in faith. This current book is an attempt to ask and answer Ferreira's question when it is applied to Kierkegaard's remarks about reason.

4. For the distinction between an "absolute paradox," which cannot be "explained," and a "relative paradox," which can, see CUP, 217–223, esp. 219.

5. Robert C. Roberts, in "Existence, Emotion, and Virtue: Classical Themes in Kierkegaard," claims that the *Postscript* is "certainly about a version of what has traditionally been called 'practical wisdom'" (182). Thus Roberts sees subjectivity—which the *Postscript* is certainly about—as practical wisdom put into practice.

6. Lessing, *Philosophical and Theological Writings,* 141.

7. George Pattison, in *The Philosophy of Kierkegaard,* presents some challenging arguments that Kierkegaard is a kind of philosopher, pp. 7–9, and throughout the book.

8. C. Stephen Evans, in *Passionate Reason: Making Sense of Kierkegaard's" Philosophical Fragments,"* presents many compelling arguments that when Climacus refers to the incarnation as a contradiction he does not mean a "formal contradiction" (97–106). My arguments in the footnoted paragraph for the same claim are drawn from Evans's work. See also *Kierkegaard on Faith and the Self: Collected Essays,* 118–124; and Merold Westphal, *Becoming a Self: A Reading of Kierkegaard's* Concluding Unscientific Postscript, 124–125 and 181–183, for similar arguments and for a good explanation of what Climacus means by "contradiction" in this context.

9. I learned the argument of this paragraph from Merold Westphal's *Kierke-gaard's Critique of Reason and Society*, 85-103.

10. *Crito*, 46b.

11. Alastair MacKinnon, *The Kierkegaard Indices; see esp.* vols. 3 and 4.

2. Paradoxical Rationality

1. In *The Concept of Anxiety*, the *demonic* is sometimes used to describe a kind of objectivity, but in *Fear and Trembling*, it seems to mean a kind of diseased subjectivity.

2. Merold Westphal, *Becoming a Self*, argues that Kierkegaard presents a fair, accurate, and even "impeccable summary of the Hegelian position," 89, and more generally, 86-92.

3. See *Repetition: A Venture in Experimenting Psychology, The Sickness Unto Death: A Christian Psychological Exposition for Upbuilding and Awakening, The Concept of Anxiety: A Simple Psychologically Orienting Deliberation on the Dog-matic Issue of Hereditary Sin*, and "Not Guilty? A Story of Suffering: An Imaginary Psychological Construction," in *Stages on Life's Way*.

4. The case of such thinkers as La Rochefoucald, who delight in cynical ob-servation of human vices and follies, does not refute the claim that no one engages in self-examination for the mere fun of it, because such thinkers do not examine themselves as single individuals, but (as part of) the human race in general; and they probably even excuse their own weakness with the questionable claim that weakness and vice are universal or unavoidable.

5. See Sylvia Walsh's *Living Christianly: Kierkegaard's Dialectic of Christian Existence* for an in-depth description and explication of Kierkegaard's "inverse dialectic."

6. I am treating *illusion* and *delusion* as near synonyms here. Presumably an illusion is more innocent, and more the effect of external causes, than a delusion, and a delusion is more willful than an illusion.

7. Paul Müller, in *"Kierkegaard's Works of Love": Christian Ethics and the Maieutic Ideal*, argues that Kierkegaard thinks the self-denial of love requires *pre-tending* that the beloved "has done nothing at all" wrong or offensive, even when he or she has done this (60). Thus Müller agrees that Kierkegaard is a pretender or that he recommends pretending, though Müller does not exactly or explicitly agree that Kierkegaard pretends to be irrational.

8. Kierkegaard presumably learned his strategy of finding learners where they are and beginning there, not only from the models of the incarnation and of Socrates' pedagogy, but also from St. Paul, who explicitly admits that he adapts his message to his audience. For example, in 1 Corinthians 1-2, he writes:

> And I, brethren, could not speak unto you as unto spiritual, but as unto carnal, even as unto babes in Christ. I have fed you with milk, and not with meat: for hitherto ye were not able to bear it, neither yet now are ye able.

Similarly, in 1 Corinthians 9:19-22, he writes:

> For though I be free from all men, yet have I made myself servant unto all, that I might gain the more. And unto the Jews I became as a Jew, that I might gain the Jews; to them that are under the law, as under the law, that I might gain them that are under

the law. To them that are without law, as without law, (being not without law to God, but under the law to Christ,) that I might gain them that are without law. To the weak became I as weak, that I might gain the weak: I am made all things to all men, that I might by all means save some.

The Acts of the Apostles shows how the pedagogical practice of St. Paul conforms to his theory, and in particular it shows how he adapted Christianity to whomever he was speaking. See especially Paul's famous speech at Athens to some philosophers in 17:19–34. See also Philip's conversation with an Ethiopian seeker in 8:26–40. For an early church father—Gregory the Great—who also saw Paul as adapting his teaching to his audience, see Mulder, *Kierkegaard and the Catholic Tradition,* 113.

9. *Gorgias,* 474a.

10. See Collingwood, *An Autobiography,* 47–50, for his description of his encounters with such philosophers.

11. Stephen Evans, who does not think that Climacus is in general unreasonable, argues very persuasively that Climacus's position on apologetics and historical evidence for Christianity is unreasonable and extreme. See *Passionate Reason,* 152–166.

12. Again, for Kierkegaard's "inverse dialectic," see note 5.

13. *Gorgias,* 513b–513c.

14. In *Faith above Reason: A Kierkegaardian Account,* C. Stephen Evans claims that "Kierkegaard is best understood as a responsible fideist" who thinks that faith is "above reason" and "against reason" (78). Presumably if Kierkegaard is best understood as a fideist, then he is better described as a fideist than as a thinker committed to reason. Thus I seem to disagree on this point with Evans, whom I regard as one of the best interpreters of Kierkegaard. But the disagreement may not be as big as it seems. Evans does not think that Kierkegaard's fideism is a "repudiation of reason" (78). Evans also thinks that Kierkegaard "believes that there is a kind of general, 'natural' awareness of God that is possible for humans" without faith in Christian revelation (116). Thus what Evans calls Kierkegaard's "responsible fideism" contains much respect for reason and for its natural capacity to know God (78).

At this point we might suspect that the disagreement between my interpretation and that of Evans is merely verbal. Both of us agree that Kierkegaard respects reason in many ways, but also denies it in some respects, but I choose to stress that Kierkegaard is rational, while Evans, at least in his book *Faith above Reason,* stresses that Kierkegaard is a fideist of sorts (in other books he stresses the rationality of Kierkegaardian faith).

It seems to me, however, that much is at stake in the choice of what label to stick on Kierkegaard. Calling Kierkegaard a fideist has the advantage of stressing that Kierkegaard in an important sense values faith more than reason. But, as Evans acknowledges, it also has the disadvantage of falsely suggesting that Kierkegaard rejects reason. And even though Evans very clearly explains what he means by calling Kierkegaard a fideist, it is nonetheless likely that the label will prove more powerful than the qualifying explanation, especially in the contemporary world that is already disposed to think that Kierkegaard rejects reason and to think that faith and reason are enemies.

The advantage of stressing that Kierkegaard is rational is that this language reveals what is surprising, challenging, and perhaps least likely to be appreciated today in the writings of Kierkegaard: his respect for reason and the alliance that he tries to forge between it and faith. In Kierkegaard's day, when mainstream thinkers were trying to arrange what he regarded as an illicit union between faith and reason, it made sense for him to stress the differences and conflicts between faith and reason. But today, when most people think that faith and reason are utter enemies, it may make more sense pedagogically and strategically to challenge the dominant mentality with the claim that Kierkegaard was deeply committed to reason and saw faith as reasonable in many ways.

Perhaps, however, it would be even more effective to label Kierkegaard as something like a rational fideist, or a fideistic rationalist, in order to make it clear that Kierkegaard's ideas about faith and reason do not fit neatly into comfortable and convenient categories.

Merold Westphal, who argues that Kierkegaard is not an irrationalist, does not call Kierkegaard a fideist (so far as I can tell), but he also does not stress Kierkegaard's commitment to *reason*. Westphal nevertheless describes Kierkegaard's goals and ideas in terms that suggest rationality. For example, in *Transcendence and Self-Transcendence: On God and the Soul,* he claims that Kierkegaard sees faith as a kind of "self-transcendence that welcomes" *revelation* (206). Since many thinkers see rationality as seeking self-transcendence, one might argue that Kierkegaard's faith as described by Westphal has a rational aim. Similarly, Westphal points out that Kierkegaard claims that Abraham, in his faith, "knows himself to be addressed from on high" (209), and since reason aims at knowledge, the faith of Westphal's Kierkegaard seems to be friendly or akin to reason.

Presumably a large part of the reason that Westphal does not stress the rationality of Kiekegaard is that Westphal thinks what goes by the name of reason is often deeply suspect. For example, he argues that much of what is called rational does not seek self-transcendence, but, instead, the reduction of "the other" to "the same." Similarly, in *Levinas and Kierkegaard in Dialogue,* he claims that because culturally specific *horizons* "of expectation" "define what is to count as 'Reason,' in going beyond and against them revelation will involve us with . . . Paradox" (4). Therefore, he says, Kierkegaard in effect says, "I have found it necessary to deny 'Reason,'" that is, what conventionally passes for reason, "in order to make room for responsibility" (6). But, I reply, responsibility—adequately or rightly responding to reality—is on many accounts the very essence of reason.

I suspect that another reason that Westphal does not stress the rationality of Kierkegaardian faith is that faith requires that God *provide* a person "with the condition for understanding" the revelation of the divine voice (PF, 14); if the condition is given from above, not immanent to human nature, perhaps there is something strange about calling it reason. Nonetheless, I respond, the gift of the condition is, according to Climacus, a restoration of human nature as it was originally received from the hand of God. Moreover, the condition and what can be known with it are not, according to Westphal, forced on a person, but must be *welcomed.* Therefore the gift of the condition must be responsibly used, like reason, by its recipient.

Thus it seems to me that it is not necessary for Kierkegaardian believers to capitulate the term *reason* to their unbelieving critics. More strongly, it is even arguable that such capitulation is an ill-advised compromise.

Westphal might reply, however, that, like Kierkegaard, he finds it useful to communicate the rationality of Kierkegaardian subjectivity and/or faith indirectly, especially since he (Westphal) tends to target postmodern readers, or readers strongly influenced by postmodernism, who would probably be put off by the overt claim that Kierkegaard is a deeply rational thinker, at least initially. With such readers I agree with what I suspect is Westphal's view that it may not only be more modest but more effective merely to argue that Kierkegaard is not an irrationalist. There perhaps will be time or opportunity enough for such readers to realize for themselves that Kierkegaardian faith is an affirmation of reason.

15. The following account of early Buddhism is taken from the *Middle Length Discourses* (MLD) of the Buddha and from the contemporary anthology *Early Buddhist Discourses* (EBD).

16. "Discourse on the Parable of the Water Snake," in MLD, 107–108.

17. "Discourse of Potthapada," in EBD, 143; cf. "The Shorter Discourse to Malankyaputta," in EBD, 99, and in MLD, 536.

18. "The Shorter Discourse to Malankyaputta," in MLD, 534. "The Exposition of the Truths," in MLD, 1097–1101.

19. The Buddha describes spiritual method and its stages over and over in a variety of ways. For a few, see "Discourse of Potthapada," in EBD, 136–138, and "The Greater Discourse at Assapura," in MLD, 362–371.

20. See "To Vacchagotta on Fire," in EBD, 122, and in MLD, 594; cf. the "Discourse of the Threefold Knowledge," in EBD, 151–163, and "The Greater Discourse to Malankyaputta," in MLD, for examples of the Buddha adapting himself to the learner.

21. See the *Lotus Sutra,* chap. 3, which contains the famous "parable of a burning house." In this parable some children, who do not understand what fire is, nor what a house is, nor even what danger is, are in a burning house. Their father, who represents the Buddha, lies to them in order to induce them to run to safety. The *Lotus Sutra,* and much of Mahayana Buddhism, calls such a beneficial lie, or distortion of the truth, *upaya.*

22. "A Discourse to the First Five Disciples," in EBD, 83–86.

3. Reverse Theology

1. To be accurate, Madhyamaka in its most famous exponent, Nagarjuna, is a "middle way" between the positive excess of essentialism and the negative excess of nihilism. But to most readers, the negative in Nagarjuna's dialectic is probably far more conspicuous than the positive is. The classic text of Madhyamaka is translated by Jay L. Garfield as *The Fundamental Wisdom of the Middle Way: Nagarjuna's* Mulamadhyamakakarika. For the *tetralemma,* see chap. 17.8, p. 250, of the same text. For *neti neti,* or "not this, not this," see Brihad-aranyaka Upanishad, 3.6.26.

2. John D. Glenn Jr., "A Highest Good . . . an Eternal Happiness": The Human *Telos* in Kierkegaard's *Concluding Unscientific Postscript,*" 258.

3. 1 Corinthians 2:9.

4. Romans 5:21, 6:17, 7:14, et alia.

5. *Treatise on Happiness*, q3.a8; *The Mystical Theology*, chap. 1:3:101a; cf. chap. 2:1025B; and *The Divine Names*, chap. 7:872B.

6. Charles H. Kahn, *The Art and Thought of Heraclitus: An Edition of the Fragments with Translation and Commentary*, fragment XXXIII, 43.

7. Matthew 13:10–13; Mark 4:11–12.

8. 1 Corinthians 3:1–2.

9. *The Shorter Discourse to Malunkyaputta*, in *Early Buddhist Discourses*, 99.

10. See Anselm's *Proslogion*, the "Prologue" and chap. 2.

11. Louis Mackey, *Kierkegaard: A Kind of Poet*, 258.

12. 2 Corinthians 6:9.

13. *Summa Theologica*, 1.1.q5.a13.

14. Merold Westphal, *Transcendence and Self-Transcendence: On God and the Soul*, 115–174.

15. Buber, *The Knowledge of Man*, 49–61.

4. The Subtle Power of Simplicity

1. Romans 7:15–20.

2. John 3:19–21.

3. Philippians 4:7–9.

4. See Alexander Dru, *The Soul of Kierkegaard: Selections from His Journals*, 126: "If you wish to be and to remain enthusiastic, then draw the silk curtains of facetiousness (irony's), and so hide your enthusiasm."

5. Matthew 7:5–7.

6. Matthew 5:15–17.

7. Matthew 6:6.

5. A Critique of Indirect Communication

1. Luke 15:3–6.

2. Revelation 3:14–17.

3. The attack took the form of newspaper articles. See *The Moment*.

4. *Phaedrus* 271c–272b.

5. *Discourse on the Parable of the Water Snake*, in *Early Buddhist Discourses*, 106–107.

6. Matthew 12:43–45; Luke 11:24–26.

7. *Phaedrus* 275d.

8. Matthew 18:7.

6. The Figure of Socrates and the Climacean Capacity of Paradoxical Reason

1. In *Kierkegaard's Thought*, Gregor Malantschuk claims that *Philosophical Fragments* "completes the sharpest possible demarcation between the human and the Christian" (245). We shall see that this "sharpest possible demarcation" is in fact a bit blurry and porous.

2. Thus Johannes Climacus is John of the Ladder or John the Climber. He is named after a seventh-century Christian monk who himself earned the title "Climacus" because he wrote *The Ladder of Divine Ascent*.

3. Word *revise* from Walter Lowrie's translation, 283.

4. George Pattison, in *The Philosophy of Kierkegaard*, shows how, in the chapter of *Works of Love* titled "The Work of Love in Praising Love," Kierkegaard repeatedly "appeals to the example of Socrates," where he might have appealed instead to the example of the "apostles," "martyrs," and "saints" in order to illustrate how to praise love correctly (178–180).

5. The phrases *art of questioning* and *modeled after* are from the Lowrie translation, 225.

6. Paul Müller, in *"Kierkegaard's Works of Love": Christian Ethics and the Maieutic Ideal*, argues that Christian love requires Socratic midwifery: "all man's striving to practice 'Works of Love' must necessarily unfold inside the scope of the maieutic, in order to be in harmony with the structure which has already been given in existence" (71). Furthermore, Müller thinks that Kierkegaard sees Socrates' practice of love as very close to Christian practice: "Kierkegaard actually lets Socrates' example" of love "condemn most of that which Kierkegaard himself attacks from the basis of a Christian understanding of love" (20). Nonetheless, Müller argues that "Socrates' insight" in the character and requirements of love "stops at the threshold of the *condition* for neighbour-love" (22).

7. Sylvia Walsh, in *Kierkegaard: Thinking Christianly in an Existential Mode*, describes another way in which Climacus indicates that Socrates anticipates Christian faith. "As a subjective thinker, Socrates sought to relate himself to eternal truth as an objective uncertainty *negatively* through ignorance. For example, he did not know whether there is an immortality of the soul but he was willing to stake his life on it, ordering his life 'with the passion of the infinite' so that upon death it might be acceptable if there is (CUP 201–2)" (41). What Walsh says about Socrates obviously mirrors what Climacus says about faith: "Faith," which Climacus thinks aims at "eternal happiness," "is the objective uncertainty with the repulsion of the absurd, held fast in the passion of inwardness, which is the relation of inwardness intensified to its highest" (CUP, 611; cf. 52).

8. By portraying Socrates as moving toward Christianity in various ways, Kierkegaard problematizes his distinction between Christianity and the merely human. Sylvia Walsh, in *Living Christianly: Kierkegaard's Dialectic of Christian Existence*, asserts that Kierkegaard is not as successful at distinguishing Christianity from its rivals and alternatives as he claims to be. Even though Walsh "doubts that the Christian life has ever been described with more precision and perspicuity than" Kierkegaard presented it (162), and even though she claims that "Kierkegaard's intent . . . was precisely to bring out the distinctiveness of Christian inwardness" (161), she also says that he often distinguishes Christianity "at the expense of not sufficiently appreciating corresponding qualifications in other religious traditions" (161). As an example of this she claims that although Judaism affirms transcendent categories in common with Christianity, Kierkegaard generally manifests a negative or lukewarm attitude toward this "religion" (161).

9. See note 6.

10. Similarly, in the *Postscript* Climacus claims that there is no analogy to faith in the highest sense of that word. And yet he also writes that "Socratic ignorance is an analogue to the category of the absurd," and that "Socratic inwardness in existing is an analog to faith *sensu eminentiori* [in the eminent sense]" (CUP, 205–206, 569).

11. Many commentators have written on particular paradoxes or ironies in *Philosophical Fragments* that involve Climacus's asserting a limit and then implying that human beings can or do surpass that limit.

Lee Barret, in "The Paradox of Faith in Kierkegaard's *Philosophical Fragments*: Gift or Task?" claims that Climacus sets up a conflict in *Fragments* between "grace and freedom," or between "gift and task," that is not amenable to a "theoretic solution" (261, 266). He says that this conflict functions as a "creative tension" beckoning and guiding readers to make a "synthesis" of these opposites in their "lives," "not on paper" (275, 283). Similarly, M. Jamie Ferreira, *in Transforming Vision: Imagination and Will in Kierkegaardian Faith,* claims that we "can live together what we cannot theoretically unite" (9). Thus both of these interpreters regard Kierkegaard or Climacus as a practical writer who ignores theoretical diversions, and who thinks that there are paradoxes that cannot be explained but can be lived. See also Louis Mackey, *Kierkegaard: A Kind of Poet,* 177: "Thus freedom is infinite, for no man can determine the extent of his capacity to act or the depth of his accountability, but must assume agency and responsibility in all cases; the task of becoming oneself is infinite, because no man can calculate his own possibilities or finally arbitrate the conflict of nature and freedom in his own person." For the conflict of freedom and nature, see pp. 133–137, and 181: "Passion . . . signifies for Climacus the contradictions of existence, particularly the root-contradiction between freedom and nature in the self, experienced in the feelings, just as paradox indicates the same contradictions experienced in thought."

George Connell and Heather Servaty, in "A Paradox of Personal Identity in Kierkegaard's *Philosophical Fragments*" reveal a "paradox" (86) of change, or of "self-identity" (107) within change, in *Philosophical Fragments.* They work out an illuminating resolution of the paradox, but do not explain why Climacus himself speaks in an apparently self-contradictory manner.

George Pattison, in "Johannes Climacus and Aurelius Augustinus on Recollecting the Truth," argues that although Climacus develops a dichotomy between Christian "revelation" and Socratic "recollection," Climacus also implicitly calls this dichotomy into question and suggests that its alternatives might be fused. In other words, Pattison argues that Climacus suggests that a human being may be able to transcend both the epistemological limits of Christianity as he himself presents them, and the epistemological dichotomy that he himself constructs.

Robert C. Roberts, in "The Grammar of Sin and the Conceptual Unity of the Sickness unto Death," claims that a "paradoxical mode of expression is sustained systematically in *The Sickness unto Death,*" (137). He says that this mode is exemplified in a *Journal* entry: "Socrates believed that he was divinely commissioned to show that all are ignorant—quite right, at that time divinity had not let itself be heard from" (JP, 4:4286). The *paradox* in the *Sickness unto Death* that Roberts has in mind is this: Anti-Climacus "speaks in Part Two as though" "Christian revelation" is required for "the self" to be "conceived as standing alone before God; and yet throughout Part One, where [Anti-Climacus] was speaking merely 'psychologically,' the self was defined by its relation to God" (138). Roberts sets out to show all this is not as paradoxical as it seems and can be explained, but he also seems to think a residue of paradox remains even after the explanation. This paradox, in short, is that "being a Christian is a fulfillment of Religiousness A" and also a "breach" with it (136).

Stephen Evans and Jan Evans, in their "Translators' Preface and Introduction" to Paul Müller's *"Kierkegaard's Works of Love": Christian Ethics and the Maieutic Ideal,* describe a paradox that pervades Kierkegaard's authorship:

> the key to understanding Kierkegaard's authorship as a whole lies in understanding his view of the relationship of the "merely human" to the "specifically Christian." There is at least an apparent tension in Kierkegaard with regard to this relationship. On the one hand Kierkegaard insists that Christianity is a mode of existence which cannot even be understood by someone who has not acquired some sense of what it means to exist humanly. Here the category "Christian" seems to differentiate itself from, but just for that reason to be grounded in, the broader category of "humanness." On the other hand the "paradoxical" character of Christianity seems to point towards a relationship of opposition between the "merely human" and the "Christian" (vii–ix).

In this chapter I have attempted to point out the common structure of these paradoxes and others like them and to explicate their common meaning and purpose.

12. *Crito,* 46b, and Martin Luther, quoted in Gerhard Ebeling, *Luther: An Introduction to His Thought,* 144; and *A Commentary on St. Paul's Epistle to the Galatians,* 1531, in *Martin Luther: Selections from His Writings,* ed. John Dillenberger, 128.

13. Cf. Jacob Howland, *Kierkegaard and Socrates: A Study in Philosophy and Faith.* Howland makes many claims about Socrates similar to those that I make about him in this chapter. He argues that the Climacean Socrates of *Fragments* exists in a middle position in which he is neither merely a philosopher nor merely a man of faith (102, 55). He also argues that this Socrates is a "self-transcending" figure, who goes beyond himself and who is therefore hard to pin down (184–185). Howland, however, is not content to leave Socrates as a middle figure and often suggests or claims that Socrates can do far more or is far greater than I think Climacus and Kierkegaard suggest. For instance, Howland (very implausibly) reads a late journal entry of Kierkegaard as suggesting that Kierkegaard thought that Socrates was "without sin," and "did not need Christianity" (213–214). He goes on to suggest a retraction or a qualification of these claims, but he makes the claims nonetheless (215–218). Despite sometimes going too far, Howland aptly shows that Socrates does more than Climacus officially claims he can do (see especially his account of "The Moral" in *Fragments,* 32, 54–55, 184–185). And since my efforts at showing the same thing scarcely ever overlap with those of Howland, our arguments for the claim that the Climacean Socrates overreaches his own limits tend to corroborate one another.

14. At least two interpreters agree that Climacus merely pretends to be objective in *Fragments.*

Stephen Evans, in "Apologetic Arguments in Kierkegaard's *Philosophical Fragments,*" suggests that in *Fragments* Climacus strikes an "ironically deceptive" "pose of neutrality with respect to Christianity" (70). In other words, Climacus feigns objective disinterestedness in *Fragments.* Evans argues for this claim in several ways. "Given the antiapologetic claims that are pervasive in Kierkegaard's authorship and prominent in *Philosophical Fragments,* it is very surprising to discover that the book contains a number of arguments that look very much like apologetic efforts" (64). More particularly, Evans claims that the "overall message of the last two chapters" of *Fragments* "seems designed to undermine one common objection to Christianity" (72). Finally, Evans notes that although Climacus claims that "the attempt to make the paradox 'probable' is wrongheaded," Climacus "actually attempts in some sense to make the incarnation plausible" (70–71).

M. Piety, in "A Little Light Music: The Subversion of Subjectivity in Kierkegaard's *Philosophical Fragments*," argues that the "Interlude" in *Fragments* is "ironic." The irony consists in Climacus's pretending to be "objective," or neutral, with regard to the decision between the "Socratic view" that "the process of coming into existence" has "merely *accidental* significance" and the "Christian" view that this process "concerns the very essence of human existence" (55). The purpose of this irony is to "subvert" the pretended "objectivity" of the work as a whole, but only "implicitly," or by suggestion. Piety argues that in the "Interlude" Climacus makes "an implicit appeal to the subjective experience of his reader in order to find out whether that experience is one of freedom or of necessity" (60). If that experience is of freedom, then the reader is nudged toward the Christian hypothesis. Piety thinks that Climacus adopts this indirect and ironic approach toward Christianity because of certain resistances that readers will have to the Christian, subjective view. Thus she thinks that Climacus tries to show his readers their commitment to "time," "freedom," "possibility," and the reality of "sin," without announcing that this is his intention. In other words, Piety thinks that Climacus pretends to be objective in *Fragments*, but uses suggestion to move his readers toward subjectivity.

15. Sylvia Walsh, in *Living Christianly: Kierkegaard's Dialectic of Christian Existence*, argues that in his later writings Kierkegaard consistently employs an "inverse dialectic" (7). In this dialectic, the "the negative is an indirect sign of the positive," and "the positive is indirectly present in or known through the negative" (168, 13). Thus the positive in this dialectic comes to be and shows itself, at least initially, in the negative. For example, one must first become sorrowfully conscious of sin in order then to become joyfully aware of and grateful for the forgiveness of sin.

Walsh claims that "Kierkegaard's understanding of Christian existence is given a one-dimensional representation in terms of the negative, whereas it should be given a dialectical construction in terms of the positive that is expressed in and through the negative" (113). This is to say that Kierkegaard often appears to readers to be saying the opposite of what he really means to communicate, because they do not appreciate his inverse dialectic.

Many of the paradoxes in Kierkegaard's authorship are a result of, or at least closely connected with, Kierkegaard's inverse dialectic, which uses the finite or limited aspects of human activity to reveal or suggest the infinite or transcending aspects of human activity. Similarly, it seems likely that inverse dialectic has something to do with Kierkegaard's revealing rationality by appearing irrational. In other words, it seems that Kierkegaard's communication of rationality through a pretense of rationality is closely related to his inverse dialectic.

16. C. Stephen Evans, *Kierkegaard's "Fragments" and "Postscript": The Religious Philosophy of Johannes Climacus*, 98–102.

17. Merold Westphal pointed this out in his Kierkegaard course at Fordham in 1992. See also his *Kierkegaard's Critique of Reason and Society*, 111.

7. The Figure of Socrates and the Downfall of Paradoxical Reason

1. John 1:51.
2. See *Symposium*, 220c–d, 175a.

3. Although there is no monolithic and unanimous interpretation of the downfall of the understanding in the secondary literature, the commentators tend to have very similar views of it, so that one may without undue distortion speak of a "standard interpretation." See Evans, *Kierkegaard's "Fragments" and "Postscript": The Religious Philosophy of Johannes Climacus*, 60–63, 77–79, 92–93, 107–109, and 140–141—where Evans begins to move beyond the standard interpretation of the downfall; Hannay, *Kierkegaard*, 97–122; Howland, *Kierkegaard and Socrates: A Study in Philosophy and Faith*, 107; Robert C. Roberts, *Faith, Reason, and History: Rethinking Kierkegaard's "Philosophical Fragments,"* ch. 3; and by implication, Westphal, *Becoming a Self: A Reading of Kierkegaard's* Concluding Unscientific Postscript, 120.

4. John Milton, *Paradise Lost*, Bk. 1, 263. See *The Norton Anthology of English Literature*, 855–857, for Blake's and Shelley's admiration of Milton's Satan.

5. Fyodor Dostoevsky, *The Brothers Karamazov*, 245.

8. The Proof of Paradoxical Reason

1. Nietzsche, *Beyond Good and Evil*, 14–15.

2. Nietzsche, *Human, All Too Human*, 208–209.

3. *Laws*, 731e–732b.

4. *Laws*, 731e.

5. *Republic*, 518c.

6. This is not to say that anxiety and despair are merely or even mainly emotions, but they at least include an important emotional component.

7. *Phaedo*, 99d.

8. Martin Buber, *Between Man and Man*, 114–120.

9. C. S. Lewis, *An Experiment in Criticism*, p. 141.

10. Richard Hooker, from the *Laws of Ecclesiastical Polity*, quoted in C. S. Lewis, *The Pilgrim's Regress*, 19.

11. A qualification is in order here. Though I do not think that Kierkegaard argues that there is a God who can help human beings in their need, I do think that he argues that we need a God and that we are capable of nothing important without God. A further suggestion of the argument may be that this need is so pressing that it is right to postulate the existence of a God who can fulfill this need, as long as such a postulate contradicts neither itself nor any firmly established truths. This argument can be found in at least two places, most fully in *The Sickness unto Death*, which Merold Westphal interprets as presenting "an argument for faith." See his "Johannes and Johannes: Kierkegaard and Difference," 17. Kierkegaard also presents arguments for the human need for God in various "Upbuilding Discourses." For an analysis of these arguments, see George Pattison's *The Philosophy of Kierkegaard*, which provides a good account of the argument of these Discourses for the claim that a human being is "powerless" and "in need of God" to fulfill its highest purposes, pp. 140–145, 136. See also Pattison's *Kierkegaard's Upbuilding Discourses: Philosophy, Literature, and Theology*.

12. *Meno*, 71b.

13. *Phaedo*, 68d.

14. *Sophist*, 230.

15. *Laws,* 731d–732b.

16. See *Phaedrus,* 242a–243e, for Socrates' explanation of the necessity of "expiation" for a "fault" "committed" "toward the divine."

17. *Phaedo,* 115b–c.

18. Hebrews 11:1,3.

BIBLIOGRAPHY

Anselm. *Monologion and Proslogion with the Replies of Gaunilo and Anselm.* Trans. by Thomas Williams. Indianapolis: Hackett Publishing Company, 2005.

Aquinas, Thomas. *Introduction to St. Thomas Aquinas.* Ed. by Anton C. Pegis. New York: The Modern Library, 1948.

———. *Treatise on Happiness.* Trans. by John A. Oesterle. Notre Dame, Ind.: University of Notre Dame Press, 1983.

Barret, Lee. "The Paradox of Faith in Kierkegaard's *Philosophical Fragments:* Gift or Task?" In Perkins, *International Kierkegaard Commentary 7: Philosophical Fragments and Johannes Climacus.* 261–283.

Buber, Martin. *Between Man and Man.* Trans. by Ronald Gregor-Smith. New York: Routledge Classics, 2006.

———. *The Knowledge of Man.* Trans. by Maurice Friedman and Ronald Gregor-Smith. Atlantic Highlands, N.J.: Humanities Press International, 1988.

Climacus, John. *The Ladder of Divine Ascent.* Trans. by Colm Luibheid and Norman Russell. New York: Paulist Press, 1982.

Collingwood, R. G. *An Autobiography.* New York: Oxford University Press, 2002.

Connell, George, and Heather Servaty. "A Paradox of Personal Identity in Kierkegaard's *Philosophical Fragments.*" In Perkins, *International Kierkegaard Commentary 7: Philosophical Fragments and Johannes Climacus.* 85–107.

Dostoevsky, Fyodor. *The Brothers Karamazov.* Trans. by Richard Pevear and Larissa Volokhonsky. New York: Alfred A. Knopf, 1992.

Dru, Alexander, editor and translator. *The Soul of Kierkegaard: Selections from His Journal.* Mineola, N.Y.: Dover Publications, 2003.

Early Buddhist Discourses. Ed. and trans. by John J. Holder. Indianapolis: Hackett, 2006.

Ebeling, Gerhard. *Luther: An Introduction to His Thought.* Trans. R. A. Wilson. Philadelphia, Pa.: Fortress Press, 1970.

Evans, C. Stephen. "Apologetic Arguments in Kierkegaard's *Philosophical Fragments.*" In Perkins, *International Kierkegaard Commentary 7: Philosophical Fragments and Johannes Climacus.* 63–83.

————. *Faith above Reason: A Kierkegaardian Account.* Grand Rapids, Mich.: William B. Eerdmans, 1998.

————. *Kierkegaard on Faith and the Self: Collected Essays.* Waco, Tex.: Baylor University Press, 2006.

————. *Kierkegaard's "Fragments" and "Postscript": The Religious Philosophy of Johannes Climacus.* Amherst, N.Y.: Humanity Books, 1999.

————. *Passionate Reason: Making Sense of Kierkegaard's "Philosophical Fragments."* Bloomington: Indiana University Press, 1992.

Ferreira, M. Jamie. *Love's Grateful Striving: A Commentary on Kierkegaard's Works of Love.* New York: Oxford University Press, 2001.

————. *Transforming Vision: Imagination and Will in Kierkegaardian Faith.* Oxford: Clarendon Press, 1991.

Garfield, Jay L. *The Fundamental Wisdom of the Middle Way: Nagarjuna's Mulamadhyamakakarika.* New York: Oxford University Press, 1995.

Glenn, John D., Jr. "A Highest Good . . . an Eternal Happiness": The Human *Telos* in Kierkegaard's *Concluding Unscientific Postscript.*" In Perkins, *International Kierkegaard Commentary 12: Concluding Unscientific Postscript to Philosophical Fragments.* 247–262.

Hannay, Alastair. *Kierkegaard.* London: Routledge, 1991.

Howland, Jacob. *Kierkegaard and Socrates: A Study in Philosophy and Faith.* New York: Cambridge University Press, 2006.

Kahn, Charles H. *The Art and Thought of Heraclitus: An Edition of the Fragments with Translation and Commentary.* Cambridge: Cambridge University Press, 1979.

Kierkegaard, Søren. *Christian Discourses, Etc.* Trans. by Walter Lowrie. Princeton, N.J.: Princeton University Press, 1974.

————. *The Concept of Anxiety: A Simple Psychologically Orienting Deliberation on the Dogmatic Issue of Hereditary Sin.* Trans. by Reidar Thomte in collaboration with Albert B. Anderson. Princeton, N.J.: Princeton University Press, 1995.

————. *The Concept of Irony.* Trans. by Howard V. and Edna H. Hong. Princeton, N.J.: Princeton University Press, 1989.

————. *Concluding Unscientific Postscript.* 2 vols. Trans. by Howard V. and Edna H. Hong. Princeton, N.J.: Princeton University Press, 1992.

————. *The Corsair Affair and Articles Related to the Writings.* Ed. and trans. by Howard V. and Edna H. Hong. Princeton, N.J.: Princeton University Press, 1982.

————. *Early Polemical Writings.* Ed. and trans. by Julia Watkins. Princeton, N.J.: Princeton University Press, 2009.

————. *Eighteen Upbuilding Discourses.* Trans. by Howard V. and Edna H. Hong. Princeton, N.J.: Princeton University Press, 1990.

————. *Either/Or.* 2 vols. Trans. by Howard V. and Edna H. Hong. Princeton, N.J.: Princeton University Press, 1987.

————. *Fear and Trembling/Repetition.* Trans. by Howard V. and Edna H. Hong. Princeton, N.J.: Princeton University Press, 1983.

————. *For Self-Examination/Judge for Yourself!* Trans. by Howard V. and Edna H. Hong. Princeton, N.J.: Princeton University Press, 1990.

———. *From the Papers of One Still Living*. In Watkins, *Early Polemical Writings*. 53–102.

———. *The Moment and Late Writings*. Trans. by Howard V. and Edna H. Hong. Princeton, N.J.: Princeton University Press, 1998.

———. *Philosophical Fragments/Johannes Climacus*. Trans. by Howard V. and Edna H. Hong. Princeton, N.J.: Princeton University Press, 1985.

———. *The Point of View for My Work as an Author*. Trans. by Howard V. and Edna H. Hong. Princeton, N.J.: Princeton University Press, 1998.

———. *Practice in Christianity*. Trans. by Howard V. and Edna H. Hong. Princeton, N.J.: Princeton University Press, 1991.

———. *The Sickness unto Death: A Christian Psychological Exposition for Upbuilding and Awakening*. Trans. by Howard V. and Edna H. Hong. Princeton, N.J.: Princeton University Press, 1980.

———. *Søren Kierkegaard's Journals and Papers*. 7 vols. Ed. and trans. by Howard V. and Edna H. Hong, assisted by Gregor Malantschuk. Bloomington: Indiana University Press, 1967–1978.

———. *Stages on Life's Way*. Trans. by Howard V. and Edna H. Hong. Princeton, N.J.: Princeton University Press, 1988.

———. *Two Ages: The Age of Revolution and the Present Age. A Literary Review*. Trans. by Howard V. and Edna H. Hong. Princeton, N.J.: Princeton University Press, 1978.

———. *Upbuilding Discourses in Various Spirits*. Trans. by Howard V. and Edna H. Hong. Princeton, N.J.: Princeton University Press, 1993.

———. *Without Authority*. Trans. by Howard V. and Edna H. Hong. Princeton, N.J.: Princeton University Press, 1997.

———. *Works of Love*. Trans. by Howard V. and Edna H. Hong. Princeton, N.J.: Princeton University Press, 1995.

Lessing, Gotthold Ephraim. *Lessing: Philosophical and Theological Writings*. Trans. and ed. by H. B. Nisbet. Cambridge: Cambridge University Press, 2005.

Lewis, C. S. *An Experiment in Criticism*. Cambridge: Cambridge University Press, 1992.

———. *The Pilgrim's Regress: An Allegorical Apology for Christianity, Reason, and Remonaticism*. Grand Rapids, Mich.: William B. Eerdmans, 1987.

The Lotus Sutra. Trans. Burton Watson. New York: Columbia University Press, 1993.

Luther, Martin. *Martin Luther: Selections from His Writings*. Ed. by John Dillenberger. New York: Doubleday, 1962.

Mackey, Louis. *Kierkegaard: A Kind of Poet*. Philadelphia: University of Pennsylvania Press, 1971.

MacKinnon, Alastair. *The Kierkegaard Indices*. 22 vols. Leiden: E. J. Brill, 1970–1975.

Malantschuk, Gregor. *Kierkegaard's Thought*. Trans. and ed. by Howard V. Hong and Edna H. Hong. Princeton, N.J.: Princeton University Press, 1971.

Marino, Gordon, and Alastair Hannay, eds. *The Cambridge Companion to Kierkegaard*. Cambridge: Cambridge University Press, 1998.

Milton, John. *Paradise Lost: An Authoritative Text, Backgrounds and Sources*. Ed. by Scott Elledge. New York: W. W. Norton, 1975.

Mulder, Jack, Jr. *Kierkegaard and The Catholic Tradition: Conflict and Dialogue.* Bloomington: Indiana University Press, 2010.

Müller, Paul. *"Kierkegaard's Works of Love": Christian Ethics and the Maieutic Ideal.* Trans. and ed. by C. Stephen Evans and Jan Evans. Copenhagen: C. A. Reitzel, 1993.

Nietzsche, Friedrich. *Beyond Good and Evil: Prelude to a Philosophy of the Future.* Trans. by Walter Kaufmann. New York: Vintage Books, 1989.

——. *Human, All Too Human: A Book for Free Spirits.* Trans. by Marion Faber, with Stephen Lehmann. Lincoln: University of Nebraska Press, 1996.

The Norton Anthology of English Literature. 3rd ed. vol. 2. New York: W. W. Norton, 1974.

Pattison, George. "Johannes Climacus and Aurelius Augustinus on Recollecting the Truth." In Perkins, *International Kierkegaard Commentary 7: Philosophical Fragments and Johannes Climacus.* 245–260.

——. *Kierkegaard's Upbuilding Discourses: Philosophy, Literature, and Theology.* London: Routledge, 2002.

——. *The Philosophy of Kierkegaard.* Montreal: McGill-Queen's University Press, 2005.

Perkins, Robert L., editor. *International Kierkegaard Commentary 7: Philosophical Fragments and Johannes Climacus.* Macon, Ga.: Mercer University Press, 1994.

——. *International Kierkegaard Commentary 8: The Concept of Anxiety.* Macon, Ga.: Mercer University Press, 1985.

——. *International Kierkegaard Commentary 12:* Concluding Unscientific Postscript *to* Philosophical Fragments. Macon, Ga.: Mercer University Press, 1997.

——. *International Kierkegaard Commentary 19:* The Sickness unto Death. Macon, Ga.: Mercer University Press, 1987.

Piety, M. "A Little Light Music: The Subversion of Subjectivity in Kierkegaard's *Philosophical Fragments*." In Perkins, *International Kierkegaard Commentary 7: Philosophical Fragments and Johannes Climacus.* 47–62.

Plato. *Four Texts on Socrates: Plato's Euthyphro, Apology, and Crito and Aristophanes' Clouds.* Rev. ed. Trans. by Thomas G. West and Grace Starry West. Ithaca, N.Y.: Cornell University Press, 1998.

——. *The Laws of Plato.* Trans. by Thomas L. Pangle. Chicago: University of Chicago Press, 1988.

——. *Plato: Gorgias.* Trans. by James H. Nichols Jr. Ithaca, N.Y.: Cornell University Press, 1998.

——. *Plato: "Protagoras" and "Meno."* Trans. with notes and interpretative essays by Robert C. Bartlett. Ithaca, N.Y.: Cornell University Press, 2004.

——. *Plato's Phaedo.* Trans. by Eva Brann, Peter Kalkavage, and Eric Salem. Newburyport, Mass.: Focus Classical Library, 1998.

——. *Plato: Phaedrus.* Trans. by James H. Nichols Jr. Ithaca, N.Y.: Cornell University Press, 1998.

——. *Plato's Sophist.* Trans. by Eva Brann, Peter Kalkavage, and Eric Salem. Newburyport, Mass.: Focus Classical Library, 1996.

——. *The Republic of Plato.* 2nd ed. Trans. by Allan Bloom. New York: Basic Books, 1991.

———. *Symposium.* Trans. Seth Benerdete. Chicago: University of Chicago Press, 1993.

Pseudo-Dionysius: The Complete Works. Trans. by Colm Kuibheid. New York: Paulist Press, 1987.

Radhakrishnan, S., ed. and trans. *The Principal Upanishads.* Amherst, N.Y.: Humanity Books, 1992.

Roberts, Robert C. "Dialectical Emotions and the Virtue of Faith." In Perkins, *International Kierkegaard Commentary 12:* Concluding Unscientific Postscript *to* Philosophical Fragments. 73–93.

———. "Existence, Emotion, and Virtue: Classical Themes in Kierkegaard." In Marino and Hannay, *The Cambridge Companion to Kierkegaard.* 177–206.

———. *Faith, Reason, and History: Rethinking Kierkegaard's "Philosophical Fragments."* Macon, Ga.: Mercer University Press, 1986.

———. "The Grammar of Sin and the Conceptual Unity of the Sickness unto Death." In Perkins, *International Kierkegaard Commentary 19:* The Sickness unto Death. 135–160.

———."The Socratic Knowledge of God." In Perkins, *International Kierkegaard Commentary 8:* The Concept of Anxiety. 133–152.

The Teachings of the Buddha, the Middle Length Discourses of the Buddha: A Translation of the Majjhima Nikaya. Trans. by Bhikkhu Nanamoli. Ed. and rev. by Bhikkhu Bodhi. Boston: Wisdom Publications, 2005.

Walsh, Sylvia. *Kierkegaard: Thinking Christianly in an Existential Mode.* New York: Oxford University Press, 2009.

———. *Living Christianly: Kierkegaard's Dialectic of Christian Existence.* University Park: Pennsylvania State University Press, 2005.

Westphal, Merold. *Becoming a Self: A Reading of Kierkegaard's* Concluding Unscientific Postscript. West Lafayette, Ind.: Purdue University Press, 1996.

———. "Johannes and Johannes: Kierkegaard and Difference." In Perkins, *International Kierkegaard Commentary 7: Philosophical Fragments and Johannes Climacus.* 13–32.

———. *Kierkegaard's Critique of Reason and Society.* Macon, Ga.: Mercer University Press, 1987.

———. *Levinas and Kierkegaard in Dialogue.* Bloomington: Indiana University Press, 2008.

———. *Transcendence and Self-Transcendence: On God and the Soul.* Bloomington: Indiana University Press, 2004.

INDEX

absolute paradox, 2, 142, 176, 212
absurd, 6, 12–13, 22, 50, 54, 137, 176
admiration, 24–27, 29–30, 155–156, 176–177. *See also* imitation
analogy, 96, 136, 137, 143, 144, 162, 163, 172, 173, 174, 185
Anselm, St., 93
apologetics, 6, 66–67, 231n14
Aquinas, St. Thomas, 85–88, 93
autopsy, 15–16, 55

Barrett, Lee, 230n11
Buber, Martin, 93–94
Buddha, the, 80–82, 85, 91, 128, 198
Buddhism, 86, 94, 107, 215–217, 227nn15–22

Christ, 17, 91, 95, 120, 128, 134, 137, 139, 141, 142, 143, 161, 164, 173, 212
Christianity, 95, 134–137, 139, 140, 144, 151, 157, 173, 175
Climacean capacity, 134, 144, 145, 148–149, 154, 157–159
Climacus. *See* Johannes Climacus
condition, 15, 137, 140, 163, 164, 168, 179, 226n14
Connell, George, 230n11
conscience, 8, 16, 34, 105–107, 191–192, 202, 215
contradiction, 6, 12–13, 152, 223n8

demonstration. *See* rational evaluation
Descartes, René, 58, 186, 205
despair, 66, 138, 168, 170–171, 213, 221
dialectic, 11–12, 35, 58–70, 90, 205; and subjectivity, 63–66; and theory of the stages, 63. *See also* logic
Dionysius the Areopagite, 87
direct communication, 73–74, 114, 116–118, 122–126, 129
Don Quixote, 155
Dostoevsky, Fyodor, 177, 193
doubt, 10, 41–42, 66, 93, 191, 213–215
downfall, 160–180; defined, 165; standard interpretation of, 165, 233n3

eros, 138–139, 141–143, 153–154, 161–163, 172, 173. *See also* passion of thought
eternal happiness, 85–86, 94–99, 164, 165, 168, 209–211
Evans, C. Stephen, 154–155, 221nn1,2, 223n8, 225nn11,14, 231nn11,14, 233n3(chap3)
Evans, Jan, 231n11

faith, 14–19, 23–31, 67, 93, 135, 138–139, 142–143, 170, 173, 176, 177, 221n1, 222n2, 225n14, 226n14; as absurd, 22; as autopsy, 15–16, 55; as perfecting reason, 16–19
Ferreira, M. Jamie, 222n3, 230n11

Richard McCombs teaches at St. John's College in Santa Fe, New Mexico.